Cooperstown by the Numbers

Cooperstown by the Numbers

An Analysis of Baseball Hall of Fame Elections

JOHN J. MCCONNELL

McFarland & Company, Inc., Publishers

Jefferson, North Carolina, and London

LIBRARY OF CONGRESS CATALOGUING-IN-PUBLICATION DATA

McConnell, John J.
    Cooperstown by the numbers : an analysis of baseball Hall of
Fame elections / John J. McConnell.
        p.   cm.
    Includes index.

    ISBN 978-0-7864-4737-4
    softcover : 50# alkaline paper ∞

    1. National Baseball Hall of Fame and Museum.   2. Baseball —
United States — History.   I. Title.
GV863.A1M225   2010
796.357'640973 — dc22   2010004380

British Library cataloguing data are available

Front cover ©2010 Shutterstock

Manufactured in the United States of America

*McFarland & Company, Inc., Publishers
    Box 611, Jefferson, North Carolina 28640
    www.mcfarlandpub.com*

This study is dedicated to the memory of David Bradley, a true Renaissance man, a brilliant statistician and scholar, a patient co-worker and, most importantly, a good friend. At the time of his untimely death, he was working on an expanded statistical analysis of the Hall of Fame data, which sadly he was unable to complete and which could not be included in this volume. David left us far too soon.

Table of Contents

PART III: ANALYSIS OF HALL OF FAME
   PLAYERS BY POSITION

Preface

The Baseball Hall of Fame has a long and storied history, mirroring the colorful history of the game itself. Between the Baseball Writers' Association elections each year and the additions to the Hall of Fame of players from the earliest decades of baseball by the special Veterans Committee, the best players have generally been inducted into the Hall of Fame. However, to my knowledge, no detailed study has been conducted of the voting history for the players nominated for Hall of Fame induction, nor of the relationship between other measures of excellence in baseball, such as annual Most Valuable Player awards and Cy Young awards, and Hall of Fame membership.

Over the years I have been intrigued by the furor that a Hall of Fame election can generate. Without fail a highly regarded player is overlooked, at least in the minds of some scribes. For years the ("Pee Wee") Reese–(Phil "The Scooter") Rizzuto controversy waged. If one can make it into the Hall of Fame, why not the other? Fortunately, that issue was finally resolved with Rizzuto's election.

Gil Hodges, during his tenure on the ballot, received the most total votes in history but has never been able to reach the magical 75 percent required by the Baseball Writers' Association and the Veterans Committee. Conversely, several Veterans Committee inductees received scant or no attention on the Baseball Writers ballot.

My background as an (amateur) baseball player, college baseball coach, sports fan, avid reader of numerous publications on the history of baseball, and visitor to the Baseball Hall of Fame in Cooperstown, New York, has led to a life-long fascination with the unique history, colorful characters, and mind-boggling statistics of America's favorite sport. I long ago developed an interest in the process of selection for Hall of Fame inductees, wondering in particular whether the most-deserving players were being elected and what other factors may have influenced the voting. This book grew out of such questions, which persisted over the 30 years that I worked on it, part-time, as a labor of love.

Part I is a straightforward history of Hall of Fame voting from the very first election, in 1936, through 2009. I have chronicled the status of every player who received 10 percent of the vote and listed every player by position who ever received a single Hall of Fame vote. In addition, I analyzed the voting patterns of the Baseball Writers' Association.

The studies that make up Part II explore the relationship between awards (Most Valuable Player, Cy Young Gold Glove, Rookie of the Year) and special recognition (selection for *The Sporting News* All-Star team, for instance) and Hall of Fame election. Also included are analyses of managers in the Hall of Fame, the status of ethnic minorities, the playing longevity of Hall of Famers, and the franchises for which the Hall of Famers played.

In Part III of this book, the voting history for each position is taken up. As in Part I, every player who has received a vote in a Baseball Writers' Association of America election is covered. In addition, there is a yearly list of the players receiving the highest percentage of votes, a general analysis of the voting, rankings by year of those who achieved at least 10 percent of the vote, a yearly list of the number of players who received at least 10 percent of the vote, the number each year which were ultimately elected to the Hall of Fame via the Baseball Writers' Association or the Veterans' Committee, and the year that each non–Hall of Famer received at least 10 percent of the vote and conclusions drawn from the preceding data.

A number of valuable and exhaustive statistical sources were utilized for the data compiled for this study. They include *The Baseball Encyclopedia* (Macmillan); *Total Baseball*, Sixth Edition (Total Sports), edited by John Thorn, Pete Palmer, Michael Gershman, and David Pietrusza; *The Sporting News* magazine, mainly the issues containing the annual All-Star Team selections as chosen by *The Sporting News* editorial team; and the websites Baseball-Reference.com and MLB.com.

There has been no specific effort to call attention to oversights or inconsistencies among the voters. This is strictly the prerogative of the reader.

PART I: A HISTORY OF HALL OF FAME VOTING

Introduction

When the Baseball Writers' Association of America elected Rickey Henderson and Jim Rice to the Baseball Hall of Fame in January 2009 it marked the sixty-fifth year of voting. Similarly, the Veterans Committee completed its fifty-seventh year of balloting in December 2008, when it inducted Joe Gordon.

The Baseball Writers' Association of America has voted for Hall of Fame candidates since the first election in 1936, although not in every year. Also, a committee variously referred to in its early years as the "Veterans Committee," the "Hall of Fame Committee," and the "Executive Committee," has voted for candidates considered "old-timers" from the earlier years of baseball and for candidates retired for specified numbers of years, who had not been selected by the Baseball Writers. This committee has undergone numerous changes in the number and composition of its membership, and it has not met every year. However, it has been consistently named the "Veterans' Committee" since 1953.

In some of the earlier years of the Hall of Fame, elections were scheduled at intervals rather than annually. This explains the lack of elections in 1940, 1941, and 1943. Also, from 1956 to 1965 (except for 1962 and 1964) the Baseball Writers' Committee and the Veterans Committee alternated in selecting candidates each year. The Baseball Writers have held elections every year since 1966. Since 2001, the Veterans Committee has met bi-annually rather than every year.

Although eligibility regulations have changed somewhat over the years, a 75 percent majority vote has remained constant in both the Baseball Writers' Association and Veterans' Committee elections. To date 106 players have been inducted by the Baseball Writers and 93 by the Veterans' Committee and its forerunners (the Hall of Fame Committee and the Executive Committee). The Baseball Writers' Association is abbreviated as "BWA" and the Veteran's Committee is abbreviated as "VC" in many of the tables that appear in this study. The rest of Part I contains a detailed chronology of the year-by-year balloting, organized by decade. The results include all those who received at least 10 percent of the votes cast.

The 1930s

1936

In this first year of voting two separate elections were held. The Veterans' Committee election was set up to consider players who performed before 1900, while the Baseball Writers' Association dealt with 20th century players. Eligibility guidelines were unclear, which resulted in several active players (Hornsby, Cochrane and Gehrig) receiving votes in the Baseball Writers' Association voting and eight players being considered on both ballots.

BASEBALL WRITERS' ASSOCIATION ELECTION

In the initial election 226 voters each cast ballots for a maximum of 10 players. Forty-seven different players received votes with five all-time greats achieving the mandatory 75 percent.

Player	Percentage of Votes	Result
Ty Cobb	98.2	Elected
Babe Ruth	95.1	Elected
Honus Wagner	95.1	Elected
Christy Mathewson	90.7	Elected
Walter Johnson	83.6	Elected
Nap Lajoie	64.6	
Tris Speaker	58.8	
Cy Young	49.1	
Rogers Hornsby	46.5	
Mickey Cochrane	35.4	
George Sisler	34.1	
Eddie Collins	26.5	
Jimmy Collins	25.7	
Grover Alexander	24.3	
Lou Gehrig	22.6	
Roger Bresnahan	20.8	
Willie Keeler	17.7	
Rube Waddell	14.6	

All 18 of the players listed above eventually were elected to the Hall of Fame.

VETERANS COMMITTEE ELECTION

A Veterans Committee of 78 voters cast ballots for 57 players with nobody coming close to the 75 percent required. Thirteen players garnered

10 percent or more of the vote and all but Herman Long were ultimately elected to the Hall of Fame.

Name	Playing Years	Percentage of Votes	Hall of Fame & Year Elected
Cap Anson	1876–1897	51.3	Executive Committee 1939
Buck Ewing	1880–1897	51.3	Executive Committee 1939
Willie Keeler	1892–1910	42.3	BWA 1939
Cy Young	1890–1911	41.0	BWA 1937
Ed Delahanty	1888–1903	28.2	Hall of Fame Committee 1945
John McGraw	1891–1906	21.8	Executive Committee 1937 as a Manager
Herman Long	1889–1904	20.5	
Hoss Radbourn	1880–1891	20.5	Executive Committee 1939
King Kelly	1878–1893	19.2	Hall of Fame Committee 1945
Amos Rusie	1889–1901	15.4	Veterans Committee 1977
Hughie Jennings	1891–1918	14.1	Hall of Fame Committee 1945
Fred Clarke	1894–1915	11.5	Hall of Fame Committee 1945
Jimmy Collins	1895–1908	10.3	Hall of Fame Committee 1945

Honus Wagner received 6.4 percent of the votes while being elected by the Baseball Writers with 95.1 percent. Cy Young was the victim of a split vote netting 41.0 percent by the Veterans and 49.1 percent by the Baseball Writers. Willie Keeler also received support on both ballots as did Nap Lajoie.

1937

BASEBALL WRITERS' ASSOCIATION ELECTION

Lajoie, Speaker and Young who were sixth, seventh and eighth the previous year moved up into the top three spots and gained election.

Number of writers voting 201
Number of players receiving votes 113
Number of players receiving 10 percent or more of the votes 22
Number of players in the Hall of Fame through 2009 21
Number of players who received 10 percent on previous ballot ... 11
Number of players elected to Hall of Fame this year 3
Cumulative total 8

Player	Percentage of Votes	Result
Lajoie	83.6	Elected
Speaker	82.1	Elected
Young	76.1	Elected
Alexander	62.2	
E. Collins	57.2	
Keeler	57.2	
Sisler	52.7	

Player	Percentage of Votes	Result
Ed Delahanty	34.8	
Waddell	33.3	
J. Collins	32.8	
Ed Walsh	27.9	
Hornsby	26.4	
Frank Chance	24.4	
Johnny Evers	21.9	
Bresnahan	21.4	
John McGraw	17.4	Elected by Executive Committee as a Manager
Mordecai Brown	15.4	
Rabbit Maranville	12.4	
Ray Schalk	11.9	
Eddie Plank	11.4	
Fred Clarke	10.9	
Johnny Kling	10.0	

The only player on the list who failed to eventually make the Hall of Fame was Johnny Kling.

Executive Committee

No players were selected but managers John McGraw and Connie Mack, and pioneer/executives Morgan G. Bulkeley, Ban Johnson and George Wright were selected. McGraw also received 17.4 percent of the votes in the Baseball Writers Association election; based on his credentials as a player he might well have qualified in that category. He also received 21.8 percent of the vote in the 1936 Veterans Election which ranked sixth.

1938

Baseball Writers' Association Election

Only Grover Cleveland Alexander acquired enough votes for election and continued the three-year pattern by moving up from fourth to first in the balloting.

Number of writers voting 262
Number of players receiving votes 119
Number of players receiving 10 percent or more of the votes 23
Number in the Hall of Fame through 2009 23
Number of players who received 10 percent on the previous ballot . 17
Number of players elected to Hall of Fame this year 1
Cumulative total 9

Player	Percentage of Votes	Result
Alexander	80.9	Elected
Sisler	68.3	
Keeler	67.6	

Player	Percentage of Votes	Result
E. Collins	66.8	
Waddell	56.5	
Chance	50.8	
Delahanty	50.4	
Walsh	42.0	
Evers	34.7	
J. Collins	30.2	
Maranville	27.9	
Bresnahan	25.6	
Clarke	24.0	
Brown	20.6	
Miller Huggins	18.3	
Hornsby	17.6	
Schalk	17.2	
Ross Youngs	15.3	
Plank	14.5	
Herb Pennock	14.1	
Joe McGinnity	13.7	
Chief Bender	12.6	
Frank Baker	12.2	

EXECUTIVE COMMITTEE

The Committee failed to elect any players. The only selections were executive Alexander Cartwright and writer-statistician Henry Chadwick.

1939

BASEBALL WRITERS' ASSOCIATION ELECTION

The voting became more widely distributed with 27 individuals receiving 10 percent or more of the votes. With twenty-one carry-overs from the previous year a consistent voting pattern was emerging. Once again the players who occupied the second, third and fourth slots in the previous election were the ones to be inducted this year. In December of 1939, Lou Gehrig was elected by acclamation of the Baseball Writers at their annual meeting.

Number of writers voting 274
Number of players receiving votes 108
Number of players receiving 10 percent or more of the votes 27
Number in the Hall of Fame through 2009 27
Number of players who received 10 percent on the previous ballot . 21
Number of players elected to the Hall of Fame this year 4
Cumulative total 13

Player	Percentage of Votes	Result
Sisler	85.8	Elected
E. Collins	77.7	Elected

Player	Percentage of Votes	Result
Keeler	75.5	Elected
Waddell	65.3	
Hornsby	64.2	
Chance	57.7	
Delahanty	52.9	
Walsh	48.2	
Evers	39.1	
Huggins	35.4	
Maranville	29.9	
J. Collins	26.3	
Bresnahan	24.5	
Clarke	21.5	
Brown	19.7	
Wilbert Robinson	16.8	
Pennock	14.6	
Bender	14.6	
Schalk	12.8	
Hugh Duffy	12.4	
Youngs	12.4	
Hughie Jennings	12.0	
McGinnity	11.7	
Baker	10.9	
Mickey Cochrane	10.2	
Plank	10.2	
Addie Joss	10.2	

EXECUTIVE COMMITTEE

A top level trio consisting of Commissioner Kenesaw Mountain Landis and League Presidents Ford Frick and William Harridge selected Charles Comiskey, Candy Cummings and A. G. Spalding in the Pioneer/Executive category. In addition, three of the top vote-getters in the 1936 Veterans Election were selected. Cap Anson and Buck Ewing who had each garnered 51.3 percent to tie for the top spot and Hoss Radbourn with 20.5 percent of the vote were selected for Hall of Fame induction.

The 1940s

1942

Only the Baseball Writers held an election in 1942. While fewer players were receiving votes, there was a more widespread distribution with only Rogers Hornsby moving up from the fifth spot in the last election to achieve Hall of Fame status.

Number of writers voting 233
Number of players receiving votes 72
Number of players receiving 10 percent or more of the votes 29
Number in the Hall of Fame through 2009 29
Number of players who received 10 percent on the previous ballot . 23
Number of players elected to the Hall of Fame this year 1
Cumulative total 14

Player	Percentage of Votes	Result
Hornsby	78.1	Elected
Chance	58.4	
Waddell	54.1	
Walsh	48.5	
Huggins	47.6	
Delahanty	44.6	
Evers	39.1	
Robinson	38.2	
Cochrane	37.8	
Frankie Frisch	36.1	
Duffy	33.1	
Pennock	30.9	
Clark Griffith	30.5	
J. Collins	29.2	
Maranville	28.3	
Jennings	27.5	
Brown	27.0	
Plank	27.0	
McGinnity	25.3	
Clarke	24.9	
Bresnahan	24.5	
Bender	23.6	
Schalk	22.7	
Youngs	18.9	
Baker	16.7	
Dazzy Vance	15.9	
Joe Tinker	15.5	
Bill Terry	15.5	
Joss	14.2	

1944

The three-man committee selected Commissioner Landis to the Hall of Fame in the Executive category.

1945

BASEBALL WRITERS ASSOCIATION ELECTION

This marked the first year in which none of the candidates could achieve the required 75 percent for election. Chance, Waddell and Walsh occupied the top three spots, each moving up one place from 1942.

Number of writers voting 247
Number of players receiving votes 94
Number of players receiving 10 percent or more of the votes 27
Number in the Hall of Fame through 2009- 27
Number of players who received 10 percent on the previous ballot . 23
Number of players elected to the Hall of Fame this year 0
Cumulative total 14

Player	Percentage of Votes	Result
Chance	72.5	
Waddell	62.3	
Walsh	55.5	
Evers	54.3	
Bresnahan	53.8	Elected by Hall of Fame Committee, 1945
Huggins	53.8	
Cochrane	50.6	
J. Collins	49.0	Elected by Hall of Fame Committee, 1945
Delahanty	44.9	Elected by Hall of Fame Committee, 1945
Griffith	43.7	
Frisch	40.9	
Jennings	37.2	Elected by Hall of Fame Committee, 1945
Robinson	32.8	Elected by Hall of Fame Committee as a Manager, 1945
Pie Traynor	32.8	
Duffy	25.9	Elected by Hall of Fame Committee, 1945
Clarke	21.5	Elected by Hall of Fame Committee, 1945
Maranville	20.6	
Tinker	19.8	
Brown	18.6	
Herb Pennock	18.2	
McGinnity	17.8	
Bender	16.2	
Schalk	13.4	
Plank	13.4	
Bill Terry	13.0	
Lefty Grove	11.3	
Baker	10.5	

HALL OF FAME COMMITTEE

A six-member committee selected nine "veteran" players and one manager who had performed between the years of 1876 and 1915. This action helped to reduce the numbers which were causing the widespread dispersion in the voting in the Baseball Writers poll. The following were elected:

Ed Delahanty	Percentage of Votes	Rank
Veterans Election 1936	28.2	5th
Rank in 1945		1st

Results of Baseball Writers Association Voting:

Year	Percentage of Votes	Rank
1936	7.1	
1937	34.8	8th
1938	50.4	7th
1939	52.9	7th
1942	44.6	6th
1945	44.9	9th

King Kelly	Percentage of Votes	Rank
Veterans Election 1936	19.2	9th
Rank in 1945		3rd

He did not receive any votes in Baseball Writers Association elections between 1936 and 1945, possibly because his career ended in 1893 and was less well known by many of the voters.

Hughie Jennings	Percentage of Votes	Rank
Veterans Election 1936	14.1	11th
Rank in 1945		5th

Results of Baseball Writers Association voting:

Year	Percentage of Votes	Rank
1936	0.0	
1937	2.0	
1938	8.8	
1939	12.0	21st
1942	27.5	16th
1945	37.2	12th

Fred Clarke	Percentage of Votes	Rank
Veterans Election 1936	11.5	12th
Rank in 1945		6th

Results of Baseball Writers Association voting:

Year	Percentage of Votes	Rank
1936	0.4	
1937	10.9	20th
1938	24.0	13th
1939	21.5	14th
1942	24.9	20th
1945	21.5	16th

Jimmy Collins	Percentage of Votes	Rank
Veterans Election 1936	10.3	13th
Rank in 1945		7th

Results of Baseball Writers Association voting

Year	Percentage of Votes	Rank
1936	25.7	13th
1937	32.8	10th
1938	30.2	10th
1939	26.3	12th
1942	29.2	14th
1945	49.0	8th

Hugh Duffy	Percentage of Votes	Rank
Veterans Election 1936	5.1	22nd (tie)
Rank in 1945		13th

Results of Baseball Writers Association voting:

Year	Percentage of Votes	Rank
1937	3.5	
1938	9.2	
1939	12.4	20th (tie)
1942	33.1	11th
1945	25.9	15th

Dan Brouthers	Percentage of Votes	Rank
Veterans Election 1936	2.6	28th
Rank in 1945		18th (tie)

Brouthers did not receive votes in any of the Baseball Writers Association elections.

Roger Bresnahan: Bresnahan was not considered in the Veterans Election of 1936 but received support in the Baseball Writers Association elections as follows:

Year	Percentage of Votes	Rank
1936	20.8	16th
1937	21.4	15th
1938	25.6	12th
1939	24.5	13th
1942	24.5	21st
1945	53.8	5th

Jim O'Rourke: O'Rourke has the unique distinction of never having received votes in the only Veterans Election or any of the five Baseball Writers Association elections held prior to his nomination.

Wilbert Robinson: The other 1945 nominee, Wilbert Robinson, was elected as a manager. He received strong support in the 1942 and 1945 Baseball Writers Association balloting as well as 7.7 percent of the vote in the 1936 Veterans Election.

	Percentage of Vote	*Rank*
Veterans Election 1936	7.7	14th (tie)
Rank in 1945		7th (tie)

Results of Baseball Writers Association voting:

Year	*Percentage of Votes*	*Rank*
1937	2.5	
1938	6.5	
1939	16.8	16th
1942	38.2	8th
1945	32.8	13th (tie)

1946

BASEBALL WRITERS ASSOCIATION ELECTION

This was the first year in which a run-off election was held. The twenty top vote-getters (including ties) were involved in a second ballot but nobody succeeded in acquiring the magic 75 percent figure.

Number of writers voting . . . . 202 (263 in run-off)
Number of players receiving votes 76
Number of players receiving 10 percent or more of the votes 28
Number of Hall of Famers through 2009 28
Number of players who received 10 percent on the previous ballot . 20
Number of players elected to the Hall of Fame this year 0
Cumulative total 14

Name	*Percentage of Votes*	*Percentage of Votes in Run Off*	*Result*
Chance	71.3	57.0	Elected by Hall of Fame Committee, 1946
Evers	64.4	41.8	Elected by Hall of Fame Committee, 1946
Huggins	63.9	40.3	
Waddell	60.4	33.1	Elected by Hall of Fame Committee, 1946
Walsh	56.9	40.3	Elected by Hall of Fame Committee, 1946
Frisch	51.5	25.5	
Carl Hubbell	50.0	28.5	
Cochrane	39.6	24.7	
Griffith	36.1	31.2	Elected by Hall of Fame Committee as an Executive, 1946
Grove	35.1	23.2	
Traynor	32.2	20.2	
Brown	27.7	18.3	
Tinker	27.2	17.1	Elected by Hall of Fame Committee, 1946

Name	Percentage of Votes	Percentage of Votes in Run Off	Result
McGinnity	26.2	17.9	Elected by Hall of Fame Committee, 1946
Maranville	24.8	11.0	
Charlie Gehringer	21.3	8.7	
Pennock	20.3	6.1	
Bill Dickey	19.8	12.1	
Dizzy Dean	19.8	17.1	
Bender	19.3	13.3	
Baker	19.3	13.7	
Schalk	17.8	—	
Plank	16.8	—	Elected by Hall of Fame Committee, 1946
Dazzy Vance	15.3	—	
Terry	15.3	—	
Jimmy Foxx	12.9	—	
Ross Youngs	12.4	—	
Harry Heilmann	11.4	—	

HALL OF FAME COMMITTEE

Ten players were selected by the six-member committee following the unsuccessful Baseball Writers Association election. Those receiving the first, second, fourth and fifth amount of votes in the Baseball Writers Association balloting were selected. Miller Huggins, third in the voting, was elected in 1964 as a manager. He won six pennants in his managerial career but his playing statistics would scarcely qualify him as a Hall of Fame candidate as a second baseman. Clark Griffith, a 240-game winner, was also selected as an executive although his pitching credentials were impressive.

Over the years there have been questions raised about the selection of the Tinker to Evers to Chance combination, but it should be pointed out that the latter two ranked first and second in the Baseball Writers Association voting.

The backgrounds of those elected:

Frank Chance—no votes in the 1936 Veterans Election
Results of Baseball Writers Association voting:

Year	Percentage of Votes	Rank
1936	2.2	
1937	24.4	13th
1938	50.8	6th
1939	57.7	6th
1942	58.4	2nd
1945	72.5	1st
1946	71.3	1st
1946 Run-Off	57.0	1st

Johnny Evers—no votes in the 1936 Veterans Election

Results of Baseball Writers Association voting:

Year	Percentage of Votes	Rank
1936	2.7	
1937	21.9	14th
1938	34.7	9th
1939	39.1	9th
1942	39.1	7th
1945	54.3	4th
1946	64.4	2nd
1946 Run-Off	41.8	2nd

Rube Waddell—no votes in the 1936 Veterans Election
Results of Baseball Writers Association voting:

Year	Percentage of Votes	Rank
1936	14.6	18th
1937	33.3	9th
1938	56.5	5th
1939	65.3	4th
1942	54.1	3rd
1945	62.3	2nd
1946	60.4	4th
1946 Run-Off	33.1	5th

Ed Walsh—no votes in the 1936 Veterans Election
Results of Baseball Writers Association voting:

Year	Percentage of Votes	Rank
1936	8.8	
1937	27.9	11th
1938	42.0	8th
1939	48.2	8th
1942	48.5	4th
1945	55.5	3rd
1946	56.9	5th
1946 Run-Off	40.3	3rd (tie)

Joe Tinker—no votes in the 1936 Veterans Election
Results of Baseball Writers Association voting:

Year	Percentage of Votes	Rank
1937	7.5	
1938	6.1	
1939	4.4	
1942	15.5	27th (tie)
1945	19.8	18th
1946	27.2	13th
1946 Run-Off	17.1	14th (tie)

Joe McGinnity—no votes in the 1936 Veterans Election
Results of Baseball Writers Association voting:

Year	Percentage of Votes	Rank
1937	6.0	
1938	13.7	21st
1939	11.7	23rd
1942	25.3	19th
1945	17.8	21st
1946	26.2	14th
1946 Run-Off	17.9	13th

Eddie Plank—no votes in the 1936 Veterans Election
Results of Baseball Writers Association voting:

Year	Percentage of Votes	Rank
1937	11.4	20th
1938	14.5	19th
1939	10.2	25th (tie)
1942	27.0	17th (tie)
1945	13.4	23rd (tie)
1946	16.8	23rd
1946 Run-Off	no votes	

Jesse Burkett	Percentage of Votes	Rank
Veterans Election, 1936	1.3	35th (tie)
Rank in 1946		17th (tie)

Results of Baseball Writers Association voting:

Year	Percentage of Votes	Rank
1937	0.5	
1938	0.8	
1939	0.0	
1942	1.7	
1945	0.8	
1946	1.0	

Tommy McCarthy	Percentage of Votes	Rank
Veterans Election, 1936	1.3	35th (tie)
Rank in 1946		17th (tie)

No votes received in Baseball Writers Association elections

Jack Chesbro—no votes in the 1936 Veterans Election
Results of Baseball Writers Association voting:

Year	Percentage of Votes	Rank
1937	0.5	
1938	0.8	
1939	2.2	
1942	0.0	
1945	0.0	
1946	0.5	

Clark Griffith—no votes in the 1936 Veterans Election Results of Baseball Writers Association voting:

Year	Percentage of Votes	Rank
1937	2.0	
1938	3.8	
1939	7.3	
1942	30.5	13th
1945	43.7	10th
1946	36.1	9th
1946 Run-Off	31.2	6th

To date the forerunner of the Veterans Committee had inducted 22 players into the Hall of Fame.

1947

The Baseball Writers' Election placed four players in the Hall of Fame, the first ones elected since 1942. Again, the top eligibles from the previous year moved up into the highest spots. This was the first year that the voting was intended for players only.

Number of writers voting 161
Number of players receiving votes 39
Number of players receiving 10 percent or more of the votes 21
Number of Hall of Famers through 2009 19
Number of players who received 10 percent on the previous ballot . 16
Number of players elected to the Hall of Fame this year 4
Cumulative total 18

Player	Percentage of Votes	Result
Hubbell	87.0	Elected
Frisch	84.5	Elected
Cochrane	79.5	Elected
Grove	76.4	Elected
Traynor	73.9	
Gehringer	65.2	
Maranville	56.5	
Dean	54.7	
Pennock	53.4	

Player	Percentage of Votes	Result
Bender	44.7	
Heilman	40.4	
Vance	31.1	
Schalk	31.1	
Baker	30.4	
Terry	28.6	
Zack Wheat	23.0	
Youngs	22.4	
Joe Wood	18.0	
Edd Roush	15.5	
Babe Adams	13.7	
Rube Marquard	11.2	

1948

Pie Traynor, who had finished fifth and just out of the money in the previous election, moved up to second position this time. Herb Pennock made the jump from ninth to first. Both barely exceeded the 75 percent requirement.

Number of writers voting 121
Number of players receiving votes 106
Number of players receiving 10 percent or more of the votes 21
Number of Hall of Famers through 2009 21
Number of players who received 10 percent on the previous ballot . 12
Number of players elected to Hall of Fame this year 2
Cumulative total 20

Player	Percentage of Votes	Result
Pennock	77.7	Elected
Traynor	76.9	Elected
Al Simmons	49.6	
Gehringer	43.0	
Terry	43.0	
Paul Waner	42.1	
Jimmy Foxx	41.3	
Dean	33.1	
Heilmann	33.1	
Bill Dickey	32.2	
Maranville	31.4	
Gabby Hartnett	27.3	
Joe Cronin	20.7	
Vance	19.0	
Schalk	18.2	
Tony Lazzeri	17.4	
Youngs	15.7	
Roush	14.0	
Lefty Gomez	13.2	
Wheat	12.4	
Ted Lyons	12.4	

1949

BASEBALL WRITERS ASSOCIATION ELECTION

With nobody able to garner 75 percent of the votes, the second run-off was held which included the top 20 vote getters. Charlie Gehringer was the only selection holding off the challenge of Mel Ott who was in his first year of eligibility.

Number of writers voting . . . . 153 (187 in run-off)
Number of players receiving votes 98
Number of players receiving 10 percent or more of the votes 22
Number of Hall of Famers through 2009 21
Number of players who received 10 percent on the previous ballot . 17
Number of players elected to the Hall of Fame this year 1
Cumulative total 21

Player	Percentage of Votes	Percentage of Votes in Run-Off	Result
Gehringer	66.7	85.0	Elected
Mel Ott	61.4	68.4	
Simmons	58.2	40.6	
Dean	57.5	43.3	
Foxx	55.6	47.6	
Terry	52.9	25.7	
P. Waner	43.8	33.7	
Hank Greenberg	43.8	23.5	
Dickey	42.5	20.9	
Heilmann	38.6	27.8	
Maranville	37.9	20.9	
Hartnett	22.9	3.7	
Vance	21.6	8.0	
Cronin	21.6	8.6	
Lyons	19.0	7.5	
Jimmie Wilson	15.7	6.4	
Schalk	15.7	9.1	
Red Ruffing	14.4	2.1	
Lazzeri	13.1	3.2	
Youngs	13.1	5.9	
Gomez	11.1	—	
Pepper Martin	10.5	—	

HALL OF FAME COMMITTEE

Two pitchers were selected. Kid Nichols, a 361-game winner, and Mordecai Brown, who notched 239 career victories, were enshrined.

Kid Nichols	*Percentage of Votes*	*Rank*
Veterans Election, 1936	3.5	24th (tie)
Rank in 1949		7th (tie)

Results of Baseball Writers Association balloting:

Year	Percentage of Votes	Rank
1938	1.1	
1939	2.6	
1942	2.1	
1945	2.0	
1946	0.5	

Mordecai Brown—no votes in the 1936 Veterans Election
Results of Baseball Writers Association balloting:

Year	Percentage of Votes	Rank
1936	2.7	
1937	15.4	17th
1938	20.6	14th
1939	19.7	15th
1942	27.0	17th (tie)
1945	18.6	19th
1946	27.7	12th
1946 Run-Off	18.3	12th

The 1950s

1950

With almost the same cast of characters as in 1949, no one could harness enough support for election. While moving from second to the top slot, Ott fell short by 6.1 percent of the vote.

Number of writers voting 167
Number of players receiving votes 99
Number of players receiving 10 percent or more of the votes 18
Number of Hall of Famers through 2009 18
Number of players who received 10 percent on the previous ballot . 17
Number of players elected to the Hall of Fame this year 0
Cumulative total 21

Player	Percentage of Votes	Result
Ott	68.9	
Terry	62.9	
Foxx	61.7	
P. Waner	56.9	
Simmons	53.9	
Heilmann	52.1	
Dean	50.9	
Dickey	46.7	
Maranville	39.5	

Player	Percentage of Votes	Result
Greenberg	38.3	
Hartnett	32.3	
Vance	31.1	
Lyons	25.1	
Cronin	19.8	
Lazzeri	12.6	
Gomez	10.8	
Zack Wheat	10.2	
Youngs	10.2	

1951

Mel Ott repeated his first place finish of the previous year but this time acquired enough votes for election. Jimmy Foxx moved up a notch from third to second place to also gain admission. At the time of their election, Foxx was second on the all-time home run list with 534 and Ott third with 511.

Number of writers voting 226
Number of players receiving votes 86
Number of players receiving 10 percent or more of the votes 21
Number of Hall of Famers through 2009 20
Number of players who received 10 percent on the previous ballot . 17
Number of players elected to the Hall of Fame this year 2
Cumulative total 23

Player	Percentage of Votes	Result
Ott	87.2	Elected
Foxx	79.2	Elected
P. Waner	71.7	
Heilmann	67.7	
Terry	65.5	
Dean	64.2	
Dickey	52.2	
Simmons	· 51.3	
Maranville	48.7	
Lyons	31.4	
Vance	31.0	
Greenberg	29.6	
Hartnett	25.2	
Cronin	19.5	
Ray Schalk	16.4	
Chief Bender	15.5	
Youngs	15.0	
Max Carey	11.9	
Lazzeri	11.9	
Hank Gowdy	11.5	
Gomez	10.2	

1952

Paul Waner and Harry Heilmann moved up from third and fourth place in 1951 into the top two positions to gain election.

Number of writers voting 234
Number of players receiving votes 75
Number of players receiving 10 percent or more of the votes 23
Number of Hall of Famers through 2009 21
Number of players who received 10 percent on the previous ballot . 17
Number of players elected to the Hall of Fame this year 2
Cumulative total 25

Player	Percentage of Votes	Result
Heilmann	86.8	Elected
P. Waner	83.3	Elected
Terry	66.2	
Dean	65.0	
Simmons	60.3	
Dickey	59.4	
Maranville	56.8	
Vance	44.9	
Lyons	43.2	
Hartnett	32.9	
Greenberg	32.1	
Bender	29.9	
Cronin	20.5	
Schalk	18.8	
Carey	15.4	
Youngs	14.5	
Gowdy	14.5	
Martin	13.2	
Wheat	12.8	
Gomez	12.4	
Lazzeri	12.4	
Casey Stengel	11.5	
Roush	10.3	

1953

BASEBALL WRITERS ASSOCIATION ELECTION

The players who occupied the third through ninth spots in 1952 moved up to take over the top seven positions in 1953. This showed a continuation of a pattern of consistency among the voters.

Number of writers voting 264
Number of players receiving votes 83
Number of players receiving 10 percent or more of the votes 23

Number of Hall of Famers through 2009 21
Number of players who received 10 percent on the previous ballot . 21
Number of players elected to the Hall of Fame this year 2
Cumulative total 27

Player	Percentage of Votes	Result
Dean	79.2	Elected
Simmons	75.4	Elected
Terry	72.3	
Dickey	67.8	
Maranville	62.1	
Vance	56.8	
Lyons	52.7	
Joe DiMaggio	44.3	
Bender	39.4	Elected by Veterans' Committee, 1953
Hartnett	39.4	
Greenberg	38.5	
Cronin	26.1	
Stengel	23.1	
Gowdy	22.0	
Carey	20.8	
Schalk	19.7	
Martin	16.3	
Hack Wilson	16.3	
Gomez	13.3	
Wheat	12.1	
Roush	12.1	
Youngs	11.7	
Lazzeri	10.6	

VETERANS' COMMITTEE

In July of 1953 an eleven-member Veterans' Committee was established which considered players who had been retired 25 years or more. The two receiving the required 75 percent vote were Chief Bender and Bobby Wallace.

Chief Bender—no votes in the 1936 Veterans Election
Results of Baseball Writers Association balloting:

Year	Percentage of Votes	Rank
1936	0.9	
1937	8.5	
1938	12.6	22nd
1939	14.6	18th
1942	23.6	22nd
1945	16.2	22nd
1946	19.3	20th (tie)
1946 Run-Off	13.3	17th
1947	44.7	10th
1948	4.1	

Year	Percentage of Votes	Rank
1949	1.3	
1949 Run-Off	0.0	
1950	3.6	
1951	15.5	16th
1952	29.9	12th
1953	39.4	9th (tie)

Bobby Wallace	Percentage of Votes	Rank
Veterans Election, 1936	1.3	35th (tie)
Rank in 1953		15th (tie)

Results of Baseball Writers Association voting:

Year	Percentage of Votes	Rank
1937	0.5	
1938	2.7	
1939	1.8	
1942	0.9	
1945	1.2	

1954

Terry, Dickey and Maranville, who finished third, fourth and fifth behind last year's two inductees, moved into the top three positions and achieved the required percentage of votes for election.

Number of writers voting 252
Number of players receiving votes 53
Number of players receiving 10 percent or more of the votes 19
Number of Hall of Famers through 2009 18
Number who received 10 percent on the previous ballot 18
Number of players elected to the Hall of Fame this year 3
Cumulative total 30

Player	Percentage of Votes	Result
Maranville	82.9	Elected
Dickey	80.2	Elected
Terry	77.4	Elected
J. DiMaggio	69.4	
Lyons	67.5	
Vance	62.7	
Hartnett	59.9	
Greenberg	38.5	
Cronin	33.7	
Carey	21.8	
Schalk	21.4	
Roush	20.6	
Gowdy	20.2	

Player	Percentage of Votes	Result
H. Wilson	19.0	
Gomez	15.1	
Youngs	13.5	
Wheat	13.1	
Lazzeri	11.9	
Red Ruffing	11.5	

1955

BASEBALL WRITERS ASSOCIATION ELECTION

The first twelve places in this election were occupied by the same players who finished fourth through fifteenth in the previous year's election, again a testimonial to the remarkable consistency shown by the Baseball Writers' Association.

Number of writers voting 251
Number of players receiving votes 65
Number of players receiving 10 percent or more of the votes 25
Number of Hall of Famers through 2009 22
Number of players who received 10 percent on the previous ballot . 16
Number of players elected to the Hall of Fame this year 4
Cumulative Total 34

Player	Percentage of Votes	Result
J. DiMaggio	88.8	Elected
Lyons	86.5	Elected
Vance	81.7	Elected
Hartnett	77.7	Elected
Greenberg	62.5	
Cronin	53.8	
Carey	47.4	
Schalk	45.0	Elected by Veterans' Committee, 1955
Roush	38.6	
Gowdy	35.9	
H. Wilson	32.3	
Gomez	28.3	
Lazzeri	26.3	
Ruffing	23.9	
Wheat	20.3	
Youngs	19.1	
Rube Marquard	13.9	
Kiki Cuyler	13.9	
Duffy Lewis	13.5	
Waite Hoyt	13.1	
Sam Rice	11.2	
Red Faber	10.8	
Jim Bottomley	10.4	

Player	Percentage of Votes	Result
Chuck Klein	10.0	
Dickie Kerr	10.0	

VETERANS' COMMITTEE

Ray Schalk and Frank "Home Run" Baker were elected after receiving Baseball Writers Association support since the initial 1936 balloting. Schalk received votes in sixteen consecutive elections as follows:

Year	Percentage of Votes	Rank
1936	1.8	
1937	11.9	19th
1938	17.2	17th
1939	12.8	19th
1942	22.7	23rd
1945	13.4	23rd
1946	17.8	22nd
1946 Run-Off	0.0	
1947	31.1	12th (tie)
1948	18.2	15th
1949	15.7	16th (tie)
1949 Run-Off	9.1	12th
1950	9.6	
1951	16.4	15th
1952	18.8	14th
1953	19.7	16th
1954	21.4	11th
1955	45.0	8th

Baker had limited support in eleven elections peaking in 1947 and then tailing off markedly, as shown in the following table:

Year	Percentage of Votes	Rank
1936	0.4	
1937	6.5	
1938	12.2	23rd
1939	10.9	24th
1942	16.7	25th
1945	10.5	27th
1946	19.3	20th (tie)
1946 Run-Off	13.7	16th
1947	30.4	14th
1948	3.3	
1949	0.0	
1949 Run-Off	0.0	
1950	2.4	
1951	3.5	

1956

Only the Baseball Writers voted in 1956. Once again, the "on deck" syndrome was repeated with Greenberg and Cronin moving up from fifth and sixth in the previous election to gain Hall of Fame entrance.

Number of writers voting 193
Number of players receiving votes 103
Number of players receiving 10 percent or more of the votes 20
Number of Hall of Famers through 2009 19
Number of players who received 10 percent on the previous ballot . 16
Number of players elected to the Hall of Fame this year 2
Cumulative total 36

Player	Percentage of Votes	Result
Greenberg	85.0	Elected
Cronin	78.8	Elected
Ruffing	50.3	
Roush	47.2	
Gomez	46.1	
H. Wilson	38.3	
Carey	33.7	
Lazzeri	33.2	
Cuyler	28.5	
Gowdy	25.4	
Rice	23.3	
Klein	22.8	
Bottomley	21.8	
Hoyt	19.2	
Faber	17.6	
Joe Medwick	16.1	
Eppa Rixey	14.0	
Wheat	13.5	
Goose Goslin	13.5	
Burleigh Grimes	13.0	

1957

The Veterans' Committee elected Sam Crawford, an outfielder, who despite imposing credentials had garnered little voting support from the Baseball Writers Association.

Year	Percentage of Votes	Rank
1936	0.4	
1937	2.5	
1938	4.2	
1939	2.2	
1942	0.9	
1945	1.6	
1946	4.5	

1958

The Baseball Writers Association failed to elect a candidate in the widest dispersion of votes to date. Max Carey led the list with only 51.1 percent of the votes. Eleven players received 10 percent of the vote in their first time on the ballot.

Number of writers voting 266
Number of players receiving votes 152
Number of players receiving 10 percent or more of the votes 28
Number of Hall of Famers through 2009 23
Number of players who received 10 percent on the previous ballot . 16
Number of players elected to the Hall of Fame this year 0
Cumulative total 36

Player	Percentage of Votes	Result
Carey	51.1	
Roush	42.1	
Ruffing	37.2	
H. Wilson	35.3	
Cuyler	33.8	
Rice	33.8	
Lazzeri	30.1	
Luke Appling	28.9	
Gomez	28.6	
Grimes	26.7	
Faber	25.6	
Lou Boudreau	24.1	
Bottomley	21.4	
Medwick	18.8	
Martin	17.3	
Gowdy	16.9	
Bucky Harris	16.9	
Dave Bancroft	16.2	
Lloyd Waner	14.7	
Hoyt	13.9	
Klein	13.5	
Johnny Vander Meer	13.2	
Stan Coveleski	12.8	
Earle Combs	12.8	
Al Lopez	12.6	
Bucky Walters	12.4	
Rixey	12.0	
Lefty O'Doul	10.2	

1959

Zack Wheat with 2,884 hits and a .317 batting average compiled over 19 seasons was the sole selection of the Veterans' Committee. He received little support for 6 years and for the next 10 years ranged between 8.4 percent and 23.0 percent of the vote.

Year	Percentage of Votes	Rank
1937	2.5	
1938	2.7	
1939	1.5	
1942	1.3	
1945	0.8	
1946	3.0	
1946 Run-Off	0.0	
1947	23.0	16th
1948	12.4	20th (tie)
1949	9.8	
1949 Run-Off	0.0	
1950	10.2	17th (tie)
1951	8.4	
1952	12.8	19th
1953	12.1	20th (tie)
1954	13.1	17th
1955	20.3	15th
1956	13.5	18th

The 1960s

1960

History repeated itself with the same number of players as in 1958 getting at least 10 percent but nobody coming close to the required 75 percent. Max Carey who led in 1958 was dropped from the ballot in 1960 and replaced by Edd Roush who had finished behind Carey in 1958.

Number of writers voting 269
Number of players receiving votes 131
Number of players receiving 10 percent or more of the vote 28
Number of Hall of Famers through 2009 22
Number of players who received 10 percent on the previous ballot . 23
Number of players elected to the Hall of Fame this year 0
Cumulative total 36

Player	Percentage of Votes	Result
Roush	54.3	
Rice	53.2	
Rixey	52.8	
Grimes	34.2	
Bottomley	33.1	
Ruffing	32.0	
Faber	30.9	
Appling	26.8	

Player	Percentage of Votes	Result
Cuyler	26.8	
H. Wilson	26.8	
Lazzeri	21.9	
Gomez	19.0	
O'Doul	16.7	
Johnny Mize	16.7	
Combs	16.0	
Gowdy	14.1	
Medwick	14.1	
Klein	13.8	
Marty Marion	13.8	
Boudreau	13.0	
Vander Meer	11.5	
Harris	11.5	
Bancroft	11.2	
Goose Goslin	11.2	
Martin	10.8	
Chick Hafey	10.8	
Hoyt	10.8	
Jimmy Dykes	10.0	

1961

Of the two players selected by the Veterans' Committee, Max Carey seemed an obvious choice because of his high placement in previous Baseball Writers Association balloting.

Year	Percentage of Votes	Rank
1937	3.0	
1938	2.3	
1939	2.6	
1942	0.0	
1945	0.4	
1946	0.0	
1947	0.0	
1948	7.4	
1949	7.8	
1950	8.4	
1951	11.9	18th (tie)
1952	15.4	15th
1953	20.8	15th
1954	21.8	10th
1955	47.4	7th
1956	33.7	7th
1958	51.1	1st

Billy Hamilton, a bona-fide old-timer (1888–1901), received scant voter support.

	Percentage of Vote	Rank
1936 Veterans Election	2.6	28th (tie)
Rank in 1961		10th (tie)

Results of Baseball Writers Association voting:

Year	Percentage of Votes
1942	0.4

1962

BASEBALL WRITERS ASSOCIATION ELECTION

When Bob Feller and Jackie Robinson were elected it marked the first time, since the original 1936 ballot, that players were inducted in their first year of eligibility. Feller, at the time, was third on the all-time strikeout list behind Walter Johnson and Cy Young. The dynamic Robinson, besides breaking the color barrier in 1947 as a 28-year-old rookie, packed a remarkable career into 10 years.

```
Number of writers voting . . . . . . . . . . . . . . . . . . . . . . . . . . . . . . . . . 160
Number of players receiving votes . . . . . . . . . . . . . . . . . . . . . . . . . . 77
Number of players receiving 10 percent or more of the votes . . . . . 17
Number of Hall of Famers through 2009 . . . . . . . . . . . . . . . . . . . . . 16
Number of players who received 10 percent on the previous ballot . 14*
Number of players elected to the Hall of Fame this year . . . . . . . . . . 2
Cumulative total . . . . . . . . . . . . . . . . . . . . . . . . . . . . . . . . . . . . . . . . . . 38
```
Feller and Robinson not eligible in 1960

Player	Percentage of Votes	Result
Bob Feller	93.8	Elected
Jackie Robinson	77.5	Elected
Rice	50.6	Elected by Veterans' Committee in 1963
Ruffing	45.0	
Rixey	30.6	Elected by Veterans' Committee in 1963
Appling	30.0	
Phil Rizzuto	27.5	
Grimes	26.9	
Wilson	24.4	
Medwick	21.3	
Cuyler	19.4	
Faber	18.8	
Gomez	12.5	
Bottomley	12.5	
Klein	11.3	
Hoyt	11.3	
Marion	10.0	

VETERANS' COMMITTEE

Edd Roush, also in his first year of eligibility for consideration by the Veterans' Committee, was the only player selected. Roush had the distinction of receiving votes in every Baseball Writers Association election through 1960 although his popularity did not grow until the last five elections.

Year	Percentage of Votes	Rank
1936	0.9	
1937	5.0	
1938	3.4	
1939	2.9	
1942	0.4	
1945	2.0	
1946	5.4	
1946 Run-Off	0.0	
1947	15.5	19th
1948	14.0	18th
1949	9.2	
1949 Run-Off	0.0	
1950	9.6	
1951	9.3	
1952	10.3	23rd
1953	12.1	20th (tie)
1954	20.6	12th
1955	38.6	9th
1956	47.2	4th
1958	42.1	2nd
1960	54.3	1st

1963

The number of years a player had to be retired before being considered by the Veterans' Committee was reduced from 30 to 20 years, which made Sam Rice and Eppa Rixey eligible for induction. John Clarkson, who finished his career in 1894 with 326 career victories, was third among all-time winners not yet in the Hall of Fame. Elmer Flick, a speedy outfielder with a career batting average of .313 over 13 seasons, was elected despite virtually no prior voter support.

Sam Rice:

Year	Percentage of Votes	Rank
1938	0.4	
1948	0.8	
1949	2.0	
1950	0.6	
1951	0.4	
1952	0.4	

Year	Percentage of Votes	Rank
1953	1.1	
1954	3.6	
1955	11.2	21st
1956	23.3	11th
1958	33.8	5th (tie)
1960	53.2	2nd
1962	50.6	3rd

Eppa Rixey:

Year	Percentage of Votes	Rank
1937	0.5	
1938	0.8	
1945	0.4	
1947	1.2	
1948	4.1	
1949	2.6	
1950	3.6	
1951	2.2	
1952	1.3	
1953	1.1	
1954	2.0	
1955	3.2	
1956	14.0	17th
1958	12.0	27th
1960	52.8	3rd
1962	30.6	5th

John Clarkson	Percentage of Votes	Rank
1936 Veterans Election	6.4	20th (tie)
Rank in 1963		6th

Baseball Writers Association balloting:

Year	Percentage of Votes
1946	0.5

Elmer Flick:

Year	Percentage of Votes
1938	0.4

1964

BASEBALL WRITERS ASSOCIATION ELECTION

In sharp contrast to previous elections only six players who achieved 10 percent on the 1962 ballot appeared on the 1964 ballot. Campanella and Reese in their first year of eligibility received strong support.

In a run-off election among the top 30, Luke Appling was elected. Although Red Ruffing received 81.4 percent of the votes, the rules provided for only one person to be selected in run-off elections.

Number of writers voting 201
Number of players receiving votes 59
Number of players receiving 10 percent or more of the votes 25
Number of Hall of Famers through 2009 19
Number of players who received 10 percent on the previous ballot . 6*
Number of players selected to the Hall of Fame this year 1
Cumulative total 39
*Campanella, Kell, Lemon and Reese not eligible in 1962.

Player	Percentage of Votes 1964	Percentage of Votes Run Off	Result
Appling	70.6	83.6	Elected
Ruffing	70.1	81.4	
Roy Campanella	57.2	61.1	
Medwick	53.7	57.5	
PeeWee Reese	36.3	20.8	
Boudreau	33.8	19.0	
Lopez	28.4	15.0	
Klein	27.9	8.0	
Mize	26.9	5.3	
Mel Harder	25.4	6.2	
Vander Meer	25.4	8.1	
Marion	24.9	7.5	
L. Waner	23.4	5.3	
Rizzuto	22.4	4.9	
Walters	17.4	3.5	
Allie Reynolds	17.4	2.7	
Ernie Lombardi	16.4	4.0	
George Kell	16.4	3.5	
Ralph Kiner	15.4	1.3	
Joe Gordon	14.9	0.4	
Billy Herman	12.9	4.0	
Hal Newhouser	12.9	1.3	
Bob Lemon	11.9	1.3	
Bobby Doerr	11.9	2.2	
Phil Cavaretta	10.9	0.4	

VETERANS' COMMITTEE

Of the five "veteran" inductees, Tim Keefe and Monte Ward completed their careers in 1893 and 1894 respectively while Faber (1933), Grimes (1934) and Manush (1939) represented a younger generation of veteran. Miller Huggins, who received strong support in the 1940's, was selected as a manager.

Monte Ward	*Percentage of Votes*	*Rank*
1936 Veterans Election	3.8	26th (tie)
Rank in 1964		7th (tie)

Tim Keefe	*Percentage of Votes*	*Rank*
1936 Veterans Election	1.3	35th (tie)
Rank in 1964		13th (tie)

Red Faber:

Year	*Percentage of Votes*	*Rank*
1937	1.5	
1938	0.4	
1939	1.1	
1942	0.4	
1948	2.5	
1949	3.9	
1950	5.4	
1951	3.5	
1952	3.8	
1953	3.4	
1954	4.8	
1955	10.8	22nd
1956	17.6	15th
1958	25.6	11th
1960	30.9	7th
1962	18.8	12th

Burleigh Grimes:

Year	*Percentage of Votes*	*Rank*
1937	0.5	
1938	0.4	
1939	0.4	
1948	5.8	
1949	5.2	
1950	3.6	
1951	2.2	
1952	3.8	
1953	3.4	
1955	1.2	
1956	13.0	20th
1958	26.7	10th
1960	34.2	4th
1962	26.9	8th

Miller Huggins:

Year	*Percentage of Votes*	*Rank*
1937	2.5	

Year	Percentage of Votes	Rank
1938	18.3	15th
1939	35.4	10th
1942	47.6	5th
1945	53.8	5th (tie)
1946	63.9	3rd
1946 Run Off	40.3	3rd (tie)
1948	3.3	
1950	1.2	

Heinie Manush:

Year	Percentage of Votes	Rank
1948	0.8	
1949	0.7	
1956	6.7	
1958	8.3	
1960	7.4	
1962	9.4	

1965

The sole Veterans' Committee selection was James "Pud" Galvin who pitched from 1879 until 1892 and notched 361 career wins. At the time of his election he had the most victories of any pitcher not already in the Hall of Fame. Galvin was ignored in the 1936 Veterans Election and was never considered by the Baseball Writers.

1966

BASEBALL WRITERS ASSOCIATION ELECTION

Despite his trials with sportswriters over a distinguished career interrupted by two stints in the Marine Air Corps, Ted Williams gained entrance in his first year of eligibility. His 93.4 percent was the largest vote received behind only Cobb, Ruth and Wagner in 1936 and Bob Feller in 1962.

```
Number of writers voting . . . . . . . . . . . . . . . . . . . . . . . . . . . . . . . . . 302
Number of players receiving votes  . . . . . . . . . . . . . . . . . . . . . . . . 49
Number of players receiving 10 percent or more of the votes  . . . . . 20
Number in Hall of Fame through 2009  . . . . . . . . . . . . . . . . . . . . . 15
Number of players receiving 10 percent on the previous ballot  . . . 17*
Number of players selected to the Hall of Fame this year . . . . . . . . . . 1
Cumulative total . . . . . . . . . . . . . . . . . . . . . . . . . . . . . . . . . . . . . . . 40
```
Williams and Slaughter not eligible in 1964

Player	Percentage of Votes	Result
Ted Williams	93.4	Elected
Ruffing	68.9	

Player	Percentage of Votes	Result
Campanella	65.2	
Medwick	61.9	
Boudreau	38.1	
Lopez	36.1	
Enos Slaughter	33.1	
Reese	31.5	
Marion	28.5	
Mize	26.8	
Kiner	24.5	
Vander Meer	23.8	
Reynolds	19.9	
Walters	18.5	
Rizzuto	17.9	
Arky Vaughan	11.9	
Harder	11.3	
Lombardi	11.3	
Newhouser	10.6	
Gordon	10.3	

VETERANS' COMMITTEE

No players in the Veterans category were able to muster the required three-fourths of the votes for election. Casey Stengel, who had received limited support, was selected as a manager.

Year	Percentage of Votes	Rank
1938	0.8	
1939	2.2	
1945	0.8	
1948	0.8	
1949	2.0	
1950	1.8	
1951	3.5	
1952	11.5	22nd
1953	23.1	13th

1967

BASEBALL WRITERS ASSOCIATION ELECTION

Red Ruffing nosed out Joe Medwick in a run-off by a scant 5.9 percent of the vote. The two had tied at 72.6 percent on the first ballot.

Number of writers voting 292
Number of players receiving votes 47
Number of players receiving 10 percent or more of the vote 24
Number in Hall of Fame through 2009 18
Number receiving 10 percent on the previous ballot 19
Number of players selected to the Hall of Fame this year 1
Cumulative total 41

Player	Percentage of Votes	Percentage of Votes in Run-Off	Result
Ruffing	72.6	86.9	Elected
Medwick	72.6	81.0	
Campanella	69.9	55.6	
Boudreau	49.0	22.2	
Kiner	42.5	13.4	
Slaughter	42.1	15.7	
Lopez	39.0	16.3	
Marion	30.8	7.2	
Mize	30.5	4.6	
Reese	30.5	5.2	
Vander Meer	29.8	11.4	
Reynolds	26.4	6.7	
Rizzuto	24.3	4.6	
Gordon	22.6	4.2	
Walters	22.3	7.8	
Newhouser	21.3	4.2	
Herman	20.2	4.6	
Harder	17.8	4.6	
Vaughan	15.8	6.2	
Lombardi	14.7	8.2	
Kell	13.7	3.6	
Alvin Dark	13.0	2.3	
Lemon	12.0	2.3	
Doerr	12.0	4.9	

VETERANS' COMMITTEE

Lloyd Waner (1927–1945) who became eligible in 1966 was the only selection in 1967. In 18 years he accumulated 2,459 hits and a .316 batting average.

Year	Percentage of Votes	Rank
1949	2.0	
1950	0.6	
1951	0.4	
1952	0.9	
1956	9.3	
1958	14.7	19th
1960	8.2	
1962	3.1	
1964	23.4	13th
1964 Run-Off	5.3	12th (tie)

1968

BASEBALL WRITERS ASSOCIATION ELECTION

Joe Medwick, after his close defeat in the 1967 run-off, this time led the voting. Over 17 years he collected 2,471 hits to go with a .324 batting average.

Number of writers voting 283
Number of players receiving votes 48
Number of players receiving 10 percent or more of the votes 20
Number in the Hall of Fame through 2009 14
Number receiving 10 percent on the previous ballot 19
Number of players selected to the Hall of Fame this year 1
Cumulative total 42

Player	Percentage of Votes	Result
Medwick	84.8	Elected
Campanella	72.4	
Boudreau	51.6	
Slaughter	45.6	
Kiner	41.7	
Mize	36.4	
Reynolds	33.6	
Marion	31.4	
Vaughan	29.0	
Reese	28.6	
Vander Meer	27.9	
Gordon	27.2	
Rizzuto	26.1	
Walters	23.7	
Newhouser	23.7	
Doerr	17.0	
Kell	16.6	
Lemon	16.6	
Dark	12.7	
Terry Moore	11.7	

VETERANS' COMMITTEE

Kiki Cuyler and Goose Goslin, a pair of 18-year outfielders, each with over 2,200 hits and .300 batting averages, were the only inductees.

Kiki Cuyler:

Year	Percentage of Votes	Rank
1948	2.5	
1949	2.6	
1950	6.6	
1951	3.5	
1952	4.3	
1953	6.8	
1954	7.9	
1955	13.9	18th (tie)
1956	28.5	9th
1958	33.8	5th
1960	26.8	8th (tie)
1962	19.4	11th

Goose Goslin:

Year	Percentage of Votes	Rank
1948	0.8	
1949	2.6	
1950	1.2	
1954	0.4	
1955	2.8	
1956	13.5	18th (tie)
1958	9.8	
1960	11.2	23rd (tie)
1962	8.8	

1969

BASEBALL WRITERS ASSOCIATION ELECTION

Stan Musial, in his first year on the ballot, received a resounding 93.2 percent of the vote. Roy Campanella, after six strong showings, was elected on his seventh try. The second through seventh positions were occupied by the same persons as the previous election although not in the same order.

Number of writers voting 340
Number of players receiving votes 46
Number of players receiving 10 percent or more of the votes 22
Number in the Hall of Fame through 2009 15
Number receiving 10 percent on the previous ballot 16*
Number of players elected to the Hall of Fame this year 2
Cumulative total 44
*Musial, Wynn, Hodges and Schoendienst not eligible in 1968.

Player	Percentage of Votes	Result
Stan Musial	93.2	Elected
Campanella	79.4	Elected
Boudreau	64.1	
Kiner	40.3	
Slaughter	37.6	
Mize	34.1	
Marion	32.9	
Reynolds	28.8	
Gordon	28.5	
Vander Meer	27.9	
Early Wynn	27.9	
Reese	26.2	
Gil Hodges	24.1	
Newhouser	24.1	
Rizzuto	22.9	
Red Schoendienst	19.1	
Doerr	18.2	
Kell	17.6	

Player	Percentage of Votes	Result
Lemon	16.5	
Tommy Henrich	14.7	
Dark	14.1	
Cavaretta	10.9	

VETERANS' COMMITTEE

Waite Hoyt and Stan Coveleski, pitchers who won 237 and 215, games respectively, were the 1969 selections.

Waite Hoyt:

Year	Percentage of Votes	Rank
1939	0.4	
1942	0.4	
1946	0.5	
1948	5.8	
1949	4.6	
1950	6.6	
1951	5.8	
1952	5.1	
1953	5.3	
1954	5.6	
1955	13.1	20th
1956	19.2	14th
1958	13.9	20th
1960	10.8	25th (tie)
1962	11.3	15th

Stan Coveleski:

Year	Percentage of Votes	Rank
1938	0.4	
1948	1.7	
1949	2.0	
1950	0.6	
1958	12.8	23rd (tie)

The 1970s

1970

BASEBALL WRITERS ASSOCIATION ELECTION

Lou Boudreau, in his tenth year on the ballot, was the only selection, moving up from a third place finish the previous year.

Number of writers voting 300
Number of players receiving votes 46

Number of players receiving 10 percent or more of the votes 21
Number in the Hall of Fame through 2009 14
Number receiving 10 percent on the previous ballot 20*
Number of players elected to the Hall of Fame this year 1
Cumulative total 45

*Snider not eligible in 1969

Player	Percentage of Votes	Result
Boudreau	77.3	Elected
Kiner	55.7	
Hodges	48.3	
Wynn	46.7	
Slaughter	44.3	
Mize	42.0	
Marion	40.0	
Reese	32.3	
Schoendienst	32.3	
Kell	30.0	
Reynolds	29.7	
Vander Meer	29.3	
Newhouser	26.7	
Rizzuto	26.3	
Gordon	26.3	
Doerr	25.0	
Lemon	23.3	
Henrich	20.7	
Dark	18.3	
Cavaretta	17.0	
Duke Snider	17.0	

VETERANS' COMMITTEE

Earle Combs, an outfielder with the fabled New York Yankees of the
'20s and '30s, with a career .325 batting average and Jesse Haines, a pitcher
who won 215 games over 19 years, were the two selections of the Veterans'
Committee.

Earle Combs:

Year	Percentage of Votes	Rank
1937	2.0	
1938	2.7	
1939	1.1	
1945	0.4	
1948	5.0	
1949	3.9	
1950	1.8	
1952	0.4	
1953	1.1	
1955	0.4	

Year	Percentage of Votes	Rank
1956	7.3	
1958	12.8	23rd (tie)
1960	16.0	15th
1962	3.8	

Jesse Haines:

Year	Percentage of Votes	Rank
1939	0.4	
1947	0.6	
1948	1.7	
1949	1.3	
1950	6.6	
1953	1.5	
1954	2.4	
1955	4.0	
1956	7.3	
1958	8.3	
1960	7.4	
1962	1.9	

1971

BASEBALL WRITERS ASSOCIATION ELECTION

Yogi Berra, in his first year on the ballot, led the voting but fell short of the 75 percent requirement. Positions two through fourteen were filled by the same thirteen players in the 1970 and 1971 elections.

Number of writers voting 360
Number of players receiving votes 48
Number of players receiving 10 percent or more of the votes 20
Number in Hall of Fame through 2009 14
Number who received 10% on the previous ballot 18*
Number of players elected to Hall of Fame this year 0
Cumulative total 45
Berra and Fox not eligible in 1970

Player	Percentage of Votes	Result
Yogi Berra	67.2	
Wynn	66.7	
Kiner	58.9	
Hodges	50.0	
Slaughter	45.8	
Mize	43.6	
Reese	35.3	
Marion	34.2	
Schoendienst	34.2	
Reynolds	30.6	

Player	Percentage of Votes	Result
Kell	29.2	
Vander Meer	27.2	
Newhouser	26.1	
Rizzuto	25.6	
Lemon	25.0	
Snider	24.7	
Cavaretta	23.1	
Doerr	21.7	
Dark	15.0	
Nelson Fox	10.8	

VETERANS' COMMITTEE

A bumper crop of six veterans were selected whose combined careers covered the years 1888 through 1937.

Jake Beckley	Percentage of votes	Rank
1936 Veterans Election	1.3	35th (tie)
Rank in 1971		12th (tie)

Baseball Writers Association voting:

Year	Percentage of Votes	Rank
1942	0.4	

Joe Kelley:

Year	Percentage of Votes	Rank
1939	0.4	
1942	0.4	

Rube Marquard:

Year	Percentage of Votes	Rank
1936	0.4	
1937	6.5	
1938	3.8	
1939	1.5	
1946	3.0	
1947	11.2	21st
1948	5.0	
1949	2.6	
1951	1.3	
1952	3.8	
1953	7.2	
1954	6.0	
1955	13.9	17th (tie)

Harry Hooper:

Year	Percentage of Votes	Rank
1937	3.0	
1938	1.5	
1939	1.8	
1948	1.7	
1950	1.2	
1951	1.3	

Dave Bancroft:

Year	Percentage of Votes	Rank
1937	1.5	
1938	1.1	
1939	0.4	
1946	0.5	
1948	3.3	
1949	3.3	
1950	5.4	
1951	4.0	
1952	4.7	
1953	3.8	
1954	4.0	
1955	7.6	
1956	7.8	
1958	16.2	18th
1960	11.2	23rd (tie)

Chick Hafey:

Year	Percentage of Votes	Rank
1948	0.8	
1949	1.3	
1950	2.4	
1951	0.4	
1952	0.4	
1953	0.8	
1954	0.8	
1955	1.6	
1956	8.3	
1958	4.5	
1960	10.8	25th (tie)
1962	4.4	

1972

BASEBALL WRITERS ASSOCIATION ELECTION

Sandy Koufax, the dominant pitcher of his era, was honored his first year on the ballot. His 2.76 earned run average, .655 winning percentage and 9.28 strikeouts per nine innings convinced the writers. Berra, elected in his second try, had collected 2,150 hits and 358 home runs at the time, highest among catchers. Early Wynn was one of two 300-game winners, then eligible, and was selected on his fifth try.

Number of writers voting 396
Number of players receiving votes 46
Number of players receiving 10 percent or more of the votes 19
Number in Hall of Fame through 2009 14
Number who received 10 percent on the previous ballot 18*
Number of players elected to the Hall of Fame this year 3
Cumulative total 48
*Koufax not eligible in 1971

Player	Percentage of Votes	Result
Sandy Koufax	86.9	Elected
Berra	85.6	Elected
Wynn	76.0	Elected
Kiner	59.3	
Hodges	40.7	
Mize	39.6	
Slaughter	37.6	
Reese	32.6	
Marion	30.3	
Lemon	29.5	
Kell	29.0	
Reynolds	26.5	
Schoendienst	26.3	
Rizzuto	26.0	
Newhouser	23.2	
Snider	21.2	
Fox	16.2	
Cavaretta	15.4	
Dark	13.9	

VETERANS' COMMITTEE

Lefty Gomez, after 15 years on the Baseball Writers Association ballot, was recognized by the Committee. Ross Youngs, after 17 years of votes extending from 1936 through 1956, was also selected.

Lefty Gomez:

Year	Percentage of Votes	Rank
1945	2.8	
1946	2.0	
1947	0.6	
1948	13.2	19th
1949	11.1	21st

Year	Percentage of Votes	Rank
1950	10.8	16th
1951	10.2	21st
1952	12.4	20th (tie)
1953	13.3	19th
1954	15.1	15th
1955	28.3	12th
1956	46.1	5th
1958	28.6	9th
1960	19.0	12th
1962	12.5	13th (tie)

Ross Youngs:

Year	Percentage of Votes	Rank
1936	4.4	
1937	8.0	
1938	15.3	18th
1939	12.4	20th
1942	18.9	24th
1945	8.9	
1946	12.4	27th
1947	22.4	17th
1948	15.7	17th
1949	13.1	20th
1949 Run-Off	5.9	17th
1950	10.2	17th (tie)
1951	15.0	17th
1952	14.5	16th (tie)
1953	11.7	22nd
1954	13.5	16th
1955	19.1	16th
1956	9.8	

1973

BASEBALL WRITERS ASSOCIATION ELECTION

In his first season on the ballot, Warren Spahn, the winningest left-handed pitcher of all time, was elected to the Hall of Fame. Another lefty of the same talent, Whitey Ford, finished second but with too few votes to qualify.

Following his tragic death in a plane crash December 31, 1972, Roberto Clemente received 92.7 percent of the vote in a special election held in March 1973.

Number of writers voting 380
Number of players receiving votes 44
Number of players receiving 10 percent or more of the votes 21

Number in Hall of Fame through 2009 14
Number who received 10 percent on the previous ballot 16*
Number of players elected to the Hall of Fame this year 2
Cumulative total 50

*Spahn, Ford and Roberts not eligible in 1972.

Player	Percentage of Votes	Result
Warren Spahn	83.2	Elected
Whitey Ford	67.1	
Kiner	61.8	
Hodges	57.4	
Robin Roberts	56.1	
Lemon	46.6	
Mize	41.3	
Slaughter	38.2	
Marion	33.4	
Reese	33.2	
Kell	30.0	
Rizzuto	29.2	
Snider	26.6	
Schoendienst	25.3	
Reynolds	24.5	
Newhouser	20.8	
Cavaretta	19.2	
Fox	19.2	
Dark	13.9	
Johnny Sain	12.4	
Dominic DiMaggio	11.3	

VETERANS' COMMITTEE

Mickey Welch, a real old-timer, who pitched from 1880 to 1892 and the only 300-game winner not yet in the Hall of Fame, was elected. The other inductee, George Kelly, batted .297 in a 16-year career.

Mickey Welch—For unknown reasons, Welch was overlooked in the 1936 Veterans Election and because he retired after the 1892 season, was never considered by the Baseball Writers.

George Kelly:

Year	Percentage of Votes	Rank
1947	0.6	
1948	1.7	
1949	0.7	
1956	1.0	
1958	0.8	
1960	1.9	
1962	0.6	

1974

BASEBALL WRITERS ASSOCIATION ELECTION

Long-time teammates Mickey Mantle and Whitey Ford entered the Hall of Fame together, Mantle on his first try and Ford on his second.

Number of writers voting 365
Number of players receiving votes 44
Number of players receiving 10 percent or more of the votes 21
Number in Hall of Fame through 2009 15
Number who received 10% on the previous ballot 17*
Number of players elected to the Hall of Fame this year 2
Cumulative total 52
Mantle, Mathews and Maris not eligible in 1973.

Player	Percentage of Votes	Result
Mickey Mantle	88.2	Elected
Ford	77.8	Elected
Roberts	61.4	
Kiner	58.9	
Hodges	54.2	
Lemon	52.1	
Slaughter	39.7	
Reese	38.6	
Eddie Mathews	32.3	
Rizzuto	30.4	
Snider	30.4	
Schoendienst	30.1	
Reynolds	27.7	
Kell	25.8	
Fox	21.6	
Roger Maris	21.4	
Newhouser	20.0	
Cavaretta	16.7	
Richie Ashburn	15.3	
Dark	14.8	
Sain	14.0	

VETERANS' COMMITTEE

Sam Thompson (1885–1906) and Jim Bottomley (1922–1937) were selected for enshrinement in 1974. Thompson had a career batting average of .331 while Bottomley batted .310 and collected 2,313 lifetime hits.

Sam Thompson—Thompson, like several others, was overlooked in the 1936 Veterans Election and was never considered in any of the Baseball Writers voting.

Jim Bottomley:

Year	Percentage of Votes	Rank
1948	3.3	
1949	5.2	
1950	4.8	
1951	2.7	
1952	3.0	
1953	3.8	
1954	6.3	
1955	10.4	23rd
1956	21.8	13th
1958	21.4	13th
1960	33.1	5th
1962	12.5	13th (tie)

1975

BASEBALL WRITERS ASSOCIATION ELECTION

Ralph Kiner, in his twelfth year on the ballot, climaxed a steady climb in popularity by winning election by a scant 0.4 percent.

Number of writers voting 362
Number of players receiving votes 37
Number of players receiving 10 percent or more of the votes 20
Number in Hall of Fame through 2009 14
Number who received 10 percent on previous ballot 18*
Number of players elected to the Hall of Fame this year 1
Cumulative total 53
*Drysdale not eligible in 1974.

Player	Percentage of Votes	Result
Kiner	75.4	Elected
Roberts	72.7	
Lemon	64.4	
Hodges	51.9	
Slaughter	48.9	
Newhouser	42.8	
Reese	42.5	
Mathews	40.9	
Cavaretta	35.6	
Snider	35.6	
Sain	34.0	
Rizzuto	32.3	
Kell	31.5	
Schoendienst	26.0	
Fox	21.0	
Ashburn	21.0	
Don Drysdale	21.0	

Player	Percentage of Votes	Result
Maris	19.3	
Dark	13.3	
Vic Raschi	10.2	

VETERANS' COMMITTEE

Earl Averill with 2,020 career hits and a .318 batting average was joined in the Hall of Fame by Billy Herman with 2,345 hits and a .304 average.

Bucky Harris, who had a 29-year managerial career, was selected to the Hall of Fame in that category.

Earl Averill:

Year	Percentage of Votes	Rank
1949	0.7	
1952	0.9	
1955	0.8	
1956	1.6	
1958	5.3	
1960	4.1	
1962	1.9	

Billy Herman:

Year	Percentage of Votes	Rank
1948	0.8	
1956	1.0	
1958	2.6	
1962	2.5	
1964	12.9	21st (tie)
1964 Run-Off	4.0	15th (tie)
1966	9.3	
1967	20.2	17th
1967 Run-Off	4.6	16th (tie)

Bucky Harris:

Year	Percentage of Votes	Rank
1938	0.4	
1939	0.4	
1948	2.5	
1949	7.2	
1949 Run-Off	no votes	
1950	2.4	
1951	4.0	
1952	5.1	
1953	8.0	

Year	Percentage of Votes	Rank
1958	16.9	16th (tie)
1960	11.5	21st

1976

BASEBALL WRITERS ASSOCIATION ELECTION

Robin Roberts, one of the greatest modern-era control pitchers with 286 career wins, and Bob Lemon, with 207 wins and a .618 winning percentage, were elected by the writers. Five players received over 10 percent of the vote on their first time on the ballot and occupied the 16th through 20th positions in the election.

Number of writers voting 388
Number of players receiving votes 32
Number of players receiving 10 percent or more of the votes 20
Number of players in the Hall of Fame through 2009 12
Number who received 10 percent on previous ballot 15
Number of players elected to the Hall of Fame this year 2
Cumulative total 55

Player	Percentage of Votes	Result
Roberts	86.9	Elected
Lemon	78.6	Elected
Hodges	60.1	
Slaughter	50.8	
Mathews	48.7	
Reese	47.9	
Fox	44.8	
Snider	41.0	
Rizzuto	38.4	
Kell	33.2	
Schoendienst	33.2	
Drysdale	29.4	
Maris	22.4	
Ashburn	21.9	
Dark	21.3	
Walker Cooper	14.4	
Elston Howard	14.2	
Mickey Vernon	13.4	
Ted Kluszewski	12.9	
Don Larsen	12.1	

VETERANS' COMMITTEE

Roger Connor (1880–1897) one of the early power hitters who collected 2,467 hits to go with a .317 batting average, was selected. The other inductee was Freddie Lindstrom who batted .311 in a 13-year career.

Roger Connor—Connor, surprisingly, received no votes in the initial Veterans Election and, because of his pre–1900 retirement, was never considered by the Baseball Writers.

Freddie Lindstrom:

Year	Percentage of Votes	Rank
1949	0.7	
1956	1.6	
1958	1.9	
1960	2.2	
1962	4.4	

1977

BASEBALL WRITERS ASSOCIATION ELECTION

"Mr. Cub" Ernie Banks was elected after 19 distinguished years in which he collected 2,583 hits and 512 home-runs. Banks was in his first year of eligibility, a tribute to his great skills as well as his personal popularity.

```
Number of writers voting ................................ 383
Number of players receiving votes ......................... 34
Number of players receiving 10 percent or more of the votes ..... 22
Number of players in Hall of Fame through 2009 .............. 11
Number who received 10 percent on previous ballot ........... 17*
Number of players elected to the Hall of Fame this year .......... 1
Cumulative total ....................................... 56
```
Banks and Bunning not eligible in 1976.

Player	Percentage of Votes	Result
Ernie Banks	83.8	Elected
Mathews	62.4	
Hodges	58.5	
Slaughter	58.0	
Snider	55.4	
Drysdale	51.4	
Reese	42.6	
Fox	39.7	
Jim Bunning	38.1	
Kell	36.8	
Ashburn	36.3	
Schoendienst	27.4	
Lew Burdette	22.2	
Maris	18.8	
Dark	17.2	
Harvey Kuenn	14.9	
Kluszewski	14.4	
Vernon	13.6	
W. Cooper	11.7	

Player	Percentage of Votes	Result
E. Howard	11.2	
Don Newcombe	11.2	
Larsen	10.2	

VETERANS' COMMITTEE

Amos Rusie (1889–1901), a 246-game winner, was elected after having been overlooked in the 1936 Veterans Election. Joe Sewell, who still is number one in fewest strikeouts per at-bat, was the other selection. Sewell batted .312 and accumulated 2,226 hits in a 14-year career. Al Lopez was elected as a manager after a 17-year tenure with the Cleveland Indians and Chicago White Sox.

Amos Rusie	Percentage of Votes	Rank
1936 Veterans Election	15.4	10th
Rank in 1977		2nd

Baseball Writers Association balloting:

Year	Percentage of Votes	Rank
1937	0.5	
1938	3.1	
1939	2.2	
1942	0.4	
1945	0.4	

Joe Sewell:

Year	Percentage of Votes	Rank
1937	0.5	
1948	0.8	
1954	0.4	
1955	0.4	
1956	1.6	
1958	0.4	
1960	8.6	

Al Lopez:

Year	Percentage of Votes	Rank
1949	0.7	
1952	0.9	
1953	0.8	
1956	0.5	
1958	12.6	25th
1960	9.7	

Year	Percentage of Votes	Rank
1962	6.9	
1964	28.4	7th
1964 Run Off	15.0	7th
1966	36.1	6th
1967	39.0	7th
1967 Run Off	16.3	5th

1978

BASEBALL WRITERS ASSOCIATION ELECTION

In his fifth year on the ballot, Eddie Mathews was inducted. A power-hitting third baseman, Mathews accumulated 512 home runs and 2,315 hits in a 17-year career.

Number of writers voting 379
Number of players receiving votes 35
Number of players receiving 10 percent or more of the votes 20
Number of players in the Hall of Fame through 2009 10
Number who received 10 percent on the previous ballot 18*
Number of players elected to the Hall of Fame this year 1
Cumulative total 57
Wilhelm and Wills not eligible in 1977

Player	Percentage of Votes	Result
Mathews	79.4	Elected
Slaughter	68.9	
Snider	67.0	
Hodges	59.6	
Drysdale	57.8	
Bunning	47.8	
Reese	44.6	
Ashburn	41.7	
Hoyt Wilhelm	41.7	
Fox	39.3	
Schoendienst	34.3	
Maury Wills	30.3	
Maris	21.9	
Burdette	20.1	
Vernon	17.4	
Dark	15.8	
Kuenn	15.3	
Kluszewski	13.5	
Newcombe	12.7	
E. Howard	10.8	

VETERANS' COMMITTEE

In a departure from protocol, the committee selected Addie Joss whose career was cut short at age 31 after only nine years in the major leagues. In that time, he collected 160 wins but, more impressively, a .623 winning percentage and a 1.88 earned run average which is second best on the all-time list.

Addie Joss:

Year	Percentage of Votes	Rank
1937	5.5	
1938	6.9	
1939	10.2	24th (tie)
1942	14.2	29th
1945	9.3	
1946	6.9	

1979

BASEBALL WRITERS ASSOCIATION ELECTION

The irrepressible Willie Mays won a resounding 94.7 percent of the vote in his first year of eligibility. His 660 home runs currently still ranks third on the all-time list and he stands high in numerous other offensive categories.

Number of writers voting 432
Number of players receiving votes 38
Number of players receiving 10 percent or more of the votes 20
Number of players in the Hall of Fame through 2009 10
Number who received 10 percent on the previous ballot 17*
Number of players elected to the Hall of Fame this year 1
Cumulative total 58
*Mays and Aparicio not eligible in 1978

Player	Percentage of Votes	Result
Willie Mays	94.7	Elected
Snider	71.3	
Slaughter	68.8	
Hodges	56.0	
Drysdale	53.9	
Fox	40.3	
Wilhelm	38.9	
Wills	38.4	
Schoendienst	36.8	
Bunning	34.0	
Ashburn	30.1	
Maris	29.4	
Luis Aparicio	27.8	
Vernon	20.4	

Player	Percentage of Votes	Result
Dark	18.5	
Kuenn	14.6	
Kluszewski	13.4	
Burdette	12.3	
Larsen	12.3	
Newcombe	12.0	

VETERANS' COMMITTEE

Hack Wilson, a powerful slugger who played for four National League teams during a 12-year career, was the only selection of the Veterans' Committee.

Hack Wilson:

Year	Percentage of Votes	Rank
1937	0.5	
1939	0.4	
1942	0.4	
1948	1.7	
1949	15.7	16th (tie)
1949 Run-Off	6.4	16th
1950	9.6	
1951	9.3	
1952	9.0	
1953	16.3	17th (tie)
1954	19.0	14th
1955	32.3	11th
1956	38.3	6th
1958	35.3	4th
1960	26.8	8th (tie)
1962	24.4	9th

The 1980s

1980

BASEBALL WRITERS ASSOCIATION ELECTION

Two great outfielders were inducted in 1980. Al Kaline in a distinguished 22 years all with the Detroit Tigers compiled 3,007 hits and 399 home runs to go with a .297 batting average. Kaline gained election in his first year of eligibility.

Duke Snider, after working his way upward, achieved election in his eleventh year on the ballot. His 407 home runs, 2,116 hits and .295 batting average helped to put him over the top.

Number of writers voting 385
Number of players receiving votes 32

Number of players receiving 10 percent or more of the votes 19
Number of players in the Hall of Fame through 2009 11
Number who received 10 percent on the previous ballot 17*
Number of players elected to the Hall of Fame this year 2
Cumulative total 60

*Kaline and Cepeda not eligible in 1979

Player	Percentage of Votes	Result
Al Kaline	88.3	Elected
Snider	86.5	Elected
Drysdale	61.8	
Hodges	59.7	
Wilhelm	54.3	
Bunning	46.0	
Schoendienst	42.6	
Fox	41.8	
Wills	37.9	
Ashburn	34.8	
Aparicio	32.2	
Maris	28.8	
Vernon	24.9	
Kuenn	21.6	
Burdette	17.1	
Newcombe	15.3	
Kluszewski	13.0	
Orlando Cepeda	12.5	
Dark	11.2	

VETERANS' COMMITTEE

Chuck Klein, after 12 years on the Baseball Writers Association ballot, was selected by the Veterans' Committee. His credentials included a .320 batting average, 2,076 hits and 300 home runs.

Chuck Klein:

Year	Percentage of Votes	Rank
1948	2.5	
1949	5.9	
1950	8.4	
1951	6.6	
1952	8.1	
1954	4.4	
1955	10.0	24th (tie)
1956	22.8	12th
1958	13.5	21st
1960	13.8	18th (tie)
1962	11.3	15th
1964	27.9	8th
1964 Run-Off	8.0	9th

1981

BASEBALL WRITERS ASSOCIATION ELECTION

Bob Gibson, second in career strikeouts when he retired, was ushered into the Hall of Fame in his first year of eligibility. His 2.91 earned run average, 56 shutouts and 251 victories attest to his ability to overpower the opposition.

Number of writers voting 401
Number of players receiving votes 32
Number of players receiving 10 percent or more of the votes 19
Number in Hall of Fame through 2009 11
Number who received 10% on the previous ballot 14*
Number of players elected to the Hall of Fame this year 1
Cumulative total 61
Gibson, Killebrew, Marichal and Munson not eligible in 1980.

Player	Percentage of Votes	Result
Bob Gibson	84.0	Elected
Drysdale	60.6	
Hodges	60.1	
Harmon Killebrew	59.6	
Wilhelm	59.4	
Juan Marichal	58.1	
Fox	41.9	
Schoendienst	41.4	
Bunning	40.9	
Wills	40.6	
Ashburn	35.4	
Maris	23.4	
Kuenn	23.2	
E. Howard	20.7	
Cepeda	19.2	
Thurman Munson	15.5	
Kluszewski	14.0	
Aparicio	12.0	
Burdette	12.0	

VETERANS' COMMITTEE

Johnny Mize, after 11 years on the Baseball Writers Association ballot, was selected three years after he became eligible for consideration by the Veterans' Committee. Although he hit with great power (359 home runs and a .562 slugging average), his batting average was a highly respectable .312.

Johnny Mize:

Year	Percentage of Votes	Rank
1960	16.7	13th (tie)

Year	Percentage of Votes	Rank
1960	16.7	13th (tie)
1962	8.8	
1964	26.9	9th
1964 Run-Off	5.3	12th (tie)
1966	26.8	10th
1967	30.5	9th (tie)
1967 Run-Off	4.6	16th (tie)
1968	36.4	6th
1969	34.1	6th
1970	42.0	6th
1971	43.6	6th
1972	39.6	6th
1973	41.3	7th

1982

BASEBALL WRITERS ASSOCIATION ELECTION

In their first year of eligibility, Henry Aaron and Frank Robinson far outdistanced the field. Aaron, the all-time home run and RBI leader, ranks in the top ten in numerous offensive categories. Robinson, currently fourth on the home run list with 586, had an illustrious 21-year career in which he collected 2,943 hits to go with a .294 batting average.

Number of writers voting 415
Number of players receiving votes 32
Number of players receiving 10 percent or more of the votes 19
Number in Hall of Fame through 2009 13
Number who received 10% on the previous ballot 15*
Number of players elected to the Hall of Fame this year 2
Cumulative total 63
*Aaron, F. Robinson, B. Williams and Oliva not eligible in 1981.

Player	Percentage of Votes	Result
Henry Aaron	97.8	Elected
Frank Robinson	89.2	Elected
Marichal	73.5	
Killebrew	59.3	
Wilhelm	56.9	
Drysdale	56.1	
Hodges	49.4	
Aparicio	41.9	
Bunning	33.3	
Schoendienst	32.5	
Fox	30.6	
Ashburn	30.4	
Billy Williams	23.4	
Wills	21.9	
Maris	16.6	
Tony Oliva	15.2	

Player	Percentage of Votes	Result
Kuenn	14.9	
Burdette	10.4	
Cepeda	10.1	

Veterans' Committee

Travis Jackson was a smooth fielding shortstop for the New York Giants who compiled a .291 batting average over 15 years.

Travis Jackson:

Year	Percentage of Votes	Rank
1948	4.1	
1949	3.9	
1950	3.6	
1951	1.8	
1952	0.4	
1953	0.8	
1954	0.4	
1955	2.0	
1956	7.3	
1958	4.1	
1960	4.1	
1962	0.6	

1983

Baseball Writers Association Election

Brooks Robinson, a 16-year Gold Glove winner, regarded by many as the prototype third baseman, was the top vote-getter in his first year.

Juan Marichal with 243 wins, 2.89 earned run average and .631 winning percentage became the other inductee in his third try.

Number of writers voting 374
Number of players receiving votes 31
Number of players receiving 10 percent or more of the votes 18
Number in Hall of Fame through 2009 12
Number who received 10 percent on the previous ballot 16*
Number of players elected to the Hall of Fame this year 2
Cumulative total 65
Brooks Robinson not eligible in 1982.

Player	Percentage of Votes	Result
Brooks Robinson	92.0	Elected
Marichal	83.7	Elected
Killebrew	71.9	
Aparicio	67.4	

Player	Percentage of Votes	Result
Wilhelm	65.0	
Drysdale	64.7	
Hodges	63.4	
Fox	46.3	
B. Williams	40.9	
Schoendienst	39.0	
Bunning	36.9	
Kuenn	20.6	
Wills	20.6	
Oliva	20.1	
Maris	18.4	
Cepeda	15.8	
Bill Mazeroski	12.8	
Burdette	11.5	

VETERANS' COMMITTEE

George Kell, after 13 years on the Baseball Writers Association ballot, was selected in his first year of eligibility for Veterans' Committee consideration. He batted .306 with 2,054 hits in a 15-year career.

George Kell:

Year	Percentage of Votes	Rank
1964	16.4	17th (tie)
1964 Run-Off	3.5	17th (tie)
1966	9.6	
1967	13.7	21st
1967 Run-Off	3.6	22nd
1968	16.6	16th (tie)
1969	17.6	18th
1970	30.0	10th
1971	29.2	11th
1972	29.0	11th
1973	30.0	11th
1974	25.8	14th
1975	31.5	13th
1976	33.2	10th (tie)
1977	36.8	10th

1984

BASEBALL WRITERS ASSOCIATION ELECTION

For the first time since 1972, three players were elected. Luis Aparicio, in his sixth year, Harmon Killebrew, in his fourth year, and Don Drysdale, in his tenth year, all exceeded the 75 percent barrier.

Number of writers voting 403
Number of players receiving votes 26
Number of players receiving 10 percent or more of the votes 17
Number in Hall of Fame through 2009 9
Number who received 10 percent on the previous ballot 14
Number of players elected to the Hall of Fame this year 3
Cumulative total 68

Player	Percentage of Votes	Result
Aparicio	84.6	Elected
Killebrew	83.1	Elected
Drysdale	78.4	Elected
Wilhelm	72.0	
Fox	61.0	
B. Williams	50.1	
Bunning	49.9	
Cepeda	30.8	
Oliva	30.8	
Maris	26.6	
Kuenn	26.3	
Wills	25.8	
Burdette	24.1	
Mazeroski	18.4	
Roy Face	16.1	
E. Howard	11.2	
Joe Torre	11.2	

VETERANS' COMMITTEE

Pee Wee Reese, the hub of the Dodger infield for 16 years, was elected in his first year of eligibility. The other inductee was Rick Ferrell, a highly regarded catcher who batted .281 over 18 seasons.

Pee Wee Reese:

Year	Percentage of Votes	Rank
1964	36.3	5th
1964 Run-Off	20.8	5th
1966	31.5	8th
1967	30.5	9th (tie)
1967 Run-Off	5.2	14th
1968	28.6	10th
1969	26.2	12th
1970	32.3	8th (tie)
1971	35.3	7th
1972	32.6	8th
1973	33.2	10th
1974	38.6	8th
1975	42.5	7th
1976	47.9	6th

Year	Percentage of Votes	Rank
1977	42.6	7th
1978	44.6	7th

Rick Ferrell:

Year	Percentage of Votes	Rank
1956	0.5	
1958	0.4	
1960	0.4	

1985

Baseball Writers Association Election

Hoyt Wilhelm was the first bona fide relief pitcher to be inducted into the Hall of Fame. His career spanned 21 years during which he appeared in 1,070 games. He was still pitching his knuckler at age 49.

Lou Brock, in his first year of eligibility, was also elected. At the time, he was the all-time leading basestealer and had accumulated 3,023 hits and a .293 batting average over 19 seasons.

Nelson Fox recorded the closest near miss in history, receiving 74.7 percent of the votes in his last year of eligibility.

```
Number of writers voting . . . . . . . . . . . . . . . . . . . . . . . . . . . . . . . . 395
Number of players receiving votes . . . . . . . . . . . . . . . . . . . . . . . . . 36
Number of players receiving 10 percent or more of the votes . . . . . 19
Number in Hall of Fame through 2009  . . . . . . . . . . . . . . . . . . . . . . . 8
Number who received 10 percent on the previous ballot  . . . . . . . . 14*
Number of players elected to the Hall of Fame this year  . . . . . . . . . . 2
Cumulative total . . . . . . . . . . . . . . . . . . . . . . . . . . . . . . . . . . . . . . . . 70
```
Brock, Hunter and Lolich not eligible in 1984.

Player	Percentage of Votes	Result
Wilhelm	83.8	Elected
Lou Brock	79.7	Elected
Fox	74.7	
B. Williams	63.8	
Bunning	54.2	
Jim Hunter	53.7	
Maris	32.4	
Kuenn	31.6	
Cepeda	28.9	
Oliva	28.9	
Wills	23.5	
Mazeroski	22.0	
Burdette	20.8	
Mickey Lolich	20.3	
Ken Boyer	17.2	

Player	Percentage of Votes	Result
Face	15.7	
E. Howard	13.7	
Ron Santo	13.4	
Torre	11.1	

VETERANS' COMMITTEE

After receiving strong support for 15 years on the Baseball Writers Association ballot, Enos Slaughter with his 2,383 hits and .300 batting average was selected for induction. Arky Vaughan, a .318 hitter with 2,103 career hits, was also selected. He collected votes in 11 Baseball Writers Association elections.

Enos Slaughter:

Year	Percentage of Votes	Rank
1966	33.1	7th
1967	42.1	6th
1967 Run-Off	15.7	6th
1968	45.6	4th
1969	37.6	5th
1970	44.3	5th
1971	45.8	5th
1972	37.6	7th
1973	38.2	8th
1974	39.7	7th
1975	48.9	5th
1976	50.8	4th
1977	58.0	4th
1978	68.9	2nd
1979	68.8	3rd

Arky Vaughan:

Year	Percentage of Votes	Rank
1953	0.4	
1954	0.8	
1955	1.6	
1956	4.7	
1958	2.3	
1960	3.7	
1962	3.8	
1964	8.5	
1964 Run-Off	2.7	
1966	11.9	16th
1967	15.8	19th
1967 Run-Off	6.2	13th
1968	29.0	9th

1986

BASEBALL WRITERS ASSOCIATION ELECTION

Willie McCovey became another first year inductee after a distinguished 22-year career featuring 521 home runs and 2,211 hits.

Number of writers voting 425
Number of players receiving votes 39
Number of players receiving 10 percent or more of the votes 20
Number in the Hall of Fame through 2009 6
Number who received 10 percent on the previous ballot 16*
Number of players elected to the Hall of Fame this year 1
Cumulative total 71
*McCovey and Minoso not eligible in 1985

Player	Percentage of Votes	Result
Willie McCovey	81.4	Elected
B. Williams	74.1	
Hunter	68.0	
Bunning	65.6	
Maris	41.6	
Oliva	36.2	
Cepeda	35.8	
Kuenn	33.9	
Wills	29.2	
Mazeroski	23.5	
Burdette	22.6	
K. Boyer	22.4	
Minnie Minoso	20.9	
Lolich	20.2	
Face	17.4	
Santo	15.1	
Torre	14.1	
E. Howard	12.0	
Curt Flood	10.6	
Vada Pinson	10.1	

VETERANS' COMMITTEE

Bobby Doerr, who had a sterling 14-year career with the Boston Red Sox, and Ernie Lombardi, the hard-hitting catcher with a career .306 batting average, were the two 1986 inductees.

Bobby Doerr:

Year	Percentage of Votes	Rank
1953	0.8	
1956	2.6	

Year	Percentage of Votes	Rank
1958	9.4	
1960	5.6	
1962	6.3	
1964	11.9	24th (tie)
1964 Run-Off	2.2	20th
1966	9.9	
1967	12.0	23rd (tie)
1967 Run-Off	4.9	15th
1968	17.0	16th
1969	18.2	17th
1970	25.0	16th
1971	21.7	18th

Ernie Lombardi:

Year	Percentage of Votes	Rank
1950	1.8	
1951	1.3	
1956	4.1	
1958	1.5	
1960	2.2	
1962	3.1	
1964	16.4	17th (tie)
1964 Run-Off	4.0	15th (tie)
1966	11.3	17th (tie)
1967	14.7	20th
1967 Run-Off	8.2	9th

1987

BASEBALL WRITERS ASSOCIATION ELECTION

Billy Williams, in his sixth try, and Jim "Catfish" Hunter, in his third, were elected by the writers. Williams compiled 426 home runs and 2,711 hits in an 18-year career, while Hunter won 224 games in 15 seasons.

Number of writers voting 413
Number of players receiving votes 26
Number of players receiving 10 percent or more of the votes 20
Number in Hall of Fame through 2009 5
Number who received 10 percent on the previous ballot 19
Number of players elected to the Hall of Fame this year 2
Cumulative total 73

Player	Percentage of Votes	Result
B. Williams	85.7	Elected
Hunter	76.3	Elected
Bunning	70.0	
Cepeda	43.3	

Player	Percentage of Votes	Result
Maris	42.6	
Oliva	38.7	
Kuenn	34.9	
Mazeroski	30.3	
Wills	27.4	
K. Boyer	23.2	
Burdette	23.2	
Lolich	20.3	
Minoso	19.9	
Face	18.9	
Santo	18.9	
Dick Allen	13.3	
Flood	12.1	
Pinson	11.6	
Torre	11.4	
E. Howard	10.7	

VETERANS' COMMITTEE

The committee failed to select a player for induction to the Hall of Fame.

1988

BASEBALL WRITERS ASSOCIATION ELECTION

Willie Stargell, in his first year of eligibility, was the only selection although Jim Bunning made his strongest showing (74.2 percent) in 15 appearances on the ballot.

Number of writers voting 427
Number of players receiving votes 30
Number of players receiving 10 percent or more of the votes 20
Number in Hall of Fame through 2009 4
Number who received 10 percent on the previous ballot 17*
Number of players elected to the Hall of Fame this year 1
Cumulative total 74
*Stargell, Tiant and Lyle not eligible in 1987.

Player	Percentage of Votes	Result
Willie Stargell	82.4	Elected
Bunning	74.2	
Oliva	47.3	
Cepeda	46.6	
Maris	43.1	
Kuenn	39.3	
Mazeroski	33.5	
Luis Tiant	30.9	
Wills	29.7	

Player	Percentage of Votes	Result
K. Boyer	25.5	
Lolich	25.5	
Santo	25.3	
Minoso	21.1	
Face	18.5	
Pinson	15.7	
Torre	14.1	
Sparky Lyle	13.1	
E. Howard	12.4	
D. Allen	12.2	
Flood	11.2	

VETERANS' COMMITTEE

For the second consecutive year, no candidates received the 75 percent required for election.

1989

BASEBALL WRITERS ASSOCIATION ELECTION

Four future Hall of Famers made their debuts on the 1989 ballot. Johnny Bench and Carl Yastrzemski were elected immediately. Gaylord Perry and Ferguson Jenkins received strong support and placed third and fifth, respectively, in the voting.

Number of writers voting 447
Number of players receiving votes 30
Number of players receiving 10 percent or more of the votes 17
Number in Hall of Fame through 2009 7
Number who received 10 percent on the previous ballot 12*
Number of players elected to the Hall of Fame this year 2
Cumulative total 76
Bench, Yastrzemski, G. Perry, Jenkins and Kaat not eligible in 1988.

Player	Percentage of Votes	Result
Johnny Bench	96.4	Elected
Carl Yastrzemski	94.6	Elected
Gaylord Perry	68.0	
Bunning	63.3	
Ferguson Jenkins	52.3	
Cepeda	39.4	
Oliva	30.2	
Mazeroski	30.0	
Kuenn	25.7	
Wills	21.3	
Jim Kaat	19.5	
Santo	16.8	
K. Boyer	13.9	

Player	Percentage of Votes	Result
Minoso	13.2	
Face	10.5	
Lolich	10.5	
Tiant	10.5	

VETERANS' COMMITTEE

Red Schoendienst, who batted .289 in 19 major league seasons and totaled 2,449 hits, was the only Veterans selection. Schoendienst completed 15 years on the Baseball Writers Association ballot in 1983.

Year	Percentage of Votes	Rank
1969	19.1	16th
1970	32.3	9th
1971	34.2	9th
1972	26.3	13th
1973	25.3	14th
1974	30.1	12th
1975	26.0	14th
1976	33.2	10th (tie)
1977	27.4	12th
1978	34.3	11th
1979	36.8	9th
1980	42.6	7th
1981	41.4	8th
1982	32.5	10th
1983	39.0	10th

The 1990s

1990

BASEBALL WRITERS ASSOCIATION ELECTION

In a repeat of the previous year, two first-time candidates, Jim Palmer and Joe Morgan, were elected. Palmer, with 268 wins and a 2.86 earned run average, spent his entire 19 years with Baltimore. Morgan, a two-time MVP, garnered 2,517 hits and 689 stolen bases in a brilliant 22-year career.

Number of writers voting 444
Number of players receiving votes 34
Number of players receiving 10 percent or more of the votes 17
Number in Hall of Fame through 2009 7
Number who received 10 percent on the previous ballot 13*
Number of players elected to the Hall of Fame this year 2
Cumulative total 78
*Morgan and Palmer not eligible in 1989.

Player	Percentage of Votes	Result
Jim Palmer	92.6	Elected
Joe Morgan	81.8	Elected
G. Perry	72.1	
Jenkins	66.7	
Bunning	57.9	
Cepeda	47.5	
Oliva	32.0	
Mazeroski	29.5	
Kuenn	24.1	
Santo	21.6	
Wills	21.4	
Kaat	17.8	
K. Boyer	17.6	
D. Allen	13.1	
Torre	12.4	
Minoso	11.5	
Face	11.3	

VETERANS' COMMITTEE

For the third time in four years, the Veterans' Committee was unable to select a candidate.

1991

BASEBALL WRITERS ASSOCIATION ELECTION

For the first time since 1984, three players gained election. Rod Carew with his .328 batting average and 3,053 hits breezed in, but pitchers Gaylord Perry (314 wins) and Ferguson Jenkins (284 wins) barely exceeded the 75 percent requirement.

Number of writers voting 443
Number of players receiving votes 34
Number of players receiving 10 percent or more of the votes 14
Number in Hall of Fame through 2009 7
Number who received 10 percent on the previous ballot 12*
Number of players elected to the Hall of Fame this year 3
Cumulative total 81
*Carew and Fingers not eligible in 1990.

Player	Percentage of Votes	Result
Rod Carew	90.5	Elected
G. Perry	77.2	Elected
Jenkins	75.4	Elected
Rollie Fingers	65.7	
Bunning	63.7	
Cepeda	43.3	
Oliva	36.1	

Player	Percentage of Votes	Result
Mazeroski	32.1	
Santo	26.2	
Kuenn	22.6	
Kaat	14.0	
Wills	13.8	
Allen	13.3	
K. Boyer	13.1	

VETERANS' COMMITTEE

The committee went back into the pre–World War II era to select Tony Lazzeri, a mainstay of the Yankee dynasty who appeared in six World Series.

Tony Lazzeri:

Year	Percentage of Votes	Rank
1945	0.4	
1947	0.6	
1948	17.4	16th
1949	13.1	19th (tie)
1949 Run-Off	3.2	19th (tie)
1950	12.6	15th
1951	11.9	18th (tie)
1952	12.4	20th (tie)
1953	10.6	23rd
1954	11.9	18th
1955	26.3	13th
1956	33.2	8th
1958	30.1	7th
1960	21.9	11th
1962	5.0	

1992

BASEBALL WRITERS ASSOCIATION ELECTION

Tom Seaver, in his first year of eligibility, received the highest percentage of votes ever recorded, 98.8 percent. In his magnificent 20-year career, he amassed 311 wins, 3,640 strikeouts and a 2.86 earned run average. He was joined by Rollie Fingers, one of the leaders in most categories of relief pitching.

Number of writers voting 430
Number of players receiving votes 30
Number of players receiving 10 percent or more of the votes 15
Number of Hall of Famers through 2009 5
Number who received 10 percent on the previous ballot 9*
Number of players elected to the Hall of Fame this year 2
Cumulative total 83
*Seaver and Perez not eligible in 1991.

Player	Percentage of Votes	Result
Tom Seaver	98.8	Elected
Fingers	81.2	Elected
Cepeda	57.2	
Tony Perez	50.0	
Mazeroski	42.3	
Oliva	40.7	
Santo	31.6	
Kaat	26.5	
Wills	25.6	
K. Boyer	16.5	
Allen	16.0	
Minoso	16.0	
Torre	14.4	
Tiant	11.6	
Lolich	10.5	

VETERANS' COMMITTEE

Hal Newhouser, a 207-game winner with a 3.06 earned run average, was elected after 12 years on the Baseball Writers' Association ballot.

Year	Percentage of Votes	Rank
1962	2.5	
1964	12.9	21st (tie)
1964 Run-Off	1.3	21st (tie)
1966	10.6	19th
1967	21.3	16th
1967 Run-Off	4.2	20th (tie)
1968	23.7	14th (tie)
1969	24.1	13th (tie)
1970	26.7	13th
1971	26.1	13th
1972	23.2	15th
1973	20.8	16th
1974	20.0	17th
1975	42.8	6th

1993

BASEBALL WRITERS ASSOCIATION ELECTION

The power-hitting (563 home runs) Reggie Jackson, in his first year of eligibility, was the only Baseball Writers Association selection.

Number of writers voting 423
Number of players receiving votes 27
Number of players receiving 10 percent or more of the votes 15
Number of Hall of Famers through 2009 4
Number who received 10 percent on the previous ballot 11*

Number of players elected to the Hall of Fame this year 1
Cumulative total 84
*Jackson, P. Niekro and Garvey not eligible in 1992.

Player	Percentage of Votes	Result
Reggie Jackson	93.6	Elected
Phil Niekro	65.7	
Cepeda	59.6	
Perez	55.1	
Steve Garvey	41.6	
Oliva	37.1	
Santo	36.6	
Kaat	29.6	
Allen	16.5	
K. Boyer	16.3	
Minoso	15.8	
Torre	14.9	
Tiant	14.7	
Bobby Bonds	10.6	
Lolich	10.2	

VETERANS' COMMITTEE

No candidates were elected for Hall of Fame induction in 1993.

1994

BASEBALL WRITERS ASSOCIATION ELECTION

Steve Carlton, in his first year, was the only selection although Orlando Cepeda in his last year of eligibility just fell short with 73.6 percent of the vote. Carlton is ninth on the career victory list with 329 and his 4,136 strikeouts rank him second only to Nolan Ryan.

Number of writers voting 455
Number of players receiving votes 33
Number of players receiving 10 percent or more of the votes 14
Number of Hall of Famers through 2009 6
Number who received 10 percent on the previous ballot 10*
Number of players elected to the Hall of Fame this year 1
Cumulative total 85
*Carlton, Sutton and Sutter not eligible in 1993.

Player	Percentage of Votes	Result
Steve Carlton	95.8	Elected
Cepeda	73.6	
P. Niekro	60.0	
Perez	57.8	
Don Sutton	56.9	

Player	Percentage of Votes	Result
Garvey	36.5	
Oliva	34.7	
Santo	33.0	
Bruce Sutter	24.0	
Kaat	21.5	
Allen	14.5	
K. Boyer	11.9	
Torre	11.6	
Pinson	10.1	

VETERANS' COMMITTEE

At long last, "The Scooter" Phil Rizzuto, after repeated comparisons with contemporaries Reese, Boudreau and Appling, was finally selected to the honor that had eluded him for many years.

Year	Percentage of Votes	Rank
1956	0.5	
1962	27.5	7th
1964	22.4	14th
1964 Run-Off	4.9	14th
1966	17.9	15th
1967	24.3	13th
1967 Run-Off	4.6	16th (tie)
1968	26.1	13th
1969	22.9	15th
1970	26.3	14th (tie)
1971	25.6	14th
1972	26.0	14th
1973	29.2	12th
1974	30.4	10th
1975	32.3	12th
1976	38.4	9th

1995

BASEBALL WRITERS ASSOCIATION ELECTION

Mike Schmidt, with 548 home runs and ten Gold Gloves in a marvelous 18-year career, was elected in his first year of eligibility. One of the great power-hitters of all time, he ranks at or near the top of the list of great third basemen.

Number of writers voting 460
Number of players receiving votes 35
Number of players receiving 10 percent or more of the votes 15
Number of Hall of Famers through 2009 6
Number who received 10 percent on the previous ballot 10*
Number of players elected to the Hall of Fame this year 1

Cumulative total 86
Schmidt, Rice and John not eligible in 1994.

Player	Percentage of Votes	Result
Mike Schmidt	96.5	Elected
P. Niekro	62.2	
Sutton	57.4	
Perez	56.3	
Garvey	42.6	
Oliva	32.4	
Santo	30.2	
Jim Rice	29.8	
Sutter	29.8	
Kaat	21.7	
Tommy John	21.3	
Allen	15.7	
Minoso	14.3	
Flood	12.8	
Torre	10.9	

VETERANS' COMMITTEE

After 15 years on the Baseball Writers Association ballot and a 15-year career, Richie Ashburn with his .308 batting average and 2,574 hits was selected. Regarded by some as the greatest defensive outfielder of all time, he ranks in the top five in several defensive categories.

Vic Willis (1898–1910) garnered 248 wins in a 13-year pitching career. He currently ranks 38th on the all-time wins list and sports a sparkling 2.63 earned run average. A durable worker, he is in 34th place in number of innings pitched.

Richie Ashburn:

Year	Percentage of Votes	Rank
1968	2.1	
1969	2.9	
1970	3.7	
1971	2.8	
1972	2.8	
1973	6.6	
1974	15.3	19th
1975	21.0	15th (tie)
1976	21.9	14th
1977	36.3	11th
1978	41.7	8th
1979	30.1	11th
1980	34.8	10th
1981	35.4	11th
1982	30.4	12th

Vic Willis:

Despite his imposing credentials, Willis did not receive any votes in the initial 1936 Veterans Election perhaps because his career ended in 1910. Neither did he garner any support in subsequent Baseball Writers Association elections.

1996

BASEBALL WRITERS ASSOCIATION ELECTION

For the first time since 1971, no one could garner enough support for election. Phil Niekro, with over 60 percent of the vote for the fourth consecutive year with 68.3 percent, was the leader. Tony Perez and Don Sutton were in close pursuit leaving the rest of the field far in arrears.

Number of writers voting 470
Number of players receiving votes 31
Number of players receiving 10 percent or more of the votes 17
Number of Hall of Famers through 2009 5
Number who received 10 percent on the previous ballot 14*
Number of players elected to the Hall of Fame this year 0
Cumulative total 86
Conception not eligible in 1995.

Player	Percentage of Votes	Result
P. Niekro	68.3	
Perez	65.7	
Sutton	63.8	
Garvey	37.2	
Santo	37.0	
Oliva	36.2	
Rice	35.3	
Sutter	29.1	
John	21.7	
Kaat	19.4	
Allen	18.9	
Flood	15.1	
Tiant	13.6	
Dave Concepcion	13.4	
Minoso	13.2	
Pinson	10.9	
Torre	10.6	

VETERANS' COMMITTEE

Jim Bunning, with 224 career victories, 40 shutouts and 2,855 strikeouts, which currently places him eleventh on the all-time list, was selected to the Hall of Fame. In 1988 he fell 0.8 percent short of election by the Baseball Writers' Association.

Ironically, Nelson Fox also received 75 percent of the votes but less than Bunning. Because the committee is allowed to select only one player, Fox must wait at least another year. In 1985, his last year for Baseball Writers Association consideration, Fox acquired 74.7 percent of the votes.

Jim Bunning:

Year	Percentage of Votes	Rank
1977	38.1	9th
1978	47.8	6th
1979	34.0	10th
1980	46.0	6th
1981	40.9	9th
1982	33.3	9th
1983	36.9	11th
1984	49.9	7th
1985	54.2	5th
1986	65.6	4th
1987	70.0	3rd
1988	74.2	2nd
1989	63.3	4th
1990	57.9	5th
1991	63.7	5th

1997

BASEBALL WRITERS ASSOCIATION ELECTION

In his fifth year on the ballot Phil Niekro was elected. He had previously finished second, third, second and first in the balloting. Don Sutton was a mere nine votes short of election. Tony Perez made his strongest bid with 66.0 percent of the vote. Ron Santo finished a distant fourth with 39.3 percent.

```
Number of writers voting  . . . . . . . . . . . . . . . . . . . . . . . . . . . . . . 473
Number of players receiving votes  . . . . . . . . . . . . . . . . . . . . . . . 30
Number of players receiving 10 percent or more of the votes  . . . . . 15
Number of Hall of Famers through 2009  . . . . . . . . . . . . . . . . . . . . . 5
Number of players who received 10 percent on the previous ballot  14*
Number of players elected to the Hall of Fame this year  . . . . . . . . . . 1
Cumulative total  . . . . . . . . . . . . . . . . . . . . . . . . . . . . . . . . . . . . . . 87
```
*Dave Parker not eligible in 1996

Player	Percentage of Votes	Result
P. Niekro	80.3	Elected
Sutton	73.2	
Perez	66.0	
Santo	39.3	

Player	Percentage of Votes	Result
Rice	37.6	
Garvey	35.3	
Sutter	27.5	
Kaat	22.6	
Torre	22.2	
John	20.5	
Minoso	17.8	
Dave Parker	17.5	
Allen	16.7	
Concepcion	12.7	
Tiant	11.2	

VETERANS' COMMITTEE

Nelson Fox was the logical choice after missing by 0.3 percent in his final year on the Baseball Writers Association ballot and then finishing a close second in last year's Veterans' Committee election. In a 19-year career he collected 2,663 hits and had a lifetime batting average of .288.

Nelson Fox:

Year	Percentage of Votes	Rank
1971	10.8	20th
1972	16.2	17th
1973	19.2	17th (tie)
1974	21.6	15th
1975	21.0	15th (tie)
1976	44.8	7th
1977	39.7	8th
1978	39.3	10th
1979	40.3	6th
1980	41.8	8th
1981	41.9	7th
1982	30.6	11th
1983	46.3	8th
1984	61.0	5th
1985	74.7	3rd

1998

BASEBALL WRITERS ASSOCIATION ELECTION

After barely falling short in 1997, Don Sutton, in his fifth year, was the only player elected. Perez, Santo and Rice all moved up one notch in the voting and Gary Carter made a strong showing in his first year on the ballot.

Number of writers voting 473
Number of players receiving votes 26
Number of players receiving 10 or more of the votes 15
Number of Hall of Famers through 2009 5
Number of players who received 10 percent on the previous ballot 12*
Number of players elected to the Hall of Fame this year 1
Cumulative total 88
*Gary Carter and Bert Blyleven not eligible in 1997.

Player	Percentage of Votes	Result
Sutton	81.6	Elected
Perez	67.9	
Santo	43.1	
Rice	42.9	
Gary Carter	42.3	
Garvey	41.2	
Sutter	31.1	
John	27.3	
Kaat	27.3	
Parker	22.4	
Bert Blyleven	17.5	
Concepción	14.8	
Minoso	14.0	
Tiant	11.0	
Keith Hernandez	10.8	

VETERANS' COMMITTEE

Larry Doby, the first African-American to play in the American League, was elected under rule 6B which reads: "Also eligible are players who played in any portion of at least ten (10) years in the Negro Baseball Leagues prior to 1946 or whose service in the Negro Baseball Leagues prior to 1946 and the Major Leagues thereafter total at least ten (10) years or portions thereof." Actually, Doby played 13 years in the American League batting .283 and hitting 253 home runs.

George Davis, a switch-hitting shortstop whose career spanned 20 years (1890–1909), was also elected. He collected 2,665 career hits and compiled a .295 batting average.

Larry Doby:

Year	Percentage of Votes	Rank
1966	2.3	
1967	3.4	
1967 Run-off	0.3	

George Davis:
Surprisingly, Davis did not receive any votes in the Veterans Election

of 1936, nor did he garner support on any subsequent Baseball Writers' elections.

1999

Baseball Writers Association Election

For the first time since the initial election in 1936, three players were inducted in their first year of eligibility. Nolan Ryan received the second highest percentage of votes of votes in history. George Brett with 3,154 hits and Robin Yount with 3,142 hits were also elected.

Number of writers voting 497
Number of players receiving votes 24
Number of players receiving 10 percent or more of the votes 17
Number of Hall of Famers through 2009 8
Number of players who received 10 percent on the previous ballot 11*
Number of players elected to the Hall of Fame this year 3
Cumulative total 91

Ryan, Brett, Yount, Fisk and Murphy not eligible in 1998.

Player	Percentage of Votes	Result
Nolan Ryan	98.8	Elected
George Brett	98.2	Elected
Robin Yount	77.5	Elected
Carlton Fisk	66.4	
Perez	60.8	
Carter	33.8	
Garvey	30.2	
Rice	29.4	
Sutter	24.3	
Kaat	20.1	
Dale Murphy	19.3	
John	18.7	
Parker	16.1	
Minoso	14.7	
Blyleven	14.1	
Concepcion	11.9	
Tiant	10.7	

Veterans' Committee

In his last year on the Baseball Writers Association ballot Orlando Cepeda missed election by the narrowest of margins. After a four-year wait he achieved the ultimate recognition. Cepeda compiled some impressive statistics in a 17-year career. A .297 batting average, .499 slugging average, 2,351 hits and 379 home runs ranked him among the leaders in these categories.

Orlando Cepeda:

Year	Percentage of Votes	Rank
1980	12.5	18th
1981	19.2	15th
1982	10.1	19th
1983	15.8	16th
1984	30.8	8th (tie)
1985	28.9	9th (tie)
1986	35.8	7th
1987	43.3	4th
1988	46.6	4th
1989	39.4	6th
1990	47.5	6th
1991	43.3	6th
1992	57.2	3rd
1993	59.6	3rd
1994	73.6	2nd

The 2000s

2000

BASEBALL WRITERS ASSOCIATION ELECTION

Carlton Fisk, who caught the most games (2,226) in the history of major league baseball, over a 24-year career, was the leading vote-getter with 79.6 percent. Tony Perez with 2,732 career hits and 379 home runs was the only other player able to receive the required 75 percent. Perez currently ranks eighteenth on the lifetime runs batted in list with 1,652.

Number of writers voting 499
Number of players receiving votes 29
Number of players receiving 10 percent or more of the votes 16
Number of Hall of Famers through 2009 6
Number of players who received 10 percent on the previous ballot 13*
Number of players elected to the Hall of Fame this year 2
Cumulative total 93
*Gossage and Morris not eligible in 1999

Player	Percentage of Votes	Result
Fisk	79.6	Elected
Perez	77.2	Elected
Rice	51.5	
Carter	49.7	
Sutter	38.5	
Rich Gossage	33.3	
Garvey	32.1	

Player	Percentage of Votes	Result
John	27.1	
Kaat	25.1	
Murphy	23.2	
Jack Morris	22.2	
Parker	20.8	
Blyleven	17.4	
Tiant	17.2	
Concepcion	13.4	
Hernandez	10.4	

VETERANS' COMMITTEE

In the year when Gil Hodges seemed to be the popular choice, the Veterans' Committee selected Bid McPhee, a nineteenth century second baseman. McPhee spent his entire career with Cincinnati (1882–1899) compiling 2,250 hits and a batting average of .271. In addition he led the league eight years in fielding percentage. Interestingly, McPhee did not receive a single vote in the Veterans Election of 1936 nor in any subsequent Baseball Writers' elections.

2001

BASEBALL WRITERS ASSOCIATION ELECTION

The long and the short of it were elected in their first year of eligibility. The rangy Dave Winfield and stubby Kirby Puckett, teammates for two years with the Minnesota Twins, were named to the Hall of Fame.

Winfield, in 22 seasons, collected 3,110 hits and 465 home runs. Puckett was forced to retire after 12 years because of eye problems but had 2,304 hits and a career .318 batting average.

```
Number of writers voting ............................... 515
Number of players receiving votes ......................... 30
Number of players receiving 10 percent or more of the votes ..... 16
Number of Hall of Famers through 2009 .................... 6
Number of players who received 10 percent on the previous ballot  13*
Number of players elected to the Hall of Fame this year .......... 2
Cumulative total ...................................... 95
```
*Winfield, Puckett and Mattingly not eligible in 2000

Player	Percentage of Votes	Result
Dave Winfield	84.5	Elected
Kirby Puckett	82.1	Elected
Carter	64.9	
Rice	57.9	
Sutter	47.6	
Gossage	44.3	

Player	Percentage of Votes	Result
Garvey	34.2	
John	28.3	
Don Mattingly	28.2	
Kaat	27.0	
Blyleven	23.5	
Morris	19.6	
Murphy	18.1	
Parker	16.3	
Concepcion	14.4	
Tiant	12.2	

VETERANS' COMMITTEE

Bill Mazeroski, regarded by many as the best fielding second baseman of all time, was selected in his sixth year of Veterans' Committee eligibility. He collected 2,016 hits in a 17-year career all with the Pittsburgh Pirates. Mazeroski is still the leader in double plays involving second basemen.

Bill Mazeroski:

Year	Percentage of Votes	Rank
1978	6.1	23rd
1979	8.3	21st
1980	8.6	20th
1981	9.5	20th
1982	6.7	22nd
1983	12.8	17th
1984	18.4	14th
1985	22.0	12th
1986	23.5	10th
1987	30.3	8th
1988	33.5	7th
1989	30.0	8th
1990	29.5	8th
1991	32.1	8th
1992	42.3	5th

2002

Ozzie Smith, "The Wizard," was elected in his first year of eligibility. Credited by many experts as having revolutionized shortstop play, Smith compiled the second highest percentage of votes behind only Honus Wagner. He currently leads all shortstops in career double plays and assists. His 580 stolen bases rank thirteenth on the all-time list. In addition he collected 2,460 hits in a 19-year career.

Number of writers voting 472
Number of players receiving votes 24

Number of players receiving 10 percent or more of the votes 17
Number of Hall of Famers through 2009 5
Number who received 10 percent on the previous ballot ...., 14*
Number of players elected to the Hall of Fame this year 1
Cumulative total 96
Smith, Dawson and Trammell not eligible in 2001

Player	Percentage of Votes	Result
Ozzie Smith	91.7	Elected
Carter	72.7	
Rice	55.1	
Sutter	50.4	
Andre Dawson	45.3	
Gossage	43.0	
Garvey	28.4	
John	26.9	
Blyleven	26.3	
Kaat	23.1	
Morris	20.6	
Mattingly	20.3	
Tiant	18.0	
Alan Trammell	15.7	
Murphy	14.8	
Parker	14.0	
Concepcion	11.9	

2003

BASEBALL WRITERS ASSOCIATION ELECTION

Eddie Murray with 3,255 career hits (currently eleventh all-time) and 504 home runs (seventeenth all-time) was elected on his first try. Gary Carter, in his sixth year, after previously finishing fourth, sixth, fourth, third and second, made it into the winner's circle. Carter, in 19 seasons, had 2,092 hits and 324 home runs.

Number of writers voting 496
Number of players receiving votes 29
Number of players receiving 10 percent or more of the votes 18
Number in Hall of Fame through 2009 6
Number who received 10% on the previous ballot 15*
Number of players elected to the Hall of Fame this year 2
Cumulative total 98
Murray, Sandberg and Smith not eligible in 2002

Player	Percentage of Votes	Result
Eddie Murray	85.3	Elected
Carter	78.0	Elected
Sutter	53.6	
Rice	52.2	

Player	Percentage of Votes	Result
Dawson	50.0	
Ryne Sandberg	49.2	
Lee Smith	42.3	
Gossage	42.1	
Blyleven	29.2	
Garvey	27.8	
Kaat	26.2	
John	23.4	
Morris	22.8	
Trammell	14.1	
Mattingly	13.7	
Murphy	11.7	
Concepcion	11.1	
Parker	10.3	

Veterans' Committee

History repeated itself when the reconstituted Veterans' Committee was unable to elect anyone to the Hall of Fame. The initial election in 1936 had the same result although 12 of the 13 who received more than 10 percent of the vote were eventually elected to the Hall of Fame. The 81 voters were unable to reach consensus among a group of highly qualified candidates.

Player	Percentage of Votes Received	Highest Percentage Received in a Baseball Writers Association Election
Gil Hodges	61.7	63.4
Tony Oliva	59.3	47.3
Ron Santo	56.8	43.1
Joe Torre	35.8	22.2
Maury Wills	29.6	40.6
Vada Pinson	25.9	15.7
Joe Gordon	23.5	28.5
Roger Maris	22.2	43.1
Marty Marion	21.0	40.0
Carl Mays	19.8	2.3
Minnie Minoso	19.8	21.1
Allie Reynolds	19.8	33.6
Dick Allen	16.0	18.9
Mickey Lolich	16.0	25.5
Wes Ferrell	14.8	3.6
Ken Boyer	13.6	25.5
Don Newcombe	13.6	15.3
Curt Flood	12.3	15.1
Ken Williams	9.9	0.5
Rocky Colavito	8.6	0.5
Elston Howard	7.4	20.7
Bob Meusel	7.4	5.0

Player	Percentage of Votes Received	Highest Percentage Received in a Baseball Writers Association Election
Bobby Bonds	6.2	10.6
Ted Kluszewski	4.9	14.4
Thurman Munson	4.9	15.5
Mike Marshall	3.7	1.5

2004

Paul Molitor and Dennis Eckersley, both in their first year of eligibility, were elected. Molitor ranks eighth on the all-time hit list with 3,319. He batted .306 over 21 major league seasons. Eckersley, who made the transition from starter to reliever, won Most Valuable Player and Cy Young awards. He is third on the career saves list and made 1,071 appearances in a remarkable 24-year career.

Number of writers voting 506
Number of players receiving votes 30
Number of players receiving 10 percent or more of the votes 16
Number of Hall of Famers through 2009 6
Number of players who received 10 percent on the previous ballot 14*
Number of players elected to the Hall of Fame this year 2
Cumulative total 100
*Molitor and Eckersley not eligible in 2003

Player	Percentage of Votes	Result
Paul Molitor	85.2	Elected
Dennis Eckersley	83.2	Elected
Sandberg	61.1	
Sutter	59.5	
Rice	54.5	
Dawson	50.0	
Gossage	40.7	
Smith	36.6	
Blyleven	35.4	
Morris	26.3	
Garvey	24.3	
John	21.9	
Trammell	13.8	
Mattingly	12.8	
Concepcion	11.3	
Parker	10.5	

2005

BASEBALL WRITERS ASSOCIATION ELECTION

Wade Boggs was elected on his first year on the ballot. His imposing credentials include 3,010 career hits and a .328 lifetime batting average. Ryne

Sandberg, elected on his third try, was a ten-time All-Star and nine-time Gold Glove winner and currently leads all second basemen with 282 home runs.

Number of writers voting 516
Number of players receiving votes 25
Number of players receiving 10 percent or more of the votes 16
Number in Hall of Fame through 2009 5
Number receiving 10 percent on the previous ballot 14*
Number of players selected to the Hall of Fame this year 2
Cumulative total 102
*Boggs not eligible in 2004

Player	Percentage of Votes	Result
Wade Boggs	91.9	Elected
Sandberg	76.2	Elected
Sutter	66.7	
Rice	59.5	
Gossage	55.2	
Dawson	52.3	
Blyleven	40.9	
Smith	38.8	
Morris	33.3	
John	23.8	
Garvey	20.5	
Trammell	16.9	
Parker	12.6	
Mattingly	11.4	
Concepcion	10.7	
Murphy	10.5	

VETERANS' COMMITTEE

Once again the 80 committee members who voted were unable to reach agreement on the 25 players comprising the final ballot.

Player	Percentage of Votes	Rank in 2003
Hodges	65.0	1st
Santo	65.0	3rd
Oliva	56.3	2nd
Jim Kaat	53.8	First year
Torre	45.0	4th
Wills	32.5	5th
Pinson	28.8	6th
Luis Tiant	25.0	First year
Maris	23.8	8th
Marion	20.0	9th
K. Boyer	18.8	16 (tie)
Gordon	17.5	7th

Player	Percentage of Votes	Rank in 2003
Mays	15.0	10th (tie)
Minoso	15.0	10th (tie)
Allen	15.0	13th (tie)
Flood	12.5	18th
W. Ferrell	11.3	15th
Lolich	11.3	13th (tie)
Newcombe	10.0	16th (tie)
Sparky Lyle	8.8	First year
E. Howard	7.5	21st (tie)
Bonds	5.0	23rd
Colavito	5.0	20th
Munson	2.5	24th (tie)
Smokey Joe Wood	2.5	First year

2006

In his thirteenth year on the ballot Bruce Sutter became the fourth relief pitcher to be elected to the Hall of Fame. He recorded 300 saves in a career that spanned 13 years.

Number of writers voting 520
Number of players receiving votes 27
Number of players receiving 10 percent of the votes 15
Number in Hall of Fame through 2009 3
Number who received 10 percent on the previous ballot 14*
Number of players elected to the Hall of Fame this year 1
Cumulative total 103
*Hershiser not eligible in 2005

Player	Percentage of Votes	Result
Sutter	76.9	Elected
Rice	64.8	
Gossage	64.6	
Dawson	61.0	
Blyleven	53.3	
Smith	45.0	
Morris	41.2	
John	29.6	
Garvey	26.0	
Trammell	17.7	
Parker	14.4	
Concepcion	12.5	
Mattingly	12.3	
Orel Hershiser	11.2	
Murphy	10.8	

2007

BASEBALL WRITERS ASSOCIATION ELECTION

Cal Ripken and Tony Gwynn were near unanimous choices in their first year of eligibility. Both are members of the exclusive 3,000 hit-club and Ripken's 2,632 consecutive games played stands alone. Gwynn's .325 career batting average currently puts him in a tie for seventeenth on the all-time list.

Number of writers voting 545
Number of players receiving votes 28
Number of players receiving 10 percent or more of the votes 14
Number of players in the Hall of Fame through 2009 4
Number who received 10 percent on the previous ballot 11*
Number of players elected to the Hall of Fame this year 2
Cumulative total 105
*Ripken, Gwynn and McGwire not eligible in 2006

Player	Percentage of Votes	Result
Ripken	98.5	Elected
Gwynn	97.6	Elected
Gossage	71.2	
Rice	63.5	
Dawson	56.7	
Blyleven	47.7	
Smith	39.8	
Morris	37.1	
Mark McGwire	23.5	
John	22.9	
Garvey	21.1	
Concepcion	13.6	
Trammell	13.4	
Parker	11.4	

VETERANS COMMITTEE

For the third successive ballot the reconstituted Veterans Committee failed to elect a candidate. It would appear that the relatively large number of highly qualified players created a problem for the voters in deciding upon the most deserving. Eighty-two ballots were cast with the following results.

Name	Percentage of Votes	Rank in 2005 Election
Ron Santo	69.5	1st (tie)
Jim Kaat	63.4	4th
Gil Hodges	61.0	1st (tie)
Tony Oliva	57.3	3rd
Maury Wills	40.2	6th
Joe Torre	31.7	5th
Don Newcombe	20.7	19th

Name	Percentage of Votes	Rank in 2005 Election
Vada Pinson	19.5	7th
Roger Maris	18.3	9th
Lefty O'Doul	18.3	First year
Luis Tiant	18.3	8th
Curt Flood	17.1	16th
Al Oliver	17.1	First year
Mickey Vernon	17.1	First year
Minnie Minoso	14.6	13th (tie)
Cecil Travis	14.6	First year
Richie Allen	13.4	13th (tie)
Marty Marion	13.4	10th
Joe Gordon	12.2	12th
Ken Boyer	11.0	11th
Mickey Lolich	9.8	17th (tie)
Wes Ferrell	8.5	17th (tie)
Sparky Lyle	7.3	20th
Carl Mays	7.3	13th (tie)
Thurman Munson	7.3	24th
Rocky Colavito	6.1	22nd (tie)
Bobby Bonds	1.2	22nd (tie)

2008

BASEBALL WRITERS' ASSOCIATION ELECTION

Rich Gossage became the fifth reliever to be elected. He accumulated 310 saves in a distinguished 22-year career. Jim Rice, on his next-to-last try, was a scant 2.8 percent short of the required 75 percent.

```
Number of writers voting  . . . . . . . . . . . . . . . . . . . . . . . . . . . . . . 543
Number of players receiving votes  . . . . . . . . . . . . . . . . . . . . . . . . 23
Number of players receiving 10 percent or more of the votes  . . . . . 14
Number in the Hall of Fame by 2009  . . . . . . . . . . . . . . . . . . . . . . 2
Number with 10 percent on the previous ballot  . . . . . . . . . . . . . . 11*
Number of players elected this year  . . . . . . . . . . . . . . . . . . . . . . . 1
Cumulative Total . . . . . . . . . . . . . . . . . . . . . . . . . . . . . . . . . . . . . 106
```
*Raines not eligible in 2007

Player	Percentage of Votes	Result
Gossage	85.8	Elected
Rice	72.2	
Dawson	65.9	
Blyleven	61.9	
Smith	43.3	
Morris	42.9	
John	29.1	
Tim Raines	24.3	
McGwire	23.6	
Trammell	18.2	
Concepcion	16.2	
Mattingly	15.8	

Player	Percentage of Votes	Result
Parker	15.1	
Murphy	13.8	

Veterans' Committee Election

After failing to elect a candidate to the Hall of Fame since 2001, the Veterans' Committee tried a new approach in an effort to break the existing log jam. Two separate committees were formed. A 12-member group voted on 10 players whose careers began before 1943. The results were:

Player	Percentage of Votes	Rank in 2007 election
Joe Gordon	83.3	19th
Allie Reynolds	66.7	
Wes Ferrell	50.0	
Mickey Vernon	41.7	
Deacon White	41.7	
Bucky Walters	33.3	
Sherry Magee	25.0	
Carl Mays	less than three votes	23rd (tie)
Bill Dahlen	less than three votes	
Vern Stephens	less than three votes	

Gordon's election comes some 50 years after his retirement. His career was shortened by two years in the military, but in 11 years he was selected to 9 All-Star teams. In addition he was the American League MVP in 1942

Joe Gordon:

Year	Percentage of Votes	Rank
1945	0.4	59th tie
1955	0.4	52nd tie
1956	2.1	43rd tie
1958	4.1	48th tie
1960	4.1	45th tie
1962	2.5	39th tie
1964	14.9	20th
1964RO	0.4	27th tie
1966	10.3	20th
1967	22.6	14th
1967RO	4.2	20th tie
1968	27.2	12th
1969	28.5	9th
1970	26.3	14th tie

The second committee was composed of the 64 living Hall of Famers who voted on 10 players who were active since 1943. This group was unable to reach the 75 percent necessary to select anyone from a highly qualified list of candidates.

Player	Percentage of Votes	Rank
Ron Santo	60.9	1st
Jim Kaat	59.4	2nd
Tony Oliva	51.6	4th
Gil Hodges	43.8	3rd
Joe Torre	29.7	6th
Maury Wills	23.4	5th
Luis Tiant	20.3	9th tie
Vada Pinson	18.8	8th
Al Oliver	14.1	12th tie
Dick Allen	10.9	17th tie

2009

Rickey Henderson was a near unanimous choice in his first year on the ballot. His career spanned 25 years and his 1,406 stolen bases currently stand alone. Jim Rice, on the other hand, gained recognition in his final year on the ballot. In 16 years he compiled a .298 batting average and 382 home runs.

Number of writers voting 539
Number of players receiving votes 20
Number receiving 10 percent or more of the votes 13
Number in the Hall of Fame through 2009 2
Number who received 10 percent on the previous ballot 12
Number of players elected to the Hall of Fame this year 2
Cumulative Total 109
*Henderson not eligible in 2008

Player	Percentage of Votes	Result
Rickey Henderson	94.8	Elected
Rice	76.4	Elected
Dawson	67.0	
Blyleven	62.7	
Smith	44.5	
Morris	44.0	
John	31.7	
Raines	22.6	
McGwire	21.9	
Trammell	17.4	
Parker	15.0	
Mattingly	11.9	
Murphy	11.5	

Summary

In analyzing Hall of Fame balloting, one factor becomes immediately apparent. The Baseball Writers Association over a 73-year period has been very consistent in the voting process. It also speaks well of the work of the Veterans' Committee in recent years in selecting candidates who had ranked high in Baseball Writers Association voting.

From 1966 through 2009, 13 to 24 players received at least 10 percent of the vote in each election. In that same period the number who failed to garner at least 10 percent of the vote in the previous year's election ranged as follows:

Number Not Receiving:

10 percent of Vote	Number of Times
0	16
1	14
2	8
3	2
4	1
5	2

These figures are adjusted to take into consideration players who were not eligible on the prior year's ballot, the assumption being that they would have achieved 10 percent had they been eligible.

In reviewing the status of those currently under consideration by the Baseball Writers, several prominent names appear:

Name	First Year Eligible	Highest Percentage Received	Last Year on Ballot
Tommy John	1995	31.7	2009
Dave Parker	1997	22.4	2011
Bert Blyleven	1998	62.7	2012
Dale Murphy	1999	23.2	2013
Jack Morris	2000	44.0	2014
Don Mattingly	2001	28.2	2015
Andre Dawson	2002	67.0	2016
Alan Trammell	2002	18.2	2016
Lee Smith	2003	44.5	2017
Mark McGwire	2007	23.6	2021
Tim Raines	2008	24.3	2022

The Veterans Committee: A Continuing Dilemma

In August of 2001 the Hall of Fame Board of Directors revised the Veterans' Committee drastically. The two areas most affected were membership and eligibility. The National Baseball Hall of Fame press release stated:

Membership: The current 15-member Veterans Committee is replaced by a group comprised of the living members of the Baseball Hall of Fame (61), the living recipients of the J.G. Taylor Spink Award (13), and the current Veterans Committee members whose terms have not yet expired (3). This group increases the size of the existing committee six-fold.

Eligible candidates: All players who played in at least 10 major league seasons, including those from the 19th century, who are not on Major League Baseball's ineligible list, and who are not being considered by the Baseball Writers Association, are eligible for election by the new Veterans Committee.

Hopefully, the new regulations will help to remedy a situation that was limiting the number of potential candidates who began their careers after 1945. One prior restriction required that players receive at least 100 votes in any one Baseball Writers' Association of America election up to and including the 1991 election. In order to see how many candidates were available to the Veterans' Committee under these regulations, all the Baseball Writers' Association elections were reviewed. Only five players whose careers began before 1946 ever received 100 or more votes in an election. They are:

Gil Hodges	14 times
Marty Marion	5 times
Allie Reynolds	3 times
Phil Cavaretta	1 time
Johnny Sain	1 time

Of those whose careers began in 1946 or later the following accumulated 100 votes:

Maury Wills	9 times (once after 1991)
Roger Maris	7 times
Tony Oliva	13 times (5 times after 1991)
Harvey Kuenn	8 times
Luis Tiant	1 time
Ken Boyer	1 time
Ron Santo	9 times (7 times after 1991)
Mickey Lolich	1 time
Jim Kaat	12 times (11 times after 1991)

The second and more restrictive phrase required 60 percent of the vote for players who began their careers after 1945. Starting with the 1992 ballot 100 votes was no longer adequate. To date every player who achieved the 60 percent standard was ultimately elected to the Hall of Fame by the Baseball Writers. The only player who exceeded 60 percent and is not yet in the Hall of Fame is Gil Hodges. He topped that number on three occasions. Currently Andre Dawson and Bert Blyleven have exceeded 60 percent. Whether this duo achieves eventual election remains to be seen.

Had the revised regulations not been put into effect only Wills, Maris, Kuenn, Santo, Boyer, Oliva, Lolich, Tiant and Kaat would have been eligible for future Veterans' Committee consideration. It seems clear that the Veterans' Committee, in a period of 5 to 10 years, would have exhausted the supply of viable candidates who began their careers after World War II (1945). While the jury will remain out until the results of the next few elections are in, at least it levels the playing field for the players of the post-war era.

Following Mazeroski's election in 2001, the Veterans' Committee was unable to make another selection. Consequently, another structural change was made before the 2008 voting occurred. Basically, the new arrangement calls for two separate elections, one for players whose careers began in 1943 or later, the other for players whose careers began in 1942 or earlier. In each case a Screening Committee selects ten players for consideration. The 12-person committee voting for the older group of players tapped Joe Gordon for election. The committee responsible for voting for the post–1942 players consists of all the living Hall of Famers, currently 61 in number. This group, again, was unable to elect a candidate. The high qualifications of the ten candidates seem to make it impossible for the committee to reach a consensus.

Hall of Famers

Decade in Which Careers Began	Baseball Writers' Association	Veterans Committee	Total
Pre–1900	4	36	40
1900–1909	5	11	16
1910–1919	9	13	22
1920–1929	16	15	31
1930–1939	9	9	18
1940–1945	3	4	7
1946–1949	6	3	9
1950–1959	18	3	21
1960–1969	20	0	20
1970–1979	13	0	13
1980–1989	5	0	5
Totals	108	94	202

It is interesting to note that the only Veterans' Committee selections whose careers began after 1945 are Richie Ashburn (1948) elected in 1995, Jim Bunning (1955) elected in 1996, Nelson Fox (1947) elected in 1997, Larry Doby (1947) elected in 1998, Orlando Cepeda (1958) elected in 1999, and Bill Mazeroski (1956) elected in 2001. Had the previous regulations remained in effect, there would have been very few post-war players elected into the Hall of Fame via the Veterans' Committee.

The following table lists the highest percentage of votes received by players who failed to obtain the required 75 percent necessary for election by the Baseball Writers:

Name/Position	Highest % of Votes	Status
Nelson Fox 2B	74.7	Veterans Committee
Jim Bunning P	74.2	Veterans Committee
Orlando Cepeda 1B	73.6	Veterans Committee
Frank Chance 1B	72.5	Veterans Committee
Enos Slaughter OF	68.9	Veterans Committee
Rube Waddell P	65.3	Veterans Committee
Johnny Evers 2B	64.4	Veterans Committee
Miller Huggins 2B	63.9	VC as a Manager
Gil Hodges 1B	63.4	Eligible
Ed Walsh P	56.9	Veterans Committee
Edd Roush OF	54.3	Veterans Committee
Roger Bresnahan C	53.8	Veterans Committee
Sam Rice OF	53.2	Veterans Committee
Ed Delahanty OF	52.9	Veterans Committee
Eppa Rixey P	52.8	Veterans Committee
Max Carey OF	51.1	Veterans Committee
Jimmy Collins 3B	49.0	Veterans Committee
Pee Wee Reese SS	47.9	Veterans Committee
Tony Oliva OF	47.3	Eligible
Lefty Gomez P	46.1	Veterans Committee
Ray Schalk C	45.0	Veterans Committee
Chief Bender P	44.7	Veterans Committee
Clark Griffith P	43.7	VC as an Executive
Johnny Mize 1B	43.6	Veterans Committee
Roger Maris OF	43.1	Eligible
Ron Santo 3B	43.1	Eligible
Hal Newhouser P	42.8	Veterans Committee
Red Schoendienst 2B	42.6	Veterans Committee
Steve Garvey 1B	42.6	Eligible
Bill Mazeroski 2B	42.3	Veterans Committee
Richie Ashburn OF	41.7	Veterans Committee
Maury Wills SS	40.6	Eligible
Marty Marion SS	40.0	Eligible
Harvey Kuenn OF	39.3	Eligible
Al Lopez C	39.0	VC as a Manager
Phil Rizzuto SS	38.4	Veterans Committee
Hack Wilson OF	38.3	Veterans Committee
Wilbert Robinson C	38.2	VC as a Manager
Hughie Jennings SS	37.2	Veterans Committee
George Kell 3B	36.8	Veterans Committee
Hank Gowdy C	35.9	Eligible
Phil Cavaretta 1B	35.6	Eligible
Burleigh Grimes P	34.2	Veterans Committee
Johnny Sain P	34.0	Eligible
Kiki Cuyler OF	33.8	Veterans Committee
Allie Reynolds P	33.6	Eligible
Tony Lazzeri 2B	33.2	Veterans Committee
Jim Bottomley 1B	33.1	Veterans Committee
Hugh Duffy OF	33.1	Veterans Committee
Tommy John P	31.7	Eligible

Name/Position	Highest % of Votes	Status
Red Faber P	30.9	Veterans Committee
Luis Tiant P	30.9	Eligible
Frank Baker 3B	30.4	Veterans Committee
Johnny Vander Meer P	29.8	Eligible
Jim Kaat P	29.6	Eligible
Arky Vaughan SS	29.0	Veterans Committee
Joe Gordon 2B	28.5	Veterans Committee
Chuck Klein OF	27.9	Veterans Committee
Mordecai Brown P	27.7	Veterans Committee
Joe Tinker SS	27.2	Veterans Committee
Eddie Plank P	27.0	Veterans Committee
Joe McGinnity P	26.2	Veterans Committee
Ken Boyer 3B	25.5	Eligible
Mickey Lolich P	25.5	Eligible
Mel Harder P	25.4	Eligible
Bobby Doerr 2B	25.0	Veterans Committee
Mickey Vernon 1B	24.9	Eligible
Fred Clarke OF	24.9	Veterans Committee
Lew Burdette P	24.1	Eligible
Bucky Walters P	23.7	Eligible
Lloyd Waner OF	23.4	Veterans Committee
Casey Stengel OF	23.1	VC as a Manager
Zack Wheat OF	23.0	Veterans Committee
Ross Youngs OF	22.4	Veterans Committee
Joe Torre C	22.2	Eligible
Alvin Dark SS	21.3	Eligible
Orestes Minoso OF	21.1	Eligible
Elston Howard C	20.7	Eligible
Tommy Henrich OF	20.7	Eligible
Billy Herman 2B	20.2	Veterans Committee
Waite Hoyt P	19.2	Veterans Committee
Roy Face P	18.9	Eligible
Dick Allen 1B	18.9	Eligible
Joe Wood P	18.0	Eligible
John McGraw 3B	17.4	VC as a Manager
Pepper Martin OF	17.3	Eligible
Bucky Harris 2B	16.9	VC as a Manager
Lefty O'Doul OF	16.7	Eligible
Ernie Lombardi C	16.4	Veterans Committee
Dave Bancroft SS	16.2	Veterans Committee
Dave Concepcion SS	16.2	Eligible
Earl Combs OF	16.0	Veterans Committee
Vada Pinson OF	15.7	Eligible
Thurman Munson C	15.5	Eligible
Don Newcombe P	15.3	Eligible
Curt Flood OF	15.1	Eligible
Walker Cooper C	14.4	Eligible
Ted Kluszewski 1B	14.4	Eligible
Addie Joss P	14.2	Veterans Committee
Rube Marquard P	13.9	Veterans Committee

Name/Position	Highest % of Votes	Status
Babe Adams P	13.7	Eligible
Goose Goslin OF	13.5	Veterans Committee
Duffy Lewis OF	13.5	Eligible
Sparky Lyle P	13.1	Eligible
Stan Coveleski P	12.8	Veterans Committee
Don Larsen P	12.3	Eligible
Terry Moore OF	11.7	Eligible
Dom DiMaggio OF	11.3	Eligible
Orel Hershiser P	11.2	Eligible
Chick Hafey OF	10.8	Veterans Committee
Keith Hernandez 1B	10.8	Eligible
Bobby Bonds OF	10.6	Eligible
Vic Raschi P	10.2	Eligible
Jimmy Dykes 3B	10.0	Eligible
Johnny Kling C	10.0	Eligible
Dickie Kerr P	10.0	Eligible

Of the 116 players who achieved between 10 percent and 74.7 percent of the vote in a Baseball Writers' Association election, 65 (56.0 percent) were elected to the Hall of Fame by the Veterans' Committee, and 51 (44.0 percent) are presently eligible or will be eligible for Veterans' Committee consideration.

Part II: Hall of Famers— Other Factors and Other Awards

Introduction

Without fail, the Baseball Hall of Fame elections spark a controversy every year. The long-suffering Nelson Fox followers were appeased when he was finally recognized after 15 years on the Baseball Writers' Association ballot, followed by an 11-year wait on the Veterans Committee list.

Earlier the Reese vs. Rizzuto battle was waged. With closely matched statistics why was "Pee Wee" in and "The Scooter" left out? A Cooperstown restaurant placed a sign in the window expressing hope that "The Scooter" would receive his just "desserts," so to speak. That dilemma was resolved when Rizzuto was elected by the Veterans Committee in 1994.

Part II of this study reviews such factors as where the Hall of Famers played, what relationship exists between other annual baseball awards such as the Most Valuable Player and Rookie of the Year awards and Hall of Fame election, the influence of a player's longevity in the game to the Hall of Fame award, and the emergence of ethnic minorities in the Hall of Fame choices.

Where Did the Hall of Famers Play?

One issue which surfaces periodically is the effect of the news media and concerted publicity campaigns upon Hall of Fame balloting. Perhaps the most celebrated case which is still being rehashed today was the 1946 vote of the Veterans Committee that inducted Joe Tinker, Johnny Evers, and Frank Chance as a double play combination. Whether the power of the Chicago press or the poem extolling the talents of the trio played a role in their election will continue to be debated.

Undoubtedly, public pressure has been brought to bear in other cases too numerous to mention. To explore the question of whether the larger cities have a disproportionate share of the voting power and hence a corner on the market, I analyzed where each Hall of Famer played throughout his career.

Some cases required no particular effort as in the following example:

MIKE SCHMIDT

City	Games	Percentage of Games	Conversion
Philadelphia	2404	100.000%	1.000

Others required a more involved breakdown:

REGGIE JACKSON

City	Games	Percentage of Games	Conversion
Kansas City	35	1.241%	0.012
Oakland	1,311	46.489%	0.465
Baltimore	134	4.752%	0.048
New York	653	23.156%	0.232
California	687	24.362%	0.244
Totals	2,820	100.000%	1.001

In the case of pitchers the same procedure was followed except that games pitched in each location was used.

STEVE CARLTON

City	Games	Percentage of Games	Conversion
St. Louis	190	25.641%	0.256
Philadelphia	499	67.341%	0.673
San Francisco	6	0.810%	0.008
Chicago	10	1.350%	0.014
Cleveland	23	3.104%	0.031
Minnesota	13	1.754%	0.018
Totals	741	100.000%	1.000

The next step was to calculate the number of years that each city had a franchise, using the following procedure.

CHICAGO

League	Years	Total Franchise Years
National	1876–2009	134
American	1901–2009	109
Union Association	1884	1
Players	1890	1
Federal	1914–1915	2
Total		247

It was necessary to subtract five years from each active franchise to coin–

cide with the waiting period required for Hall of Fame consideration. Because Chicago has two franchises, a total of 10 years were subtracted from the total of 247 franchise years.

The following table shows the results of the computation. "BWA" again refers to the Baseball Writers' Association elections, and "VC" to the Veterans Committee selections.

HALL OF FAMERS BY CITY
ACTIVE FRANCHISES

Franchises	No. Years	Wait Net	Years	BWA	VC	Total
N.Y./Brooklyn (2)	315	−10	305	21.140	23.511	44.651
Chicago (2)	247	−10	237	10.915	12.928	23.843
Philadelphia (1)	194	−5	189	6.608	9.030	15.638
Boston (1)	189	−5	184	9.104	8.735	17.839
St. Louis (1)	187	−5	182	8.418	8.327	16.745
Cincinnati (1)	135	−5	130	3.028	5.311	8.339
Pittsburgh (1)	131	−5	126	5.874	6.829	12.703
Cleveland (1)	129	−5	124	5.800	6.552	12.352
Detroit (1)	117	−5	112	5.068	3.951	9.019
L.A./Anaheim (2)	101	−10	91	4.239	0.042	4.281
S.F./Oakland (2)	94	−10	84	6.031	0.525	6.556
Washington, D.C. (1)	91	−5	86	2.043	2.631	4.674
Baltimore (1)	79	−5	74	4.886	1.587	6.473
Kansas City (1)	60	−5	55	1.268	0.208	1.476
Milwaukee (1)	56	−5	51	4.061	0.202	4.263
Minnesota (1)	49	−5	44	2.707		2.707
Houston (1)	48	−5	43	0.884	0.065	0.949
Atlanta (1)	44	−5	39	1.494	0.189	1.683
San Diego (1)	41	−5	36	2.411		2.411
Texas (1)	38	−5	33	0.645		0.645
Seattle (1)	34	−5	29	0.128		0.128
Toronto (1)	33	−5	28	0.220		0.220
Colorado (1)	17	−5	12			
Florida (1)	17	−5	12			
Tampa Bay (1)	12	−5	7	0.087		0.087
Arizona (1)	12	−5	7			
Totals (30)	2,470			107.059	90.623	197.682

INACTIVE FRANCHISES

City	Years	BWA	VC	Total
Montreal	36	0.811		0.811
Louisville	20	0.128	0.646	0.774
Buffalo	10		1.063	1.063
Providence	8		0.812	0.812
Indianapolis	6		0.109	0.109
Columbus	5			
Troy	4		0.680	0.680

City	Years	BWA	VC	Total
Worcester	3		0.006	0.006
Hartford	2			
Syracuse	2			
Toledo	2			
Newark	1		0.074	0.074
Richmond	1			
Rochester	1			
Totals	101	.939	3.390	4.329
Cumulative Totals	2,571	107.998	94.013	202.011

Managers and the Hall of Fame

Name	First/Last Year	Years Managed	Pct.	Won	Lost	Status
Joe McCarthy	1926–1950	24	.615	2125	1333	HF Mgr.
Charles Comiskey	1883–1894	12	.608	840	541	HF Exec
Frank Selee	1890–1905	16	.598	1284	862	HF Mgr
Billy Southworth	1929–1951	13	.597	1044	704	HF Mgr
Frank Chance	1905–1923	11	.593	946	648	HF Player
John McGraw	1899–1932	33	.586	2763	1948	HF Mgr
Al Lopez	1951–1969	17	.584	1410	1004	HF Mgr
Earl Weaver	1968–1986	17	.583	1480	1060	HF Mgr
Cap Anson	1879–1898	20	.578	1292	945	HF Player
Fred Clarke	1897–1915	19	.576	1602	1181	HF Player
Davey Johnson	1984–2000	14	.564	1148	888	
Steve O'Neill	1935–1954	14	.559	1040	821	
Walter Alston	1954–1976	23	.558	2040	1613	HF Mgr
Bobby Cox	1978–2009	28	.556	2413	1930	Active 2009
Mike Scioscia	2000–2009	10	.556	900	720	Active 2009
Miller Huggins	1913–1929	17	.555	1413	1134	HF Mgr
Bill Terry	1932–1941	10	.555	823	661	HF Player
Patsy Tebeau	1890–1900	11	.555	726	583	
Billy Martin	1969–1988	16	.553	1253	1013	
Harry Wright	1876–1893	18	.548	1000	825	HF Exec
Charlie Grimm	1932–1960	19	.547	1287	1067	
Sparky Anderson	1970–1995	26	.545	2194	1834	HF Mgr
Hughie Jennings	1907–1925	16	.543	1184	995	HF Player
Joe Cronin	1933–1947	15	.540	1236	1055	HF Player
Leo Durocher	1939–1973	24	.540	2008	1709	HF Mgr
Fielder Jones	1904–1918	10	.540	683	582	
Danny Murtaugh	1957–1976	15	.540	1115	950	
Joe Torre	1977–2009	28	.540	2246	1915	Active 2009
Jimy Williams	1986–2004	12	.535	910	790	
Tony LaRussa	1979–2009	31	.535	2552	2217	Active 2009
Whitey Herzog	1973–1990	18	.532	1281	1125	HF Mgr.
Ned Hanlon	1889–1907	19	.530	1313	1164	HF Mgr
Tommy Lasorda	1976–1996	21	.526	1599	1439	HF Mgr
Terry Francona	1997–2009	10	.525	850	770	Active 2009
Bill McKechnie	1915–1946	25	.524	1896	1723	HF Mgr

Name	First/Last Year	Years Managed	Pct.	Won	Lost	Status
Red Schoendienst	1965–1990	14	.522	1041	955	HF Player
Clark Griffith	1901–1920	20	.522	1491	1367	HF Exec
Lou Piniella	1986–2009	22	.521	1784	1639	Active 2009
Dusty Baker	1993–2009	16	.520	1314	1213	Active 2009
Dick Williams	1967–1988	21	.520	1571	1451	HF Mgr
Bill Virdon	1972–1984	13	.519	995	921	
Jack McKeon	1973–2005	15	.518	1011	940	
Johnny Oates	1991–2001	11	.517	797	746	
Cito Gaston	1989–2009	11	.516	809	760	Active 2009
Birdie Tebbetts	1954–1966	11	.515	748	705	
Buck Showalter	1992–2006	11	.514	882	833	
Frankie Frisch	1933–1951	16	.514	1138	1078	HF Player
Ralph Houk	1961–1984	20	.514	1619	1531	
Bobby Valentine	1985–2002	15	.510	1117	1072	
Alvin Dark	1961–1977	13	.510	994	954	
Charlie Dressen	1934–1966	16	.509	1008	973	
Don Zimmer	1972–1991	13	.508	885	858	
Casey Stengel	1934–1965	25	.508	1905	1842	HF Mgr
Paul Richards	1951–1976	12	.506	923	901	
Buck Rodgers	1980–1994	13	.503	784	774	
Felipe Alou	1992–2006	14	.503	1033	1021	
Mike Hargrove	1991–2007	16	.503	1188	1173	
Fred Hutchinson	1952–1964	12	.501	830	827	
Roger Craig	1978–1992	10	.500	738	737	
Wilbert Robinson	1902–1931	19	.500	1399	1398	HF Mgr
Art Howe	1989–2004	14	.498	1129	1137	
Jim Leyland	1986–2009	18	.496	1412	1436	Active 2009
Chuck Tanner	1970–1988	19	.495	1352	1381	
George Stallings	1897–1920	13	.495	879	898	
Bucky Harris	1924–1956	29	.493	2157	2218	HF Mgr
Bruce Bochy	1995–2009	15	.490	1182	1230	Active 2009
Lou Boudreau	1942–1960	16	.487	1162	1224	HF Player
Connie Mack	1894–1950	53	.486	3731	3948	HF Mgr
Luke Sewell	1941–1952	10	.485	606	644	
John McNamara	1969–1996	19	.485	1160	1233	
Bill Rigney	1956–1976	18	.484	1239	1321	
Jim Fregosi	1978–2000	15	.484	1028	1095	
Phil Garner	1992–2007	15	.483	985	1054	
Gene Mauch	1960–1987	26	.483	1902	2037	
Tom Kelly	1986–2001	16	.478	1140	1244	
Jimmy Dykes	1934–1961	21	.477	1406	1541	
Burt Shotton	1928–1950	11	.477	697	764	
Frank Robinson	1975–2006	16	.475	1065	1176	HF Player
Lee Fohl	1915–1926	11	.474	713	792	
Branch Rickey	1913–1925	10	.473	597	664	HF Exec
Gus Schmelz	1884–1897	11	.470	624	703	
Jeff Torborg	1977–2003	11	.469	634	718	
Rogers Hornsby	1925–1953	14	.463	701	812	HF Player
Dave Bristol	1966–1980	11	.462	657	764	
Fred Haney	1939–1959	10	.454	629	757	

Name	First/Last Year	Years Managed	Pct.	Won	Lost	Status
Jimmy McAleer	1901–1911	11	.453	735	889	
Bob Ferguson	1876–1887	11	.445	299	373	
Jim Riggleman	1992–2009	10	.444	555	694	Active 2009
Billie Barnie	1883–1898	14	.438	632	810	
Patsy Donovan	1897–1911	11	.438	684	879	
Jack Chapman	1876–1892	11	.411	351	502	
Total		16.5	.520	109,943	101,356	

Ninety-one individuals were identified who had managed for ten or more seasons. Of that number, 34 (37.4 percent) are in the Hall of Fame—19 as managers, 11 as players, and 4 as executives.

Only two managers have winning percentages greater than .600, while 31 (34.1 percent) are below .500. The winning percentage of the 91 managers is only .520, a mark somewhat lower than would be expected of a select group. Losing managers would usually not survive a minimum of ten years. It is interesting to note the homogeneous nature of the records:

Range of Winning Pct.	Number of Cases	Pct. of Sample
.480 to .520	36	39.6%
.470 to .530	50	54.9%
.460 to .540	61	67.0%
.450 to .550	67	73.6%
.440 to .560	77	84.6%
.430 to .570	80	87.9%
.420 to .580	82	90.1%
.410 to .590	86	94.5%
.400 to .600	89	97.8%

To see if any relationships existed between longevity and the Hall of Fame, I generated the following table:

No. of Years as a Manager	No. of Managers	Status
53	1	One HF Mgr
33	1	One HF Mgr
31	1	One active
29	1	One HF Mgr
28	2	Two active
26	2	One HF Mgr
25	2	Two HF Mgrs
24	2	Two HF Mgrs
23	1	One HF Mgr
22	1	One active
21	3	Two HF Mgrs
20	3	One HF Exec; One HF Player
19	6	Two HF Mgrs; One HF Player
18	4	One HF Exec; One active; One HF Mgr

No. of Years as a Manager	No. of Managers	Status
17	3	Three HF Mgrs
16	10	Four HF Players; One HF Mgr One active
15	7	One HF Player; One active
14	7	Two HF Players
13	6	One HF Mgr
12	4	One HF Exec
11	15	One HF Player; One active
10	9	One HF Exec; One HF Player; Three active

Total No. of Managers   91

Twenty Managers have 20 or more years of service; thirteen are in the Hall of Fame (65.0 percent).

Fifty Managers have 15 or more years of service; twenty-seven are in the Hall of Fame (54.0 percent).

Ninety-one Managers have 10 or more years of service; thirty-four are in the Hall of Fame (37.4 percent).

Sixteen Managers were either active during the 2009 season or not yet retired five years, which lowers the eligible number from 91 to 75. Frank Robinson is excluded from the count because he is already in the Hall of Fame.

The 19 Hall of Famers selected as managers were all active a minimum of 13 years.

Gold Glove Award and the Hall of Fame

The Gold Glove Awards was initiated in 1957 to recognize defensive excellence. There has always been some controversy among baseball writers as to exactly how much attention is given to fielding skills in Hall of Fame voting. With that issue in mind, I reviewed Gold Glove recipients by position. An asterisk (*) indicates the player is ineligible for consideration by the Veterans Committee.

PITCHERS

Name	Number of Awards	Current Status
Greg Maddux	18	Eligible in 2014
Jim Kaat	16	Fifteen years on BWA ballot; high of 29.6% in 1993

Name	Number of Awards	Current Status
Bob Gibson	9	Hall of Fame; 84.0% on first ballot
Bobby Shantz	8	Five BWA elections; 2.3% highest
Mark Langston	7	No votes in BWA elections
Mike Mussina	7	Eligible in 2014
Phil Niekro	5	Hall of Fame; 80.3% on fifth ballot
Ron Guidry	5	Nine BWA elections; 7.9% highest
Kenny Rogers	5	Eligible in 2014
Jim Palmer	4	Hall of Fame; 92.6% on first ballot
Harvey Haddix	3	Nine BWA elections; 3.8% highest
Andy Messersmith	2	Two BWA elections; 0.8% highest
Mike Norris	2	No votes in BWA elections
Rick Reuschel	2	One BWA election; 0.4%
Steve Carlton	1	Hall of Fame; 95.8% on first ballot
Frank Lary	1	No votes in BWA elections
Joaquin Andujar	1	No votes in BWA elections
Mike Boddicker	1	No votes in BWA elections
Ron Darling	1	One BWA election; 0.2%
Orel Hershiser	1	Two BWA elections; 11.2% highest
Bret Saberhagen	1	One BWA election; 1.3%
Fernando Valenzuela	1	Two BWA elections; 6.3% highest
Mike Hampton	1	Active 2009
Johan Santana	1	Active 2009
Mark Buehrle	1	Active 2009
Adam Wainwright	1	Active 2009

CATCHERS

Name	Number of Awards	Current Status
Ivan Rodriguez	13	Active 2009
Johnny Bench	10	Hall of Fame; 96.4% on first ballot
Bob Boone	7	Five BWA elections; 7.7% highest
Jim Sundberg	6	One BWA election; 0.2%
Bill Freehan	5	One BWA election; 0.5%
Del Crandall	4	Four BWA elections; 3.9% highest
Tony Pena	4	One BWA election; 0.4%
Charles Johnson	4	Eligible in 2011
Mike Matheny	4	Eligible in 2012
Earl Battey	3	No votes in BWA elections
Sherman Lollar	3	No votes in BWA elections
Gary Carter	3	Hall of Fame; 78.0% on sixth ballot
Lance Parrish	3	One BWA election; 1.7%
Thurman Munson	3	Fifteen BWA elections; 15.5% highest
Benito Santiago	3	Eligible in 2010
Tom Pagnozzi	3	No votes in BWA elections
Brad Ausmus	3	Active 2009
Johnny Edwards	2	No votes in BWA elections
Ray Fosse	2	No votes in BWA elections
Elston Howard	2	Fifteen BWA elections; 20.7% highest
John Roseboro	2	No votes in BWA elections

Name	Number of Awards	Current Status
Bengie Molina	2	Active 2009
Joe Mauer	2	Active 2009
Yadier Molina	2	Active 2009
Joe Torre	1	Fifteen BWA elections; 22.2% highest
Carlton Fisk	1	Hall of Fame; 79.6% on second ballot
Jody Davis	1	No votes in BWA elections
Mike LaValliere	1	No votes in BWA elections
Sandy Alomar	1	Eligible in 2013
Randy Hundley	1	No votes in BWA elections
Mike Lieberthal	1	Eligible in 2013
Jason Varitek	1	Active 2009
Russell Martin	1	Active 2009

FIRST BASEMEN

Name	Number of Awards	Current Status
Keith Hernandez	11	Nine BWA elections; high of 10.8% in 1998
Don Mattingly	9	Ninth year on BWA ballot; high of 28.2% in 2001
George Scott	8	One BWA election; 0.2%
Vic Power	7	Two BWA elections; 0.8% highest
Bill White	7	Three BWA elections; 1.9% highest
Wes Parker	6	*Nine years in majors
J. T. Snow	6	Eligible in 2014
Steve Garvey	4	Fifteen BWA elections; 42.6% highest
Mark Grace	4	One BWA election; 4.1%
Gil Hodges	3	Fifteen BWA elections; 63.4% highest
Joe Pepitone	3	No votes in BWA elections
Rafael Palmeiro	3	Eligible in 2011
Eddie Murray	3	Hall of Fame; 85.3% on first ballot
John Olerud	3	Eligible in 2011
Todd Helton	3	Active 2009
Derrek Lee	3	Active 2009
Mark Teixeira	3	Active 2009
Cecil Cooper	2	No votes in BWA elections
Jim Spencer	2	No votes in BWA elections
Andres Galarraga	2	Eligible in 2010
Adrian Gonzalez	2	Active 2009
Chris Chambliss	1	No votes in BWA elections
Mike Jorgenson	1	One BWA election; 0.2%
Mike Squires	1	No votes in BWA elections
Jeff Bagwell	1	Eligible in 2011
Will Clark	1	One BWA election; 4.4%
Mark McGwire	1	Third year on BWA ballot; high of 23.6% in 2008
Doug Mientkiewicz	1	Active 2009
Darin Erstad	1	Active 2009
Albert Pujols	1	Active 2009
Kevin Youkillis	1	Active 2009
Carlos Pena	1	Active 2009

SECOND BASEMEN

Name	Number of Awards	Current Status
Roberto Alomar	10	Eligible in 2010
Ryne Sandberg	9	Hall of Fame; 76.2% on third ballot
Bill Mazeroski	8	Hall of Fame VC 2001; Fifteen BWA elections; 42.3% highest
Frank White	8	One BWA election; 3.8%
Joe Morgan	5	Hall of Fame; 81.8% on first ballot
Bobby Richardson	5	Three BWA elections; 2.0% highest
Bobby Grich	4	One BWA election; 2.6%
Craig Biggio	4	Eligible in 2013
Bret Boone	4	Eligible in 2011
Orlando Hudson	4	Active 2009
Nelson Fox	3	Hall of Fame VC 1997; Fifteen BWA elections; 74.7% highest
Davey Johnson	3	One BWA election; 0.7%
Bobby Knoop	3	No votes in BWA elections
Harold Reynolds	3	No votes in BWA elections
Manny Trillo	3	No votes in BWA elections
Lou Whitaker	3	One BWA election; 2.9%
Luis Castillo	3	Active 2009
Tommy Helms	2	One BWA election; 0.3%
Felix Millan	2	One BWA election; 0.3%
Pokey Reese	2	*Eight years in majors
Fernando Vina	2	Eligible in 2010
Placido Polanco	2	Active 2009
Glenn Beckert	1	One BWA election; 0.2%
Frank Bolling	1	No votes in BWA elections
Doug Flynn	1	No votes in BWA elections
Doug Griffin	1	*Eight years in majors
Ken Hubbs	1	*Three years in majors
Jose Lind	1	*Nine years in majors
Davy Lopes	1	One BWA election; 0.5%
Charley Neal	1	*Eight years in majors
Robby Thompson	1	No votes in BWA elections
Chuck Knoblauch	1	One BWA election; 0.2%
Mark Grudzielanek	1	Eligible in 2014
Dustin Pedroia	1	Active 2009
Brandon Phillips	1	Active 2009

THIRD BASEMEN

Name	Number of Awards	Current Status
Brooks Robinson	16	Hall of Fame; 92.0% on first ballot
Mike Schmidt	10	Hall of Fame; 96.5% on first ballot
Scott Rolen	7	Active 2009
Buddy Bell	6	One BWA election; 1.7%
Robin Ventura	6	Eligible in 2010
Eric Chavez	6	Active 2009

Name	Number of Awards	Current Status
Ken Boyer	5	Fifteen BWA elections; 25.5% highest
Doug Rader	5	No votes in BWA elections
Ron Santo	5	Fifteen BWA elections; 43.1% highest
Gary Gaetti	4	One BWA election; 0.8%
Matt Williams	4	One BWA election; 1.3%
Frank Malzone	3	No votes in BWA elections
Terry Pendleton	3	One BWA election; 0.2%
Tim Wallach	3	One BWA election; 0.2%
Ken Caminiti	3	One BWA election; 0.4%
Wade Boggs	2	Hall of Fame; 91.9% on first ballot
Graig Nettles	2	Four BWA elections; 8.4% highest
David Wright	2	Active 2009
Adrian Beltre	2	Active 2009
Clete Boyer	1	Two BWA elections; 0.7% highest
George Brett	1	Hall of Fame; 98.2% on first ballot
Jim Davenport	1	No votes in BWA elections
Kelly Gruber	1	No votes in BWA elections
Ken Reitz	1	No votes in BWA elections
Aurelio Rodriguez	1	No votes in BWA elections
Scott Brosius	1	No votes in BWA elections
Travis Fryman	1	One BWA election; 0.4%
Mike Lowell	1	Active 2009
Evan Longoria	1	Active 2009
Ryan Zimmerman	1	Active 2009

SHORTSTOPS

Name	Number of Awards	Current Status
Ozzie Smith	13	Hall of Fame; 91.7% on first ballot
Omar Vizquel	11	Active 2009
Luis Aparicio	9	Hall of Fame; 84.6% on sixth ballot
Mark Belanger	8	One BWA election; 3.7%
Dave Concepcion	5	Fifteen BWA elections; 16.2% highest
Tony Fernandez	4	One BWA election; 0.7%
Alan Trammell	4	Eighth year on BWA ballot; high of 18.2% in 2008
Derek Jeter	4	Active 2009
Roy McMillan	3	Three BWA elections; 2.3% highest
Barry Larkin	3	Eligible in 2010
Rey Ordonez	3	*Nine years in majors
Jimmy Rollins	3	Active 2009
Gene Alley	2	No votes in BWA elections
Larry Bowa	2	One BWA election; 2.5%
Don Kessinger	2	One BWA election; 0.5%
Cal Ripken	2	Hall of Fame; 98.5% on first ballot
Zoilo Versalles	2	No votes in BWA elections
Maury Wills	2	Fifteen BWA elections; 40.6% highest
Alex Rodriguez	2	Active 2009

Name	Number of Awards	Current Status
Edgar Renteria	2	Active 2009
Orlando Cabrera	2	Active 2009
Ruben Amaro	1	No votes in BWA elections
Ernie Banks	1	Hall of Fame; 83.8% on first ballot
Eddie Brinkman	1	No votes in BWA elections
Rick Burleson	1	No votes in BWA elections
Leo Cardenas	1	Two BWA elections; 0.2% highest
Jay Bell	1	One BWA election; 0.4%
Jim Fregosi	1	One BWA election; 1.0%
Alfredo Griffin	1	No votes in BWA elections
Ozzie Guillen	1	One BWA election; 1.0%
Bud Harrelson	1	One BWA election; 0.2%
Dal Maxvill	1	No votes in BWA elections
Roger Metzger	1	No votes in BWA elections
Bobby Wine	1	No votes in BWA elections
Robin Yount	1	Hall of Fame; 77.5% on first ballot
Neifi Perez	1	Eligible in 2013
Cesar Izturis	1	Active 2009
Michael Young	1	Active 2009

LEFT FIELDERS

Name	Number of Awards	Current Status
Barry Bonds	8	Eligible in 2013
Carl Yastrzemski	7	Hall of Fame; 94.6% on first ballot
Minnie Minoso	3	Fifteen BWA elections; 21.1% highest
Joe Rudi	3	No votes in BWA elections
Pete Rose	2	*Ineligible for consideration
Wally Moon	1	One BWA election; 0.6%
Dusty Baker	1	One BWA election; 0.9%
Norm Siebern	1	No votes in BWA elections
Tom Tresh	1	*Nine Years in majors
Rickey Henderson	1	Hall of Fame; 94.8% on first ballot

*indicates ineligible for consideration by the Veteran's Committee

CENTER FIELDERS

Name	Number of Awards	Current Status
Willie Mays	12	Hall of Fame; 94.7% on first ballot
Ken Griffey, Jr.	10	Active 2009
Andruw Jones	10	Active 2009
Paul Blair	8	One BWA election; 1.9%
Garry Maddox	8	No votes in BWA elections
Jim Edmonds	8	Eligible in 2014
Torii Hunter	8	Active 2009
Curt Flood	7	Fifteen BWA elections; 15.1% highest
Devon White	7	No votes in BWA elections

Name	Number of Awards	Current Status
Dwayne Murphy	6	No votes in BWA elections
Kirby Puckett	6	Hall of Fame; 82.1% on first ballot
Cesar Cedeno	5	One BWA election; 0.5%
Jim Landis	5	No votes in BWA elections
Dale Murphy	5	Eleventh year on BWA ballot; high of 23.2% in 2000
Gary Pettis	5	No votes in BWA elections
Andy Van Slyke	5	No votes in BWA elections
Steve Finley	5	Eligible in 2013
Cesar Geronimo	4	No votes in BWA elections
Fred Lynn	4	Two BWA elections; 5.5% highest
Mickey Stanley	4	One BWA election; 0.5%
Marquis Grissom	4	Eligible in 2011
Kenny Lofton	4	Eligible in 2013
Bernie Williams	4	Eligible in 2012
Willie Davis	3	No votes in BWA elections
Willie McGee	3	Two BWA elections; 5.0% highest
Eric Davis	3	One BWA election; 0.6%
Amos Otis	3	No votes in BWA elections
Mike Cameron	3	Active 2009
Vernon Wells	3	Active 2009
Tommy Agee	2	No votes in BWA elections
Jimmy Piersall	2	No votes in BWA elections
Ken Berry	2	No votes in BWA elections
Darin Erstad	2	Active 2009
Grady Sizemore	2	Active 2009
Carlos Beltran	2	Active 2009
Shane Victorino	2	Active 2009
Jackie Brandt	1	No votes in BWA elections
Vada Pinson	1	Fifteen BWA elections; 15.7% highest
Bill Virdon	1	Two BWA elections; 0.8% highest
Darren Lewis	1	No votes in BWA elections
Bob Dernier	1	No votes in BWA elections
Mickey Mantle	1	Hall of Fame; 88.2% on first ballot
Vic Davalillo	1	No votes in BWA elections
Rick Manning	1	No votes in BWA elections
Juan Beniquez	1	No votes in BWA elections
Rick Miller	1	No votes in BWA elections
Willie Wilson	1	One BWA election; 2.0%
Ellis Burks	1	Eligible in 2010
Jose Cruz, Jr.	1	Eligible in 2014
Aaron Rowand	1	Active 2009
Nate McLouth	1	Active 2009
Adam Jones	1	Active 2009
Michael Bourn	1	Active 2009
Matt Kemp	1	Active 2009

RIGHT FIELDERS

Name	Number of Awards	Current Status
Roberto Clemente	12	Hall of Fame; 92.7% in special election
Al Kaline	10	Hall of Fame; 88.3% on first ballot
Ichiro Suzuki	9	Active 2009
Andre Dawson	8	Eighth year on BWA ballot; high of 67.0% in 2009
Dwight Evans	8	Three BWA elections; 8.2% highest
Dave Winfield	7	Hall of Fame; 84.5% on first ballot
Larry Walker	7	Eligible in 2011
Tony Gwynn	5	Hall of Fame; 97.6% on first ballot
Henry Aaron	3	Hall of Fame; 97.8% on first ballot
Bobby Bonds	3	Eleven BWA elections; 10.6% highest
Dave Parker	3	Thirteenth year on BWA ballot; high of 22.4% in 1998
Jesse Barfield	2	No votes in BWA elections
Raul Mondesi	2	Eligible in 2011
Frank Robinson	1	Hall of Fame; 89.2% on first ballot
Ellis Valentine	1	One BWA election; 0.2%
Jackie Jensen	1	Six BWA elections; 1.1% highest
Roger Maris	1	Fifteen BWA elections; 43.1% highest
Tony Oliva	1	Fifteen BWA elections; 47.3% highest
Al Cowens	1	No votes in BWA elections
Sixto Lezcano	1	No votes in BWA elections
Reggie Smith	1	One BWA election; 0.7%
Jay Buhner	1	One BWA election; 0.2%
Shawn Green	1	Eligible in 2013
Bobby Murcer	1	No votes in BWA elections
Jermaine Dye	1	Active 2009
Bobby Abreu	1	Active 2009
Jeff Francoeur	1	Active 2009

Summary of Gold Glove Award Winners by Position

Position	No.	# in Hall of Fame	Players Under Consideration	Active 2009	Not Yet Eligible	Eligible for VC	Ineligible
Pitchers	26	4	0	4	3	15	0
Catchers	33	3	0	7	5	18	0
First Basemen	32	1	2	9	5	14	1
Second Basemen	35	4	0	5	5	16	5
Third Basemen	30	4	0	7	1	18	0
Shortstops	38	5	1	8	2	21	1
Left Fielders	10	2	0	0	1	5	2
Center Fielders	54	3	1	14	7	29	0
Right Fielders	27	6	2	4	3	12	0
Totals	285	32	6	58	32	148	9

Of the 285 players who have received a Gold Glove Award, only 32 (11.2 percent) are currently in the Hall of Fame. When the 99 players who are either still active, not yet retired for five years or technically ineligible are factored out, the percentage in the Hall of Fame increases to 17.2 percent.

Cy Young Award and the Hall of Fame

From 1956 through 1966, the Cy Young Award recognized the outstanding pitcher in the major leagues. Beginning in 1967, the award was expanded to recognize the most valuable pitcher in each league. A summary of the winners is contained in the following list. An asterisk (*) indicates the player is ineligible for consideration by the Veterans Committee.

Name	Number of Awards	Current Status
Roger Clemens	7	Eligible in 2013
Randy Johnson	5	Active 2009
Steve Carlton	4	Hall of Fame; 95.8% on first ballot
Greg Maddux	4	Eligible in 2014
Sandy Koufax	3	Hall of Fame; 86.9% on first ballot
Tom Seaver	3	Hall of Fame; 98.8% on first ballot
Jim Palmer	3	Hall of Fame; 92.6% on first ballot
Pedro Martinez	3	Active 2009
Denny McLain	2	Three BWA elections; 0.7% highest
Bob Gibson	2	Hall of Fame; 84.0% on first ballot
Gaylord Perry	2	Hall of Fame; 77.2% on third ballot
Brett Saberhagen	2	One BWA election; 1.3%
Tom Glavine	2	Eligible in 2014
Johan Santana	2	Active 2009
Tim Lincecum	2	Active 2009
Don Newcombe	1	Fifteen BWA elections; 15.3% highest
Warren Spahn	1	Hall of Fame; 83.2% on first ballot
Bob Turley	1	No votes in BWA elections
Early Wynn	1	Hall of Fame; 76.0% on fourth ballot
Vernon Law	1	Seven BWA elections; 2.4% highest
Whitey Ford	1	Hall of Fame; 77.8% on second ballot
Don Drysdale	1	Hall of Fame; 78.4% on tenth ballot
Dean Chance	1	No votes in BWA elections
Mike McCormick	1	No votes in BWA elections
Jim Lonborg	1	Two BWA elections; 0.8% highest
Mike Cuellar	1	No votes in BWA elections
Jim Perry	1	Two BWA elections; 1.9% highest
Ferguson Jenkins	1	Hall of Fame; 75.4% on third ballot
Vida Blue	1	Four BWA elections; 8.7% highest

Name	Number of Awards	Current Status
Mike Marshall	1	One BWA election; 1.5%
Jim Hunter	1	Hall of Fame; 76.3% on third ballot
Randy Jones	1	No votes in BWA elections
Sparky Lyle	1	Four BWA elections; 13.1% highest
Ron Guidry	1	Nine BWA elections; 8.8% highest
Bruce Sutter	1	Hall of Fame; 76.9% on thirteenth ballot
Mike Flanagan	1	One BWA election; 0.4%
Steve Stone	1	No votes in BWA elections
Fernando Valenzuela	1	Two BWA elections; 6.3% highest
Rollie Fingers	1	Hall of Fame; 82.1% on second ballot
John Denny	1	No votes in BWA elections
Rick Sutcliffe	1	One BWA election; 1.8%
Dwight Gooden	1	One BWA election; 3.3%
Mike Scott	1	One BWA election; 0.4%
Steve Bedrosian	1	One BWA election; 0.2%
Orel Hershiser	1	Two BWA elections; 11.2% highest
Mark Davis	1	One BWA election; 0.2%
Doug Drabek	1	One BWA election; 0.4%
Pete Vuckovich	1	No votes in BWA elections
*La Marr Hoyt	1	*Eight years in majors
Willie Hernandez	1	One BWA election; 0.4%
Frank Viola	1	One BWA election; 0.4%
Bob Welch	1	One BWA election; 0.2%
Dennis Eckersley	1	Hall of Fame; 83.2% on first ballot
Jack McDowell	1	One BWA election; 0.8%
David Cone	1	One BWA election; 3.9%
John Smoltz	1	Active 2009
Pat Hentgen	1	Eligible in 2010
Barry Zito	1	Active 2009
Roy Halladay	1	Active 2009
Eric Gagne	1	Eligible in 2014
Bartolo Colon	1	Active 2009
Chris Carpenter	1	Active 2009
Brandon Webb	1	Active 2009
C. C. Sabathia	1	Active 2009
Jake Peavy	1	Active 2009
Cliff Lee	1	Active 2009
Zack Greinke	1	Active 2009

SUMMARY

	Summary
Hall of Famers	15
Under Consideration by BWA	0
Active 2009	14
Not Yet Eligible	5
Ineligible	1
Eligible for VC consideration	32
Total	67

Of the 67 pitchers who have received the Cy Young Award, 15 (22.4 percent) are in the Hall of Fame. When the 20 pitchers who are still active, not yet eligible or ineligible are subtracted from the total, the percentage of Hall of Famers rises to 31.9 percent.

Fifteen pitchers have won the award more than once. Six are in the Hall of Fame, four are still active, three are not yet eligible and two are Veterans Committee candidates.

Rookie of the Year Award and the Hall of Fame

Between 1940 and 1946 the Chicago chapter of the Baseball Writer's Association selected the outstanding rookie. In 1947 the award became nationally recognized with broader voting representation. The following list shows each award winner. An asterisk (*) indicates the player is ineligible for consideration by the Veterans Committee.

Name	Year of Award	Current Status
Jackie Robinson	1947	Hall of Fame; 77.5% on first ballot
Alvin Dark	1948	Fifteen BWA elections; 21.3% highest
Don Newcombe	Nat. 1949	Fifteen BWA elections; 15.3% highest
Roy Sievers	Am. 1949	Two BWA elections; 1.1% highest
Sam Jethroe	Nat. 1950	*Four years in majors
Walt Dropo	Am. 1950	One BWA election; 0.3%
Willie Mays	Nat. 1951	Hall of Fame; 94.7% on first ballot
Gil McDougald	Am. 1951	Nine BWA elections; 1.7% highest
Joe Black	Nat. 1952	*Six years in majors
Harry Byrd	Am. 1952	*Seven years in majors
Jim Gilliam	Nat. 1953	No votes in BWA elections
Harvey Kuenn	Am. 1953	Fifteen BWA elections; 39.3% highest
Wally Moon	Nat. 1954	One BWA election; 0.6%
Bob Grim	Am. 1954	*Eight years in majors
Bill Virdon	Nat. 1955	Two BWA elections; 0.8% highest
Herb Score	Am. 1955	*Eight years in majors
Frank Robinson	Nat. 1956	Hall of Fame; 89.2% on first ballot
Luis Aparicio	Am. 1956	Hall of Fame; 84.6% on sixth ballot
Jack Sanford	Nat. 1957	No votes in BWA elections
Tony Kubek	Am. 1957	*Nine years in majors
Orlando Cepeda	Nat. 1958	Hall of Fame Veteran's Committee; Fifteen BWA elections; 73.6% highest
Albie Pearson	Am. 1958	*Nine years in majors
Willie McCovey	Nat. 1959	Hall of Fame; 81.4% on first ballot
Bob Allison	Am. 1959	No votes in BWA elections
Frank Howard	Nat. 1960	One BWA election; 1.4%
Ron Hansen	Am. 1960	No votes in BWA elections
Billy Williams	Nat. 1961	Hall of Fame; 85.7% on sixth ballot

Name	Year of Award	Current Status
Don Schwall	Am. 1961	*Seven years in majors
Ken Hubbs	Nat. 1962	*Three years in majors
Tom Tresh	Am. 1962	*Nine years in majors
Pete Rose	Nat. 1963	*Ineligible for consideration
Gary Peters	Am. 1963	No votes in BWA elections
Dick Allen	Nat. 1964	Fourteen BWA elections; 18.9% highest
Tony Oliva	Am. 1964	Fifteen BWA elections; 47.3% highest
Jim Lefebvre	Nat. 1965	*Eight years in majors
Curt Blefary	Am. 1965	*Eight years in majors
Tommy Helms	Nat. 1966	One BWA election; 0.3%
Tommy Agee	Am. 1966	No votes in BWA elections
Tom Seaver	Nat. 1967	Hall of Fame; 98.8% on first ballot
Rod Carew	Am. 1967	Hall of Fame; 90.5% on first ballot
Johnny Bench	Nat. 1968	Hall of Fame; 96.4% on first ballot
Stan Bahnsen	Am. 1968	No votes in BWA elections
Ted Sizemore	Nat. 1969	No votes in BWA elections
Lou Piniella	Am. 1969	One BWA election; 0.5%
Carl Morton	Nat. 1970	*Eight years in majors
Thurman Munson	Am. 1970	Fifteen BWA elections; 15.5% highest
Earl Williams	Nat. 1971	*Eight years in majors
Chris Chambliss	Am. 1971	No votes in BWA elections
Jon Matlock	Nat. 1972	No votes in BWA elections
Carlton Fisk	Am. 1972	Hall of Fame; 79.6% on second ballot
Gary Matthews	Nat. 1973	No votes in BWA elections
Al Bumbry	Am. 1973	No votes in BWA elections
Bake McBride	Nat. 1974	No votes in BWA elections
Mike Hargrove	Am. 1974	One BWA election; 0.2%
John Montefusco	Nat. 1975	No votes in BWA elections
Fred Lynn	Am. 1975	Two BWA elections; 5.5% highest
Butch Metzger	Nat. 1976	*Five years in majors
Pat Zachry	Nat. 1976	No votes in BWA elections
Mark Fidrych	Am. 1976	*Five years in majors
Andre Dawson	Nat. 1977	Eighth year on BWA ballot; 67.0% in 2009
Eddie Murray	Am. 1977	Hall of Fame; 85.3% on first ballot
Bob Horner	Nat. 1978	No votes in BWA elections
Lou Whitaker	Am. 1978	One BWA election; 2.9%
Rick Sutcliffe	Nat. 1979	One BWA election; 1.8%
John Castino	Am. 1979	*Six years in majors
Alfredo Griffin	Am. 1979	No votes in BWA elections
Steve Howe	Nat. 1980	No votes in BWA elections
Joe Charboneau	Am. 1980	*Three years in majors
Fernando Valenzuela	Nat. 1981	Two BWA elections; 6.3% highest
Dave Righetti	Am. 1981	One BWA election; 0.4%
Steve Sax	Nat. 1982	One BWA election; 0.4%
Cal Ripken	Am. 1982	Hall of Fame; 98.5% on first ballot
Darryl Strawberry	Nat. 1983	One BWA election; 1.2%
Ron Kittle	Am. 1983	No votes in BWA elections
Dwight Gooden	Nat. 1984	One BWA election; 3.3%
Alvin Davis	Am. 1984	*Nine years in majors
Vince Coleman	Nat. 1985	One BWA election; 0.6%
Ozzie Guillen	Am. 1985	One BWA election; 1.0%

Name	Year of Award	Current Status
Todd Worrell	Nat. 1986	No votes in BWA elections
Jose Canseco	Am. 1986	One BWA election; 1.1%
Benito Santiago	Nat. 1987	Eligible in 2010
Mark McGwire	Am. 1987	Third year on BWA ballot; 23.6% in 2008
Chris Sabo	Nat. 1988	*Nine years in majors
Walt Weiss	Am. 1988	One BWA election; 0.2%
Jerome Walton	Nat. 1989	No votes in BWA elections
Gregg Olson	Am. 1989	No votes in BWA elections
David Justice	Nat. 1990	One BWA election; 0.2%
Sandy Alomar, Jr.	Am. 1990	Eligible in 2013
Jeff Bagwell	Nat. 1991	Eligible in 2011
Chuck Knoblauch	Am. 1991	One BWA election; 0.2%
Eric Karros	Nat. 1992	Eligible in 2010
Pat Listach	Am. 1992	*Six years in majors
Mike Piazza	Nat. 1993	Eligible in 2013
Tim Salmon	Am. 1993	Eligible in 2012
Raul Mondesi	Nat. 1994	Eligible in 2011
Bob Hamelin	Am. 1994	*Six years in majors
Hideo Nomo	Nat. 1995	Eligible in 2011
Marty Cordova	Am. 1995	*Nine years in majors
Todd Hollandsworth	Nat. 1996	Eligible in 2012
Derek Jeter	Am. 1996	Active 2009
Scott Rolen	Nat. 1997	Active 2009
Nomar Garciaparra	Am. 1997	Active 2009
Kerry Wood	Nat. 1998	Active 2009
Ben Grieve	Am. 1998	*Nine years in majors
Scott Williamson	Nat. 1999	Eligible in 2013
Carlos Beltran	Am. 1999	Active 2009
Rafael Furcal	Nat. 2000	Active 2009
Kazuhiro Sasaki	Am. 2000	*Four years in majors
Albert Pujols	Nat. 2001	Active 2009
Ichiro Suzuki	Am. 2001	Active 2009
Jason Jennings	Nat. 2002	Active 2009
Eric Hinske	Am. 2002	Active 2009
Dontrelle Willis	Nat. 2003	Active 2009
Angel Berroa	Am. 2003	Active 2009
Jason Bay	Nat. 2004	Active 2009
Bobby Crosby	Am. 2004	Active 2009
Ryan Howard	Nat. 2005	Active 2009
Huston Street	Am. 2005	Active 2009
Hanley Ramirez	Nat. 2006	Active 2009
Justin Verlander	Am. 2006	Active 2009
Ryan Braun	Nat. 2007	Active 2009
Dustin Pedroia	Am. 2007	Active 2009
Geovany Soto	Nat. 2008	Active 2009
Evan Longoria	Am. 2008	Active 2009
Chris Coghlan	Nat. 2009	Active 2009
Andrew Bailey	Am. 2009	Active 2009

The typical Rookie of the Year has not gone on to rack up Hall of Fame credentials. Only 13 of the 126 (10.3 percent) have achieved election. When the 34 players not currently eligible are subtracted, the Hall of Fame percentage becomes 14.1 percent. Surprisingly, 25 players did not participate in ten seasons, the minimum for Hall of Fame consideration. An additional 22, although technically qualified, never received a vote in a BWA election. This means that 51.1 percent of the Rookies of the Year either have not gotten one vote in a Hall of Fame election or have not met the minimum 10 year standard for Hall of Fame consideration.

SUMMARY

	Summary
Hall of Famers	13
Eligible for Consideration by Veterans Committee	51
Active through 2009	24
Not Yet Eligible	10
Ineligible	26
Currently on BWA ballot	2
Total	126

Most Valuable Player Award and the Hall of Fame

The Most Valuable Player Award has gone through three phases. From 1911 through 1914 the Chalmers Award was presented. Between 1922 and 1929 league awards were made. In 1931 the Baseball Writers' Association of America voted for MVPs in both leagues, a practice which is still in effect.

Name	*Number of Awards*	*Current Status*
Barry Bonds	7	Eligible in 2013
Jimmy Foxx	3	Hall of Fame; 79.2% on eighth ballot
Joe DiMaggio	3	Hall of Fame; 88.8% on fourth ballot
Stan Musial	3	Hall of Fame; 93.2% on first ballot
Roy Campanella	3	Hall of Fame; 79.4% on fifth ballot
Yogi Berra	3	Hall of Fame; 85.6% on second ballot
Mickey Mantle	3	Hall of Fame; 88.2% on first ballot
Mike Schmidt	3	Hall of Fame; 96.5% on first ballot
Alex Rodriguez	3	Active 2009
Albert Pujols	3	Active 2009
Walter Johnson	2	Hall of Fame; 83.6% on first ballot
Rogers Hornsby	2	Hall of Fame; 78.1% on fifth ballot
Lou Gehrig	2	Hall of Fame; by acclamation of BWA in 1939
Mickey Cochrane	2	Hall of Fame; 79.5% on sixth ballot
Carl Hubbell	2	Hall of Fame; 87.0% on third ballot

Name	Number of Awards	Current Status
Hank Greenberg	2	Hall of Fame; 85.0% on ninth ballot
Hal Newhouser	2	Hall of Fame Veteran's Committee; twelve BWA elections, high of 42.8%
Ted Williams	2	Hall of Fame; 93.4% on first ballot
Willie Mays	2	Hall of Fame; 94.7% on first ballot
Ernie Banks	2	Hall of Fame; 83.8% on first ballot
Roger Maris	2	Fifteen BWA elections; 43.1% highest
Frank Robinson	2	Hall of Fame; 89.2% on first ballot
Johnny Bench	2	Hall of Fame; 96.4% on first ballot
Joe Morgan	2	Hall of Fame; 81.8% on first ballot
Dale Murphy	2	Eleventh year on BWA ballot; 23.2% highest in 2000
Robin Yount	2	Hall of Fame; 77.5% on first ballot
Cal Ripken	2	Hall of Fame; 98.5% on first ballot
Frank E. Thomas	2	Eligible in 2014
Juan Gonzalez	2	Eligible in 2011
Frank Schulte	1	One BWA election; 0.5%
Ty Cobb	1	Hall of Fame; 98.2% on first ballot
Larry Doyle	1	Three BWA elections; 1.5% highest
Tris Speaker	1	Hall of Fame; 82.1% on second ballot
Jake Daubert	1	Five BWA elections; 1.0% highest
Johnny Evers	1	Hall of Fame Veteran's Committee; seven BWA elections, 64.4% highest
Eddie Collins	1	Hall of Fame; 77.7% on fourth ballot
George Sisler	1	Hall of Fame; 85.8% on fourth ballot
Babe Ruth	1	Hall of Fame; 95.1% on first ballot
Dazzy Vance	1	Hall of Fame; 81.7% on sixteenth ballot
Roger Peckinpaugh	1	Nine BWA elections; 1.5% highest
Bob O'Farrell	1	Three BWA elections; 2.4% highest
George Burns	1	No votes in BWA elections
Paul Waner	1	Hall of Fame; 83.3% on sixth ballot
Jim Bottomley	1	Hall of Fame Veteran's Committee; twelve BWA elections, 33.1% highest
Frankie Frisch	1	Hall of Fame; 84.5% on fourth ballot
Lefty Grove	1	Hall of Fame; 76.4% on fourth ballot
Chuck Klein	1	Hall of Fame Veteran's Committee; twelve BWA elections, 27.9% highest
Dizzy Dean	1	Hall of Fame; 79.2% on ninth ballot
Gabby Hartnett	1	Hall of Fame; 77.7% on eleventh ballot
Joe Medwick	1	Hall of Fame; 84.8% on tenth ballot
Charlie Gehringer	1	Hall of Fame; 85.0% on fifth ballot
Ernie Lombardi	1	Hall of Fame Veteran's Committee; nine BWA elections, 16.4% highest
Bucky Walters	1	Thirteen BWA elections; 23.7% highest
Frank McCormick	1	Four BWA elections; 3.0% highest
Dolf Camilli	1	Four BWA elections; 1.5% highest
Mort Cooper	1	Four BWA elections; 1.1% highest
Joe Gordon	1	Hall of Fame Veteran's Committee; fourteen BWA elections; 28.5%
Spud Chandler	1	Five BWA elections; 3.0% highest
Marty Marion	1	Twelve BWA elections; 40.0% highest

Name	Number of Awards	Current Status
Phil Cavaretta	1	Twelve BWA elections; 35.6% highest
Bob Elliott	1	Three BWA elections; 2.0% highest
Lou Boudreau	1	Hall of Fame; 77.3% on tenth ballot
Jackie Robinson	1	Hall of Fame; 77.5% on first ballot
Jim Konstanty	1	No votes in BWA elections
Phil Rizzuto	1	Hall of Fame Veteran's Committee; fourteen BWA elections, 38.4% highest
Hank Sauer	1	One BWA election; 1.3%
Bobby Shantz	1	Five BWA elections; 2.3% highest
Al Rosen	1	No votes in BWA elections
Don Newcombe	1	Fifteen BWA elections; 15.3% highest
Henry Aaron	1	Hall of Fame; 97.8% on first ballot
Jackie Jensen	1	Six BWA elections; 1.1% highest
Nelson Fox	1	Hall of Fame Veteran's Committee; fifteen BWA elections, 74.7% highest
Dick Groat	1	Six BWA elections; 1.8% highest
Maury Wills	1	Fifteen BWA elections; 40.6% highest
Sandy Koufax	1	Hall of Fame; 86.9% on first ballot
Elston Howard	1	Fifteen BWA elections; 20.7% highest
Ken Boyer	1	Fifteen BWA elections; 25.5% highest
Brooks Robinson	1	Hall of Fame; 92.0% on first ballot
Zoilo Versalles	1	No votes in BWA elections
Roberto Clemente	1	Hall of Fame; 92.7% in special election held in 1973
Orlando Cepeda	1	Hall of Fame Veteran's Committee; Fifteen BWA elections; 73.6% highest
Carl Yastrzemski	1	Hall of Fame; 94.6% on first ballot
Bob Gibson	1	Hall of Fame; 84.0% on first ballot
Denny McLain	1	Three BWA elections; 0.7% highest
Willie McCovey	1	Hall of Fame; 81.4% on first ballot
Harmon Killebrew	1	Hall of Fame; 83.1% on fourth ballot
Boog Powell	1	One BWA election; 1.3%
Joe Torre	1	Fifteen years on BWA ballot; 22.2% highest
Vida Blue	1	Four BWA elections; 8.7% highest
Dick Allen	1	Fourteen years on BWA ballot; 18.9% highest
Pete Rose	1	*Ineligible for consideration
Reggie Jackson	1	Hall of Fame; 93.6% on first ballot
Steve Garvey	1	Fifteen years on BWA ballot; 42.6% highest
Jeff Burroughs	1	One BWA election; 0.2%
Fred Lynn	1	Two BWA elections; 5.5% highest
Thurman Munson	1	Fifteen BWA elections; 15.5% highest
George Foster	1	Four BWA elections; 6.9% highest
Rod Carew	1	Hall of Fame; 90.5% on first ballot
Dave Parker	1	Thirteenth year on BWA ballot; highest 22.4% in 1998
Jim Rice	1	Hall of Fame; 76.4% on fifteenth ballot
Willie Stargell	1	Hall of Fame; 82.4% on first ballot
Keith Hernandez	1	Nine BWA elections; 10.8% highest
Don Baylor	1	Two BWA elections; 2.6% highest
George Brett	1	Hall of Fame; 98.2% on first ballot
Rollie Fingers	1	Hall of Fame; 82.1% on second ballot

Name	Number of Awards	Current Status
Ryne Sandberg	1	Hall of Fame; 76.2% on third ballot
Willie Hernandez	1	One BWA election; 0.4%
Willie McGee	1	Two BWA elections; 5.0% highest
Don Mattingly	1	Ninth year on BWA ballot; highest 28.2% in 2001
Roger Clemens	1	Eligible in 2013
Andre Dawson	1	Eighth year on BWA ballot; highest 67.0% in 2009
George Bell	1	One BWA election; 1.2%
Kirk Gibson	1	One BWA election; 2.5%
Jose Canseco	1	One BWA election; 1.1%
Kevin Mitchell	1	One BWA election; 0.4%
Rickey Henderson	1	Hall of Fame; 94.8% on first ballot
Terry Pendleton	1	One BWA election; 0.2%
Dennis Eckersley	1	Hall of Fame; 83.2% on first ballot
Jeff Bagwell	1	Eligible in 2011
Barry Larkin	1	Eligible in 2010
Mo Vaughn	1	One BWA election; 1.1%
Ken Caminiti	1	One BWA election; 0.4%
Ken Griffey, Jr.	1	Active 2009
Larry Walker	1	Eligible in 2011
Sammy Sosa	1	Eligible in 2013
Ivan Rodriguez	1	Active 2009
Chipper Jones	1	Active 2009
Jason Giambi	1	Active 2009
Jeff Kent	1	Eligible in 2014
Ichiro Suzuki	1	Active 2009
Miguel Tejada	1	Active 2009
Vladimir Guerrero	1	Active 2009
Ryan Howard	1	Active 2009
Justin Morneau	1	Active 2009
Jimmy Rollins	1	Active 2009
Dustin Pedroia	1	Active 2009
Joe Mauer	1	Active 2009

SUMMARY

	Summary
Hall of Famers	62
Under Consideration by BWA	4
Eligible for Consideration by VC	47
Active 2009	14
Not Yet Eligible	9
Ineligible	1
Total	137

Through the 2009 season, 137 different players had received the Most Valuable Player Award. Of that number 62 (45.3 percent) are currently in the Hall of Fame. Twenty-four players are either still active, not yet retired five years or are ineligible. Excluding that group raises the percentage of Hall of Famers to 54.9 percent.

Seven of the ten players who have won three or more MVP awards are in the Hall of Fame. Barry Bonds, the only player with seven, is not yet eligible and Alex Rodriguez and Albert Pujols with three are still active. Among the 19 who have garnered two awards, 15 are Hall of Famers. Gonzalez and Thomas have not been retired for five years. Murphy is on the BWA ballot and Maris is eligible for Veterans Committee consideration.

Status of the Top Ten Vote-Getters in Each Baseball Writers' Association Election

In the 65 elections conducted from 1936 through 2009, 176 different players ranked among the top ten (including ties). Theoretically, had there been no continuity in the voting, 650 individuals might have occupied those spots, which indicates a high degree of consistency among the voters. The following table illustrates what has happened to the "Top Ten" vote-getters.

Period	No. of Elections Held	No. of Different Individs. in Top Ten	No. Now in Hall of Fame	Pct. in Hall of Fame	Cum. No. in Top Ten	Cum. No. Now in Hall of Fame	Cum. Pct. Now in Hall of Fame
1936–1962	20	65	64	98.5%			
1964–1986	22	56	46	82.1%	121	110	90.9%
1987–2009	23	55	35	63.6%	176	145	82.4%
Totals	65	176	145				

One hundred-seven of the Hall of Famers received the 75 percent vote necessary for election. Two others, Lou Gehrig and Roberto Clemente, were enshrined in special elections. The 39 elected by the Veterans Committee and their highest rank in the Baseball Writers Association voting are shown in the following list.

Name	Highest Rank	Year	Year Elected
Roger Bresnahan	5th	1945	1945
Jimmy Collins	8th	1945	1945
Ed Delahanty	9th	1945	1945
Wilbert Robinson	8th	1942	1945 as a manager
Frank Chance	1st	1946	1946
Johnny Evers	2nd	1946	1946
Rube Waddell	2nd	1945	1946
Ed Walsh	3rd	1945	1946

Name	Highest Rank	Year	Year Elected
Clark Griffith	9th	1946	1946 as an executive
Chief Bender	9th–10th tie	1953	1953
Ray Schalk	8th	1955	1955
Max Carey	1st	1958	1961
Edd Roush	1st	1960	1962
Sam Rice	3rd	1962	1963
Eppa Rixey	3rd	1960	1963
Red Faber	7th	1960	1964
Burleigh Grimes	4th	1960	1964
Miller Huggins	3rd	1946	1964 as a manager
Kiki Cuyler	5th	1958	1968
Lefty Gomez	5th	1956	1972
Jim Bottomley	5th	1960	1974
Al Lopez	6th	1966	1977 as a manager
George Kell	10th	1970, 1976 (tie), 1983	1977
Hack Wilson	4th	1958	1979
Chuck Klein	8th	1964	1980
Johnny Mize	6th	1968, 1972	1981
PeeWee Reese	6th	1976	1984
Enos Slaughter	2nd	1978	1985
Arky Vaughan	9th	1968	1985
Red Schoendienst	7th	1980	1989
Tony Lazzeri	7th	1958	1991
Hal Newhouser	6th	1975	1992
Phil Rizzuto	9th	1976	1994
Richie Ashburn	8th	1978	1995
Jim Bunning	4th	1989	1996
Nelson Fox	3rd	1985	1997
Orlando Cepeda	2nd	1994	1999
Bill Mazeroski	5th	1992	2001
Joe Gordon	9th	1969	2008

An additional 58 Hall of Famers elected by the Veterans Committee never ranked in the top ten in a Baseball Writers' Association election.

Status of Non–Hall of Famers Who Ranked in the Top Ten

Name	Times in Top Ten	Highest Rank	Status
Hank Gowdy	2	10th	VC Eligible
Mel Harder	1	Tie 10th & 11th	VC Eligible
Johnny Vander Meer	2	10th	VC Eligible
Marty Marion	8	7th	VC Eligible
Allie Reynolds	3	7th	VC Eligible
Gil Hodges	14	3rd	VC Eligible
Phil Cavaretta	1	Tie 9th & 10th	VC Eligible
Maury Wills	7	8th	VC Eligible

Name	Times in Top Ten	Highest Rank	Status
Tony Oliva	13	6th	VC Eligible
Roger Maris	5	5th	VC Eligible
Harvey Kuenn	7	6th	VC Eligible
Ken Boyer	4	10th	VC Eligible
Lew Burdette	1	Tie 10th & 11th	VC Eligible
Dick Allen	1	9th	VC Eligible
Joe Torre	1	9th	VC Eligible
Luis Tiant	1	8th	VC Eligible
Mickey Lolich	1	Tie 10th & 11th	VC Eligible
Ron Santo	9	3rd	VC Eligible
Jim Kaat	11	8th	VC Eligible
Steve Garvey	13	4th	VC Eligible
Tommy John	11	7th	VC Eligible
Dave Parker	1	10th	On BWA ballot
Dale Murphy	1	10th	On BWA ballot
Don Mattingly	1	9th	On BWA ballot
Andre Dawson	8	3rd	On BWA ballot
Bert Blyleven	8	4th	On BWA ballot
Lee Smith	7	5th	On BWA ballot
Jack Morris	6	6th	On BWA ballot
Alan Trammell	3	10th	On BWA ballot
Mark McGwire	3	9th	On BWA ballot
Tim Raines	2	8th	On BWA ballot

Of the 31 non–Hall of Famers who finished among the top ten in the Baseball Writers' Association balloting, 10 are still under consideration. Nine of those who are eligible for Veterans Committee balloting have never ranked above ninth in an election. The apparent front-runners for future selection are Gil Hodges and Ron Santo.

The Sporting News All-Star Team Selections and the Hall of Fame

From 1925 through 1960 *The Sporting News* selected an All-Star team that included players from both leagues. Beginning in 1961 an All-Star team representing each of the leagues has been selected, a practice which continued through the 2009 season.

In 1974 the American League added a designated hitter (DH). In 1991 and 1992 the position was omitted from All-Star selections but was reinstated in 1993. In 1999 and 2000 no DH was selected. From 2001 through 2006 a DH was included. In 2007 no DH was selected. Again in 2008 and 2009 a DH was included.

The following lists tabulated by position show the number of times each player was selected and his status relative to the Hall of Fame. An asterisk

(*) indicates the player is ineligible for consideration by the Veterans Committee.

PITCHERS

Name	Times Selected	Status
Steve Carlton	7	Hall of Fame
Lefty Grove	5	Hall of Fame
Bob Feller	5	Hall of Fame
Warren Spahn	5	Hall of Fame
Jim Palmer	5	Hall of Fame
Greg Maddux	5	Eligible in 2014
Roger Clemens	5	Eligible in 2013
Carl Hubbell	4	Hall of Fame
Robin Roberts	4	Hall of Fame
Whitey Ford	4	Hall of Fame
Sandy Koufax	4	Hall of Fame
Juan Marichal	4	Hall of Fame
Tom Seaver	4	Hall of Fame
Ron Guidry	4	Nine BWA elections; 8.8% highest
Tom Glavine	4	Eligible in 2014
Pedro Martinez	4	Active 2009
Randy Johnson	4	Active 2009
Dizzy Dean	3	Hall of Fame
Red Ruffing	3	Hall of Fame
Mort Cooper	3	Four BWA elections; 1.1% highest
Hal Newhouser	3	Hall of Fame VC
Bob Lemon	3	Hall of Fame
Ferguson Jenkins	3	Hall of Fame
Jimmy Key	3	One BWA election; 0.6%
Lefty Gomez	2	Hall of Fame VC
Bucky Walters	2	Thirteen BWA elections; 23.7% highest
Boo Ferris	2	*Six years in majors
Allie Reynolds	2	Thirteen BWA elections; 33.6%highest
Johnny Antonelli	2	No votes in BWA elections
Don Newcombe	2	Fifteen BWA elections; 15.3% highest
Billy Pierce	2	Five BWA elections; 1.9% highest
Jim Bunning	2	Hall of Fame VC
Gary Peters	2	No votes in BWA elections
Jim Kaat	2	Fifteen BWA elections; 29.6% highest
Earl Wilson	2	No votes in BWA elections
Denny McLain	2	Three BWA elections; 0.7% highest
Bob Gibson	2	Hall of Fame
Mike Cuellar	2	No votes in BWA elections
Vida Blue	2	Four BWA elections; 8.7% highest
Gaylord Perry	2	Hall of Fame
Randy Jones	2	No votes in BWA elections
Frank Tanana	2	No votes in BWA elections
Fernando Valenzuela	2	Two BWA elections; 6.3% highest
Rick Sutcliffe	2	One BWA election; 1.8%
Brett Saberhagen	2	One BWA election; 1.3%
Mike Scott	2	One BWA election; 0.4%

Name	Times Selected	Status
Frank Viola	2	One BWA election; 0.4%
Danny Jackson	2	No votes in BWA elections
Chuck Finley	2	One BWA election; 0.2%
Jack McDowell	2	One BWA election; 0.8%
David Wells	2	Eligible in 2013
Curt Schilling	2	Eligible in 2013
Andy Pettitte	2	Active 2009
Johan Santana	2	Active 2009
Tim Lincecum	2	Active 2009
Mariano Rivera (Reliever)	2	Active 2009
Walter Johnson	1	Hall of Fame
Ed Rommel	1	Eight BWA elections; 4.5% highest
Dazzy Vance	1	Hall of Fame
Herb Pennock	1	Hall of Fame
George Uhle	1	Three BWA elections; 1.5% highest
Grover Alexander	1	Hall of Fame
Charley Root	1	Six BWA elections; 2.5% highest
Ted Lyons	1	Hall of Fame
Waite Hoyt	1	Hall of Fame VC
Burleigh Grimes	1	Hall of Fame VC
Wes Ferrell	1	Five BWA elections; 3.6% highest
George Earnshaw	1	Five BWA elections; 2.5% highest
Lon Warneke	1	Five BWA elections; 6.5% highest
Alvin Crowder	1	Two BWA elections; 0.4% highest
Schoolboy Rowe	1	Four BWA elections; 5.0% highest
Johnny Vander Meer	1	Twelve BWA elections; 29.8% highest
Paul Derringer	1	Seven BWA elections; 6.2% highest
Whitlow Wyatt	1	One BWA election; 0.4%
Thornton Lee	1	No votes in BWA elections
Tiny Bonham	1	No votes in BWA elections
Tex Hughson	1	*Eight years in majors
Spud Chandler	1	Five BWA elections; 3.0% highest
Rip Sewell	1	Three BWA elections; 0.6% highest
Dizzy Trout	1	One BWA election; 0.5%
Hank Borowy	1	No votes in BWA elections
Ewell Blackwell	1	Three BWA elections; 4.7% highest
Ralph Branca	1	No votes in BWA elections
Johnny Sain	1	Ten BWA elections; 34.0% highest
Harry Brecheen	1	Seven BWA elections; 2.6% highest
Mel Parnell	1	No votes in BWA elections
Ellis Kinder	1	One BWA election; 1.5%
Joe Page	1	*Eight years in majors
Vic Raschi	1	Nine BWA elections; 10.2% highest
Jim Konstanty	1	No votes in BWA elections
Sal Maglie	1	Two BWA elections; 6.5% highest
Preacher Roe	1	Six BWA elections; 0.8% highest
Bobby Shantz	1	Five BWA elections; 2.3% highest
Bob Porterfield	1	One BWA election; 0.3%
Bob Turley	1	No votes in BWA elections
Bob Friend	1	No votes in BWA elections
Early Wynn	1	Hall of Fame

Name	Times Selected	Status
Sam "Toothpick" Jones	1	No votes in BWA elections
Vernon Law	1	Seven BWA elections; 2.4% highest
Ernie Broglio	1	*Eight years in majors
Frank Lary	1	No votes in BWA elections
Joey Jay	1	No votes in BWA elections
Ralph Terry	1	No votes in BWA elections
Dick Donovan	1	No votes in BWA elections
Don Drysdale	1	Hall of Fame
Bob Purkey	1	No votes in BWA elections
Dean Chance	1	No votes in BWA elections
Jim Grant	1	No votes in BWA elections
Mel Stottlemyre	1	One BWA election; 0.8%
Jim Lonberg	1	Two BWA elections; 0.8% highest
Mike McCormick	1	No votes in BWA elections
Dave McNally	1	Four BWA elections; 2.8% highest
Jim Perry	1	Two BWA elections; 1.9% highest
Sam McDowell	1	No votes in BWA elections
Jim Merritt	1	No votes in BWA elections
Wilbur Wood	1	Six BWA elections; 7.0% highest
Ken Holtzman	1	Two BWA elections; 1.2% highest
Ron Bryant	1	*Eight years in majors
Jim Hunter	1	Hall of Fame
Andy Messersmith	1	Two BWA elections; 0.8% highest
Don Gullet	1	*Nine years in majors
Don Sutton	1	Hall of Fame
Nolan Ryan	1	Hall of Fame
Rick Reuschel	1	One BWA election; 0.4%
Jim Kern	1	No votes in BWA elections
Mike Flanagan	1	One BWA election; 0.4%
Joe Niekro	1	One BWA election; 1.3%
Steve Stone	1	No votes in BWA elections
Tommy John	1	Fifteen BWA elections; 31.7% highest
Jim Bibby	1	One BWA election; 0.2%
Jack Morris	1	Tenth year on BWA ballot; highest 44.0% in 2009
Dave Stieb	1	One BWA election; 0.4%
Geoff Zahn	1	No votes in BWA elections
Steve Rogers	1	No votes in BWA elections
LaMarr Hoyt	1	*Eight years in majors
John Denny	1	No votes in BWA elections
Larry McWilliams	1	No votes in BWA elections
Mike Boddicker	1	No votes in BWA elections
Willie Hernandez	1	One BWA election; 0.4%
Mark Thurmond	1	*Eight years in majors
Dwight Gooden	1	One BWA election; 3.3%
John Tudor	1	One BWA election; 0.4%
Teddy Higuera	1	*Nine years in majors
Zane Smith	1	No votes in BWA elections
Dave Stewart	1	Two BWA elections; 7.4% highest
Orel Hershiser	1	Two BWA elections; 11.2% highest
Mark Davis	1	One BWA election; 0.2%

Name	Times Selected	Status
Bob Welch	1	*One BWA election; 0.2%
Doug Drabek	1	One BWA election; 0.4%
Jim Abbott	1	One BWA election; 2.5%
Jose Rijo	1	One BWA election; 0.2%
Dave Fleming	1	*Five years in majors
Steve Avery	1	No votes in BWA elections
David Cone	1	One BWA election; 3.9%
Mike Mussina	1	Eligible in 2014
Pete Schourek	1	No votes in BWA elections
Pat Hentgen	1	Eligible in 2010
John Smoltz	1	Active 2009
Al Leiter	1	Eligible in 2011
Denny Neagle	1	No votes in BWA elections
Kevin Brown	1	Eligible in 2011
Mike Hampton	1	Eligible in 2011
Jose Lima	1	Eligible in 2012
Jamie Moyer	1	Active 2009
Mark Mulder	1	Eligible in 2014
Derek Lowe	1	Active 2009
Barry Zito	1	Active 2009
Roy Halladay	1	Active 2009
Eric Gagne (Reliever)	1	Eligible in 2014
Randy Wolf	1	Active 2009
Jason Schmidt	1	Active 2009
Joe Nathan (Reliever)	1	Active 2009
Chad Cordero (Reliever)	1	Eligible in 2014
Chris Carpenter	1	Active 2009
C.C. Sabathia	1	Active 2009
Jake Peavy	1	Active 2009
Joe Borowski (Reliever)	1	Eligible in 2014
Jose Valverde	1	Active 2009
Cliff Lee	1	Active 2009
Francisco Rodriguez (Reliever)	1	Active 2009
Brad Lidge (Reliever)	1	Active 2009
Ryan Franklin (Reliever)	1	Active 2009
Zack Greinke	1	Active 2009

CATCHERS

Name	Times Selected	Status
Mike Piazza	10	Eligible in 2013
Mickey Cochrane	7	Hall of Fame
Johnny Bench	7	Hall of Fame
Ivan Rodriguez	7	Active 2009
Bill Dickey	6	Hall of Fame
Gary Carter	6	Hall of Fame
Yogi Berra	5	Hall of Fame
Carlton Fisk	5	Hall of Fame
Jorge Posada	5	Active 2009
Roy Campanella	4	Hall of Fame

Name	Times Selected	Status
Bill Freehan	4	One BWA election; 0.5%
Thurman Munson	4	Fifteen BWA elections; 15.5% highest
Walker Cooper	3	Ten BWA elections; 14.4% highest
Del Crandall	3	Four BWA elections; 3.9% highest
Elston Howard	3	Fifteen BWA elections; 20.7% highest
Joe Torre	3	Fifteen BWA elections; 22.2% highest
Ted Simmons	3	One BWA election; 3.7%
Benito Santiago	3	Eligible in 2010
Mickey Tettleton	3	No votes in BWA elections
Joe Mauer	3	Active 2009
Gabby Hartnett	2	Hall of Fame
Earl Battey	2	No votes in BWA elections
Jim Sundberg	2	One BWA election; 0.2%
Lance Parrish	2	One BWA election; 1.7%
Bob O'Farrell	1	Three BWA elections; 2.4% highest
Harry Danning	1	Two BWA elections; 0.4% highest
Mickey Owen	1	No votes in BWA elections
Paul Richards	1	*Eight years in majors
Aaron Robinson	1	*Eight years in majors
Birdie Tebbetts	1	Two BWA elections; 3.0% highest
Sherm Lollar	1	*No votes in BWA elections
Smokey Burgess	1	Two BWA elections; 0.5% highest
Johnny Edwards	1	No votes in BWA elections
Paul Casanova	1	No votes in BWA elections
Tim McCarver	1	One BWA election; 3.8%
Ray Fosse	1	No votes in BWA elections
Manny Sanguillen	1	One BWA election; 0.5%
Bob Boone	1	Five BWA elections; 7.7% highest
Darrell Porter	1	No votes in BWA elections
Rick Cerone	1	No votes in BWA elections
Tony Pena	1	One BWA election; 0.4%
Rich Gedman	1	No votes in BWA elections
Matt Nokes	1	No votes in BWA elections
Ernie Whitt	1	No votes in BWA elections
Mike LaValliere	1	No votes in BWA elections
Mike Scioscia	1	No votes in BWA elections
Darren Daulton	1	One BWA election; 0.2%
Mike Stanley	1	No votes in BWA elections
Javy Lopez	1	Eligible in 2012
Johnny Estrada	1	Eligible in 2014
Jason Varitek	1	Active 2009
Paul LoDuca	1	Eligible in 2014
Brian McCann	1	Active 2009
Russell Martin	1	Active 2009
Geovany Soto	1	Active 2009
Yadier Molina	1	Active 2009

FIRST BASEMEN

Name	Times Selected	Status
Lou Gehrig	6	Hall of Fame

Name	Times Selected	Status
Jimmie Foxx	5	Hall of Fame
Keith Hernandez	5	Nine BWA elections; highest 10.8%
Willie McCovey	4	Hall of Fame
Orlando Cepeda	4	Hall of Fame VC
Boog Powell	4	One BWA election; 1.3%
Steve Garvey	4	Fifteen BWA elections; 42.6% highest
Cecil Cooper	4	No votes in BWA elections
Don Mattingly	4	Ninth year on BWA ballot; highest 28.2% in 2001
Jeff Bagwell	4	Eligible in 2011
Todd Helton	4	Active 2009
Albert Pujols	4	Active 2009
Johnny Mize	3	Hall of Fame VC
Stan Musial	3	Hall of Fame
Ted Kluszewski	3	Fifteen BWA elections; 14.4% highest
Will Clark	3	One BWA election; 4.4%
Fred McGriff	3	Eligible in 2010
Mark McGwire	3	Third year on BWA ballot; highest 23.6% in 2008
Ferris Fain	2	*Nine years in majors
Norm Cash	2	One BWA election; 1.6%
Bill White	2	Three BWA elections; 1.9% highest
Dick Allen	2	Fourteen BWA elections; 18.9% highest
John Mayberry	2	No votes in BWA elections
Rod Carew	2	Hall of Fame
Eddie Murray	2	Hall of Fame
Cecil Fielder	2	One BWA election; 0.2%
Frank E. Thomas	2	Eligible in 2014
Rafael Palmeiro	2	Eligible in 2011
Carlos Delgado	2	Active 2009
Justin Morneau	2	Active 2009
Mark Teixeira	2	Active 2009
Jim Bottomley	1	Hall of Fame VC
Chris Chambliss	1	No votes in BWA elections
George Burns	1	No votes in BWA elections
Bill Terry	1	Hall of Fame
Hank Greenberg	1	Hall of Fame
Frank McCormick	1	Four BWA elections; 3.0% highest
Dolf Camilli	1	Four BWA elections; 1.5% highest
Rudy York	1	Two BWA elections; 5.0% highest
Ray Sanders	1	*Seven years in majors
Phil Cavarretta	1	Twelve BWA elections; 35.6% highest
Tommy Henrich	1	Ten BWA elections; 20.7% highest
Walt Dropo	1	One BWA election; 0.3%
Mickey Vernon	1	Fifteen BWA elections; 24.9% highest
Bill Skowron	1	No votes in BWA elections
Norm Siebern	1	No votes in BWA elections
Joe Pepitone	1	No votes in BWA elections
Dick Stuart	1	No votes in BWA elections
Fred Whitfield	1	*Nine years in majors

Name	Times Selected	Status
Felipe Alou	1	One BWA election; 0.8%
Harmon Killebrew	1	Hall of Fame
Lee May	1	One BWA election; 0.5%
Willie Stargell	1	Hall of Fame
Tony Perez	1	Hall of Fame
Willie Montanez	1	No votes in BWA elections
Pete Rose	1	*Ineligible for Hall of Fame consideration
Al Oliver	1	No votes in BWA elections
George Hendrick	1	No votes in BWA elections
Jack Clark	1	One BWA election; 1.5%
George Brett	1	Hall of Fame
Mo Vaughn	1	One BWA election; 1.1%
Eric Karros	1	Eligible in 2010
Tino Martinez	1	Eligible in 2011
Jim Thome	1	Active 2009
Jason Giambi	1	Active 2009
Paul Konerko	1	Active 2009
Ryan Howard	1	Active 2009
Carlos Pena	1	Active 2009
Prince Fielder	1	Active 2009

SECOND BASEMEN

Name	Times Selected	Status
Rod Carew	7	Hall of Fame
Charley Gehringer	6	Hall of Fame
Joe Gordon	6	Hall of Fame VC
Bobby Richardson	6	Three BWA elections; 2.0% highest
Ryne Sandberg	6	Hall of Fame
Rogers Hornsby	5	Hall of Fame
Joe Morgan	5	Hall of Fame
Roberto Alomar	5	Eligible in 2010
Craig Biggio	5	Eligible in 2013
Jackie Robinson	4	Hall of Fame
Nelson Fox	4	Hall of Fame VC
Chase Utley	4	Active 2009
Bill Mazeroski	3	Hall of Fame VC
Glenn Beckert	3	One BWA election; 0.2%
Bobby Grich	3	One BWA election; 2.6%
Willie Randolph	3	One BWA election; 1.1%
Manny Trillo	3	No votes in BWA elections
Julio Franco	3	Eligible in 2013
Jeff Kent	3	Eligible in 2014
Frankie Frisch	2	Hall of Fame
Bobby Doerr	2	Hall of Fame VC
Red Schoendienst	2	Hall of Fame VC
Pete Rose	2	*Ineligible for Hall of Fame consideration
Dave Johnson	2	One BWA election; 0.7%
Davey Lopes	2	One BWA election; 0.5%

Name	Times Selected	Status
Damaso Garcia	2	No votes in BWA elections
Lou Whitaker	2	One BWA election; 2.9%
Carlos Baerga	2	Eligible in 2011
Chuck Knoblauch	2	One BWA election; 0.2%
Bret Boone	2	Eligible in 2011
Alfonso Soriano	2	Active 2009
Tony Lazzeri	1	Hall of Fame VC
Billy Herman	1	Hall of Fame VC
George Stirnweiss	1	No votes in BWA elections
Bobby Avila	1	No votes in BWA elections
Frank Bolling	1	No votes in BWA elections
Jim Gilliam	1	No votes in BWA elections
Ron Hunt	1	No votes in BWA elections
Tommy Helms	1	One BWA election; 0.3%
Cookie Rojas	1	No votes in BWA elections
Frank White	1	One BWA election; 3.8%
Glenn Hubbard	1	No votes in BWA elections
Tom Herr	1	No votes in BWA elections
Tony Bernazard	1	No votes in BWA elections
Steve Sax	1	One BWA election; 0.4%
Juan Samuel	1	One BWA election; 0.4%
Johnny Ray	1	No votes in BWA elections
Robby Thompson	1	No votes in BWA elections
Eric Young	1	Eligible in 2012
Edgardo Alfonzo	1	Eligible in 2012
Marcus Giles	1	*Seven seasons in majors
Mark Loretta	1	Active 2009
Brian Roberts	1	Active 2009
Robinson Cano	1	Active 2009
Placido Polanco	1	Active 2009
Dustin Pedroia	1	Active 2009
Aaron Hill	1	Active 2009

THIRD BASEMEN

Name	Times Selected	Status
Mike Schmidt	10	Hall of Fame
Brooks Robinson	9	Hall of Fame
Pie Traynor	7	Hall of Fame
Wade Boggs	7	Hall of Fame
George Kell	6	Hall of Fame VC
Ken Boyer	5	Fifteen BWA elections; 25.5% highest
Ron Santo	5	Fifteen BWA elections; 43.1% highest
Eddie Mathews	4	Hall of Fame
Matt Williams	4	One BWA election; 1.3%
Red Rolfe	3	Eight BWA elections; 4.9% highest
Stan Hack	3	Seven BWA elections; 4.8% highest
Graig Nettles	3	Four BWA elections; 8.4% highest
George Brett	3	Hall of Fame
Vinny Castilla	3	Eligible in 2012
Chipper Jones	3	Active 2009

Name	Times Selected	Status
Scott Rolen	3	Active 2009
Alex Rodriguez	3	Active 2009
David Wright	3	Active 2009
Fred Lindstrom	2	Hall of Fame VC
Mike Higgins	2	No votes in BWA elections
Bob Elliott	2	Three BWA elections; 2.0% highest
Al Rosen	2	No votes in BWA elections
Harmon Killebrew	2	Hall of Fame
Sal Bando	2	One BWA election; 0.7%
Buddy Bell	2	One BWA election; 1.7%
Tim Wallach	2	One BWA election; 0.2%
Jim Thome	2	Active 2009
Travis Fryman	2	One BWA election; 0.4%
Pepper Martin	1	Fourteen BWA elections; 17.3% highest
Billy Johnson	1	*Nine years in majors
Whitey Kurowski	1	*Nine years in majors
Frank Thomas	1	No votes in BWA elections
Frank Malzone	1	No votes in BWA elections
Deron Johnson	1	No votes in BWA elections
Tony Perez	1	Hall of Fame
Joe Torre	1	Fifteen BWA elections; 22.2% highest
Darrell Evans	1	One BWA election; 1.7%
Bill Madlock	1	One BWA election; 4.5%
Pete Rose	1	*Ineligible for Hall of Fame consideration
Doug DeCinces	1	One BWA election; 0.5%
Bobby Bonilla	1	One BWA election; 0.4%
Carney Lansford	1	One BWA election; 0.6%
Howard Johnson	1	No votes in BWA elections
Kelly Gruber	1	No votes in BWA elections
Terry Pendleton	1	One BWA election; 0.2%
Edgar Martinez	1	Eligible in 2010
Gary Sheffield	1	Active 2009
Ken Caminiti	1	One BWA election; 0.4%
Scott Brosius	1	No votes in BWA elections
Dean Palmer	1	No votes in BWA elections
Troy Glaus	1	Active 2009
Eric Chavez	1	Active 2009
Bill Mueller	1	Eligible in 2012
Melvin Mora	1	Active 2009
Morgan Ensberg	1	Eligible in 2014
Joe Crede	1	Active 2009
Mark Reynolds	1	Active 2009
Evan Longoria	1	Active 2009

SHORTSTOPS

Name	Times Selected	Status
Barry Larkin	9	Eligible in 2010
Cal Ripken	8	Hall of Fame

Name	Times Selected	Status
Joe Cronin	7	Hall of Fame
Alex Rodriguez	6	Active 2009
Luis Aparicio	5	Hall of Fame
Ozzie Smith	5	Hall of Fame
Phil Rizzuto	4	Hall of Fame VC
Ernie Banks	4	Hall of Fame
Edgar Renteria	4	Active 2009
Derek Jeter	4	Active 2009
Travis Jackson	3	Hall of Fame VC
Luke Appling	3	Hall of Fame
Maury Wills	3	Fifteen BWA elections; 40.6% highest
Don Kessinger	3	One BWA election; 0.5%
Dave Concepcion	3	Fifteen BWA elections; 16.2% highest
Garry Templeton	3	One BWA election; 0.4%
Robin Yount	3	Hall of Fame
Alan Trammell	3	Eighth year on BWA ballot; high of 18.2% in 2008
Hanley Ramirez	3	Active 2009
Johnny Pesky	2	One BWA election; 0.4%
Marty Marion	2	Twelve BWA elections; 40.0% highest
Lou Boudreau	2	Hall of Fame
Dick Groat	2	Six BWA elections; 1.8% highest
Jim Fregosi	2	One BWA election; 1.0%
Gene Alley	2	No votes in BWA elections
Bert Campaneris	2	One BWA election; 3.1%
Larry Bowa	2	One BWA election; 2.5%
Rick Burleson	2	No votes in BWA elections
Nomar Garciaparra	2	Active 2009
Glenn Wright	1	Twelve BWA elections; 6.7% highest
Joe Sewell	1	Hall of Fame VC
Arky Vaughan	1	Hall of Fame VC
Dick Bartell	1	Four BWA elections; 0.8% highest
Cecil Travis	1	No votes in BWA elections
Pee Wee Reese	1	Hall of Fame VC
Alvin Dark	1	Fifteen BWA elections; 21.3% highest
Harvey Kuenn	1	Fifteen BWA elections; 39.3% highest
Gil McDougald	1	Nine BWA elections; 1.7% highest
Tony Kubek	1	*Nine years in majors
Tom Tresh	1	*Nine years in majors
Zoilo Versalles	1	No votes in BWA elections
Rico Petrocelli	1	One BWA election; 0.7%
Leo Cardenas	1	Two BWA elections; 0.2% highest
Bud Harrelson	1	One BWA election; 0.2%
Chris Speier	1	No votes in BWA elections
Bill Russell	1	One BWA election; 0.7%
Toby Harrah	1	No votes in BWA elections
Mark Belanger	1	One BWA election; 3.7%
Roy Smalley, Jr.	1	No votes in BWA elections
Dickie Thon	1	No votes in BWA elections
Tony Fernandez	1	One BWA election; 0.7%
Shawon Dunston	1	One BWA election; 0.2%

Name	Times Selected	Status
Travis Fryman	1	One BWA election; 0.4%
Jay Bell	1	One BWA election; 0.4%
Jeff Blauser	1	No votes in BWA elections
Rich Aurilia	1	Active 2009
Miguel Tejada	1	Active 2009
Michael Young	1	Active 2009
Felipe Lopez	1	Active 2009
Jose Reyes	1	Active 2009

Left Fielders

Name	Times Selected	Status
Ted Williams	13	Hall of Fame
Barry Bonds	12	Eligible in 2013
Stan Musial	9	Hall of Fame
Al Simmons	6	Hall of Fame
Jim Rice	6	Hall of Fame
Joe Medwick	5	Hall of Fame
Albert Belle	5	Two BWA elections; 7.7% highest
Ralph Kiner	4	Hall of Fame
Billy Williams	4	Hall of Fame
George Foster	4	Four BWA elections; 6.9% highest
Carl Yastrzemski	3	Hall of Fame
Willie Stargell	3	Hall of Fame
Frank Howard	3	One BWA election; 1.4%
Joe Rudi	3	No votes in BWA elections
Rickey Henderson	3	Hall of Fame
Goose Goslin	2	Hall of Fame VC
Dick Wakefield	2	*Nine years in majors
Minnie Minoso	2	Fifteen BWA elections; 21.1% highest
Tommy Davis	2	One BWA election; 1.2%
Pete Rose	2	*Ineligible for Hall of Fame consideration
Greg Luzinski	2	One BWA election; 0.2%
Tim Raines	2	Second year on BWA ballot; highest 24.3% in 2008
George Bell	2	One BWA election; 1.2%
Joe Carter	2	One BWA election; 3.8%
Moises Alou	2	Eligible in 2014
Garret Anderson	2	Active 2009
Matt Holliday	2	Active 2009
Ryan Braun	2	Active 2009
Heinie Manush	1	Hall of Fame VC
Lefty O'Doul	1	Ten BWA elections; 16.7% highest
Hank Greenberg	1	Hall of Fame
Hank Sauer	1	One BWA election; 1.3%
Leon Wagner	1	No votes in BWA elections
Harmon Killebrew	1	Hall of Fame
Willie Horton	1	One BWA election; 0.9%
Cleon Jones	1	No votes in BWA elections
Lou Brock	1	Hall of Fame

Name	Times Selected	Status
Ben Oglivie	1	No votes in BWA elections
Dusty Baker	1	One BWA election; 0.9%
Lonnie Smith	1	One BWA election; 0.2%
Jose Cruz	1	One BWA election; 0.4%
Phil Bradley	1	*Eight years in majors
Mike Greenwell	1	One BWA election; 0.4%
Kevin McReynolds	1	No votes in BWA elections
Kevin Mitchell	1	One BWA election; 0.4%
Ron Gant	1	No votes in BWA elections
Greg Vaughn	1	No votes in BWA elections
Luis Gonzalez	1	Eligible in 2014
Albert Pujols	1	Active 2009
Miguel Cabrera	1	Active 2009
Lance Berkman	1	Active 2009
Alfonso Soriano	1	Active 2009
Carlos Lee	1	Active 2009
Carlos Quentin	1	Active 2009
Jason Bay	1	Active 2009

CENTER FIELDERS

Name	Times Selected	Status
Willie Mays	11	Hall of Fame
Joe DiMaggio	8	Hall of Fame
Ken Griffey, Jr.	8	Active 2009
Mickey Mantle	6	Hall of Fame
Kirby Puckett	6	Hall of Fame
Earl Averill	4	Hall of Fame VC
Cesar Cedeno	4	One BWA election; 0.5%
Dale Murphy	4	Eleventh year on BWA ballot; highest 23.2% in 2000
Duke Snider	3	Hall of Fame
Fred Lynn	3	Two BWA elections; 5.5% highest
Hack Wilson	2	Hall of Fame VC
Jimmy Wynn	2	No votes in BWA elections
Paul Blair	2	One BWA election; 1.9%
Larry Hisle	2	No votes in BWA elections
Eric Davis	2	One BWA election; 0.6%
Andy Van Slyke	2	No votes in BWA elections
Ellis Burks	2	Eligible in 2010
Bernie Williams	2	Eligible in 2012
Jim Edmonds	2	Eligible in 2014
Vernon Wells	2	Active 2009
Andruw Jones	2	Active 2009
Torii Hunter	2	Active 2009
Max Carey	1	Hall of Fame VC
Johnny Mostil	1	Two BWA elections; 0.5% highest
Wally Berger	1	Two BWA elections; 0.8% highest
Doc Cramer	1	Five BWA elections; 6.0% highest
Pete Reiser	1	Two BWA elections; 3.0% highest
Andy Pafko	1	Two BWA elections; 0.7% highest

Name	Times Selected	Status
Goody Rosen	1	*Six years in majors
Dom DiMaggio	1	Nine BWA elections; 11.3% highest
Larry Doby	1	Hall of Fame VC
Albie Pearson	1	*Nine years in majors
Jimmie Hall	1	*Eight years in majors
Curt Flood	1	Fifteen BWA elections; 15.1% highest
Matty Alou	1	No votes in BWA elections
Bobby Tolan	1	No votes in BWA elections
Willie Davis	1	No votes in BWA elections
Amos Otis	1	No votes in BWA elections
Al Oliver	1	One BWA election; 4.3%
Mickey Rivers	1	One BWA election; 0.5%
Omar Moreno	1	No votes in BWA elections
Al Bumbry	1	No votes in BWA elections
Dwayne Murphy	1	No votes in BWA elections
Gorman Thomas	1	No votes in BWA elections
Lloyd Moseby	1	No votes in BWA elections
Willie McGee	1	Two BWA elections; 5.0% highest
Robin Yount	1	Hall of Fame
Mike Devereaux	1	No votes in BWA elections
Lenny Dykstra	1	One BWA election; 0.2%
Darin Erstad	1	Active 2009
Johnny Damon	1	Active 2009
Carlos Beltran	1	Active 2009
Aaron Rowand	1	Active 2009
Josh Hamilton	1	Active 2009
Grady Sizemore	1	Active 2009
Matt Kemp	1	Active 2009

RIGHT FIELDERS

Name	Times Selected	Status
Hank Aaron	9	Hall of Fame
Babe Ruth	6	Hall of Fame
Tony Gwynn	6	Hall of Fame
Sammy Sosa	6	Eligible in 2013
Vladimir Guerrero	6	Active 2009
Al Kaline	5	Hall of Fame
Roberto Clemente	5	Hall of Fame
Tony Oliva	5	Fifteen BWA elections; 47.3% highest
Reggie Jackson	5	Hall of Fame
Dave Parker	5	Thirteenth year on BWA ballot; highest 22.4% in 1998
Mel Ott	4	Hall of Fame
Frank Robinson	4	Hall of Fame
Dave Winfield	4	Hall of Fame
Juan Gonzalez	4	Eligible in 2011
Manny Ramirez	4	Active 2009
Ichiro Suzuki	4	Active 2009
Paul Waner	3	Hall of Fame
Bobby Murcer	3	One BWA election; 0.7%

Name	Times Selected	Status
Andre Dawson	3	Eighth year on BWA ballot; highest 67.0% in 2009
Dwight Evans	3	Two BWA elections; 8.2% highest
Jose Canseco	3	One BWA election; 1.1%
Larry Walker	3	Eligible in 2011
Magglio Ordonez	3	Active 2009
Chuck Klein	2	Hall of Fame VC
Enos Slaughter	2	Hall of Fame VC
Roger Maris	2	Fifteen BWA elections; 43.1% highest
Bobby Bonds	2	Eleven BWA elections; 10.6% highest
Tony Armas	2	No votes in BWA elections
Pedro Guerrero	2	One BWA election; 1.3%
Darryl Strawberry	2	One BWA election; 1.2%
Bobby Bonilla	2	One BWA election; 0.4%
David Justice	2	One BWA election; 0.2%
Tim Salmon	2	Eligible in 2012
Gary Sheffield	2	Active 2009
Kiki Cuyler	1	Hall of Fame VC
Bill Nicholson	1	One BWA election; 0.4%
Dixie Walker	1	Four BWA elections; 3.0% highest
Tommy Holmes	1	Two BWA elections, 0.8% highest
Carl Furillo	1	Five BWA elections; 1.4% highest
Rocky Colavito	1	Two BWA elections; 0.5% highest
Ken Harrelson	1	*Nine years in majors
Reggie Smith	1	One BWA election; 0.7%
Merv Rettenmund	1	No votes in BWA elections
Richie Scheinblum	1	*Eight years in majors
Jeff Burroughs	1	One BWA election; 0.2%
Richie Zisk	1	No votes in BWA elections
Ken Griffey, Sr.	1	One BWA election; 4.7%
Jack Clark	1	One BWA election; 1.5%
Ken Singleton	1	No votes in BWA elections
Dave Kingman	1	One BWA election; 0.7%
George Hendrick	1	No votes in BWA elections
Harold Baines	1	Third year on BWA ballot; highest 5.9% in 2009
Ruben Sierra	1	Eligible in 2012
Reggie Sanders	1	Eligible in 2013
Dante Bichette	1	One BWA election; 0.6%
Shawn Green	1	Eligible in 2013
JD Drew	1	Active 2009
Jermaine Dye	1	Active 2009
Ryan Ludwick	1	Active 2009
Jayson Werth	1	Active 2009

DESIGNATED HITTERS

Name	Times Selected	Status
Paul Molitor	4	Hall of Fame
Hal McRae	3	No votes in BWA elections
Don Baylor	3	Two BWA elections; 2.6% highest

Name	Times Selected	Status
Edgar Martinez	3	Eligible in 2010
David Ortiz	3	Active 2009
Harold Baines	2	Third year on BWA ballot; highest 5.9% in 2009
Tommy Davis	1	One BWA election; 1.2%
Willie Horton	1	One BWA election; 0.9%
Rusty Staub	1	Seven BWA elections; 7.9% highest
Reggie Jackson	1	Hall of Fame
Richie Zisk	1	No votes in BWA elections
Greg Luzinski	1	One BWA election; 0.2%
Dave Kingman	1	One BWA election; 0.7%
Dave Parker	1	Thirteenth year on BWA ballot; highest 22.4% in 1998
Manny Ramirez	1	Active 2009
Frank E. Thomas	1	Eligible in 2014
Jose Canseco	1	One BWA election; 1.1%
Aubrey Huff	1	Active 2009
Hideki Matsui	1	Active 2009

NUMBER OF HALL OF FAMERS SELECTED TO ALL-STAR TEAMS

Position	BWA	VC	No. of Cases
Pitcher	27	5	183
Catcher	8	0	56
First Base	12	3	69
Second Base	7	7	57
Third Base	8	2	58
Shortstop	8	5	60
Left Field	13	2	55
Center Field	6	4	56
Right Field	10	3	60
Designated Hitter	2	0	19
Totals	101	31	673
Adjustment	91	31	642 19.0% in Hall of Fame

The adjustment was necessary because eight Hall of Famers were selected at two different positions and one was selected at three different positions. In addition eighteen other players were selected at two positions and one was selected at four positions.

STATUS BASED ON NUMBER OF TIMES SELECTED TO THE ALL-STAR TEAM

No. of Years Selected	No. Selected	No. in Hall of Fame	Active 2009	Currently on BWA Ballot	Retired but Not Yet Elig.	Eligible for VC Consider.	Inelig. for Future Consider.
13	1	1					

No. of Years Selected	No. Selected	No. in Hall of Fame	Active 2009	Currently on BWA Ballot	Retired but Not Yet Elig.	Eligible for VC Consider.	Inelig. for Future Consider.
12	2	1			1		
11	1	1					
10	2	1			1		
9	5	3	1		1		
8	3	2	1				
7	7	6	1				
6	19	14	1	1	1	1	1
5	27	15	3		4	5	
4	48	24	7	2	4	11	
Totals	115	68	14	3	12	17	1

Twenty-one players were selected to an All-Star team seven or more times. Fifteen are now in the Hall of Fame. Three players (Alex Rodriguez, Ivan Rodriguez and Ken Griffey, Jr.) are still active. Barry Larkin becomes eligible in 2010 and Barry Bonds and Mike Piazza will be eligible in 2013.

Players who have been selected at two or more positions:

Player	Positions-Number of Times Selected
Musial	OF-9, 1B-3
Carew	2B-7, 1B-2
Rose	OF-2, 2B-2, 1B-1, 3B-1
Jackson	OF-5, DH-1
Parker	OF-5, DH-1
Torre	C-3, 3B-1
Stargell	OF-3, 1B-1
Killebrew	3B-2, 1B-1, OF-1
Brett	3B-3, 1B-1
Yount	SS-3, OF-1
E. Martinez	DH-3, 3B-1
Bonilla	OF-2, 3B-1
Baines	DH-2, OF-1
Luzinski	OF-2, DH-1
T. Davis	OF-2, DH-1
Fryman	SS-1, 3B-2
Greenberg	1B-1, OF-1
Horton	OF-1, DH-1
Kingman	OF-1, DH-1
Perez	1B-1, 3B-1
Zisk	OF-1, DH-1
Thome	3B-2, 1B-1
Thomas	1B-2, DH-1
Canseco	OF-3, DH-1
Pujols	OF-1, 1B-4
A. Rodriguez	SS-6, 3B-3
M. Ramirez	OF-4, DH-1
Soriano	2B-2, OF-1
Sheffield	3B-1, OF-1

	No. of Years Selected	No. Selected	No. in Hall of Fame	Active 2009	Currently on BWA Ballot	Retired but Not Yet Elig.	Eligible for VC Consider.	Inelig. for Future Consider.
Pitcher	183	32	22	1	18	100	10
Catcher	56	8	8	0	5	33	2
First Base	69	15	11	2	6	31	4
Second Base	57	14	8	0	8	25	2
Third Base	58	10	12	0	5	28	3
Shortstop	60	13	10	1	1	33	2
Left Field	55	15	10	1	3	23	3
Center Field	56	10	11	1	3	28	3
Right Field	60	13	9	3	7	26	2
Designated Hitter	19	2	4	2	2	9	0
Totals	673	132	105	11	58	336	31

This table is not adjusted to account for players who were selected at two or more positions. As an example, Pete Rose appears in the tabulations four times because he was selected once as a first baseman, twice as a second baseman, once as a third baseman and twice as an outfielder.

HALL OF FAMERS NEVER SELECTED TO AN ALL-STAR TEAM

(*Completed career before the first *The Sporting News* All-Star Team was selected in 1925.)

Pitchers	Last Year
*Christy Mathewson	1916
Hoyt Wilhelm	1972
Rollie Fingers	1985
Phil Niekro	1987
*Cy Young	1911
*Rube Waddell	1910
*Ed Walsh	1917
Eppa Rixey	1933
Chief Bender	1925
Red Faber	1933
*Mordecai Brown	1916
*Eddie Plank	1917
*Joe McGinnity	1908
*Addie Joss	1910
Rube Marquard	1925
Stan Coveleski	1928
Jesse Haines	1937
*Amos Rusie	1901
*Kid Nichols	1906
*Jack Chesbro	1909
*John Clarkson	1894

Pitchers	Last Year
*Mickey Welch	1892
*Hoss Radbourn	1891
*Pud Galvin	1892
*Tim Keefe	1893
*Vic Willis	1910
Dennis Eckersley	1998
Bruce Sutter	1988
Rich Gossage	1994

Catchers	Last Year
*Roger Bresnahan	1915
Ray Schalk	1929
Ernie Lombardi	1947
*Buck Ewing	1897
Rick Ferrell	1947

First Base	Last Year
George Sisler	1930
*Frank Chance	1914
George Kelly	1932
*Jake Beckley	1907
*Cap Anson	1897
*Dan Brouthers	1904
*Roger Connor	1897

Second Base	Last Year
*Nap Lajoie	1916
Eddie Collins	1930
Johnny Evers	1929
*Bid McPhee	1899

Third Base	Last Year
*Jimmy Collins	1908
*Frank Baker	1922

Shortstop	Last Year
*Honus Wagner	1917
Rabbit Maranville	1935
*Hughie Jennings	1918
*Joe Tinker	1916
Dave Bancroft	1930
*Bobby Wallace	1918
*Monte Ward	1894
*George Davis	1909

Outfield		Last Year
Ty Cobb	CF	1928
Harry Heilmann	RF	1932
Tris Speaker	CF	1928
*Willie Keeler	RF	1910

Outfield		Last Year
Edd Roush	CF	1931
Sam Rice	RF	1934
*Ed Delahanty	LF	1903
Richie Ashburn	CF	1962
*Hugh Duffy	CF	1906
*Fred Clarke	LF	1915
Lloyd Waner	CF	1945
Zack Wheat	LF	1927
Ross Youngs	RF	1926
Earl Combs	CF	1935
Chick Hafey	LF	1937
*Sam Crawford	RF	1917
Harry Hooper	RF	1925
*Jesse Burkett	LF	1905
*Elmer Flick	RF	1910
*Joe Kelley	LF	1908
*Billy Hamilton	CF	1901
*James O'Rourke	LF	1904
*Thomas McCarthy	RF	1896
*Sam Thompson	RF	1906
*King Kelly	RF	1893

The Longevity Factor

Obviously, the majority of Hall of Famers enjoy long, productive careers. In order to see what relationship exists between longevity and Hall of Fame election we looked at the career leaders in games played, at-bats and hits. Not surprisingly, most of the same names rank high in all three categories. A total of 155 players rank among the top 200 in each of the three categories.

ANALYSIS OF PLAYERS RANKING IN THE
TOP 200 IN GAMES, AT-BATS AND HITS

Category	No. of Players	No. in Hall of Fame [BWA-VC]	Currently on BWA Ballot	Active or Not Yet Elig.	Elig. for VC Consid.	Ineligible	Pct. in Hall of Fame*
Top 50	29	22 [21–1]	2	4	0	1	100%
Top 100	72	45 [37–8]	4	13	9	1	83.3%
Top 150	116	61 [46–15]	5	22	27	1	69.3%
Top 200	155	75 [56–19]	5	31	43	1	63.6%

*Omits those players who were active in 2009, are currently on the ballot, are not yet eligible for the Baseball Writers' Association ballot or are ineligible by administrative edict.

Currently there are 141 position players in the Hall of Fame. The 75 who rank among the top 200 in all three categories represent 53.2 percent of the Hall of Fame membership. An additional 24 Hall of Famers rank among the top 200 in one or two categories. When this group is added it brings the total to 99 (70.2 percent) of the Hall of Fame.

It is interesting to note of the 42 Hall of Famers who do not appear in the "top 200" in any of the three categories, 33 are Veterans Committee selections. Nine (21.4 percent) of the group are catchers. Among the nine elected by the Baseball Writers' Association, Roy Campanella's career was ended after 10 years by his tragic car accident. Bill Dickey lost two years to military service while Hank Greenberg lost the equivalent of four years. Jackie Robinson made his historic debut as a 28-year-old rookie.

PLAYERS IN THE TOP 50 IN ALL THREE CATEGORIES

Player	Rank in Games Played	Rank in At-Bats	Rank in Hits	Status
Pete Rose	1	1	1	Ineligible for consideration
Carl Yastrzemski	2	3	6	BWA
Hank Aaron	3	2	3	BWA
Rickey Henderson	4	10	20	BWA
Ty Cobb	5	5	2	BWA
Eddie Murray	6.5	6	11	BWA
Stan Musial	6.5	9	4	BWA
Cal Ripken	8	4	13	BWA
Willie Mays	9	11	10	BWA
Barry Bonds	10	29	31	Eligible in 2013
Dave Winfield	11	8	18	BWA
Brooks Robinson	13	14	42	BWA
Robin Yount	14	7	16	BWA
Craig Biggio	15	12	19	Eligible in 2013
Al Kaline	16	21	25	BWA
Rafael Palmeiro	17	15	23	Eligible in 2011
Harold Baines	18	27	40	Currently on BWA ballot
Eddie Collins	19	24	9	BWA
Frank Robinson	21	23	30	BWA
Honus Wagner	22	16	7	BWA
Tris Speaker	23	20	5	BWA
Mel Ott	26	38	38	BWA
George Brett	27	17	14	BWA
Paul Molitor	30	13	8	BWA
Ken Griffey Jr.	33	32	46	Active 2009
Andre Dawson	34	25	45	Currently on BWA ballot
Lou Brock	35	18	22	BWA
Paul Waner	43	37	15	BWA
Sam Crawford	46.5	35	29	VC

Players in the Top 100
in All Three Categories

Player	Rank in Games Played	Rank in At-Bats	Rank in Hits	Status
Rusty Staub	12	31	55	Eligible for VC consideration
Reggie Jackson	20	28	78	BWA
Tony Perez	24	30	52	BWA
Omar Vizquel	25	26	61	Active 2009
Rabbit Maranville	31	22	72.5	BWA
Joe Morgan	32	49	87	BWA
Luis Aparicio	37	19	63	BWA
Luis Gonzalez	38	55	76	Eligible in 2014
Steve Finley	40	41.5	83	Eligible in 2013
Gary Sheffield	41	52	62	Active 2009
Ozzie Smith	42	43	100	BWA
Ernie Banks	44	40	79	BWA
Julio Franco	45	85	78	Eligible in 2013
Bill Buckner	46.5	41.5	56	Eligible for VC consideration
Tim Raines	50	71	72.5	Currently on BWA ballot
Billy Williams	52.5	46	58.5	BWA
Nap Lajoie	54	34	12	BWA
Max Carey	55	44	65	VC
Rod Carew	56.5	47	21	BWA
Vada Pinson	56.5	33	47	Eligible for VC consideration
Dave Parker	58	45	57	Currently on BWA ballot
Fred McGriff	59	79	92	Eligible in 2010
Ted Simmons	60	84	93	Eligible for VC consideration
Tony Gwynn	63	48	17	BWA
Wade Boggs	64	53	24	BWA
Roberto Clemente	67	39	26	BWA
Willie Davis	68	54	81	Eligible for VC consideration
Luke Appling	69	73	48	BWA
Zack Wheat	70	58	36	VC
Mickey Vernon	71	81	90	Eligible for VC consideration
Buddy Bell	72	67	87	Eligible for VC consideration
Sam Rice	73.5	50	28	VC
Ivan Rodriguez	78	62	58.5	Active 2009
Jake Beckley	79	36	33.5	VC
Roberto Alomar	82	60	53	Eligible in 2010
George Davis	83.5	64.5	67.5	VC

Player	Rank in Games Played	Rank in At-Bats	Rank in Hits	Status
Al Oliver	83.5	63	50	Eligible for VC consideration
Nellie Fox	85	51	66	VC
Steve Garvey	90	74	74	Eligible for VC consideration
Charlie Gehringer	93	72	43	BWA
Frankie Frisch	97	57	37	BWA
Harry Hooper	98	77	97	VC
Jeff Kent	99	94	98	Eligible in 2014

PLAYERS IN THE TOP 150 IN ALL THREE CATEGORIES

Player	Rank in Games Played	Rank in At-Bats	Rank in Hits	Status
Dwight Evans	36	66	104	Eligible for VC consideration
Gary Gaetti	48	70	142	Eligible for VC consideration
Babe Ruth	49	101	39	BWA
Carlton Fisk	51	80	120	BWA
Dave Concepcion	52.5	82	129	Eligible for VC consideration
Bill Dahlen	61	64.5	101	Eligible for VC consideration
Chili Davis	65.5	86	115	Eligible for VC consideration
Mickey Mantle	75	122	109	BWA
Eddie Mathews	76	93	131	BWA
Lou Whitaker	77	91	118	Eligible for VC consideration
Bobby Wallace	80	89	134	VC
Enos Slaughter	81	137	114	VC
Sammy Sosa	87	75	110	Eligible in 2013
Jose Cruz	88	141.5	149.5	Eligible for VC consideration
Frank E. Thomas	94	112	95	Eligible in 2014
Jimmy Foxx	95	120	70	BWA
B. J. Surhoff	96	110	129	Eligible in 2011
Alan Trammell	101	107	119	Currently on BWA ballot
Goose Goslin	104	88	51	VC
Jimmy Dykes	106	127	144	Eligible for VC consideration
Cap Anson	107	59	27	VC
Lave Cross	108	61	71	Eligible for VC consideration
Rogers Hornsby	111	116	33.5	BWA
Andres Galarraga	112	124	127	Eligible in 2010
Mark Grace	114	125	105	Eligible for VC consideration
Ron Santo	115	119	145.5	Eligible for VC consideration
Fred Clarke	116	92	64	VC
Doc Cramer	117	56	60	Eligible for VC consideration
Red Schoendienst	119	96	103	VC
Al Simmons	120	78	35	BWA
Brett Butler	121	115	117	Eligible for VC consideration
Joe Torre	123	145	124	Eligible for VC consideration
Manny Ramirez	124	134	91	Active 2009

Player	Rank in Games Played	Rank in At-Bats	Rank in Hits	Status
Tommy Corcoran	127	76	148	Eligible for VC consideration
Richie Ashburn	129.5	103	80	VC
Barry Larkin	133.5	138	125	Eligible in 2010
Joe Judge	136	144	121	Eligible for VC consideration
Alex Rodriguez	138.5	105	84	Active 2009
Chipper Jones	138.5	149	111	Active 2009
Charlie Grimm	138.5	141.5	137.5	Eligible for VC consideration
Marquis Grissom	141	108	149.5	Eligible in 2011
Lou Gehrig	142.5	131	54	BWA
Ryne Sandberg	142.5	102	113	BWA
Tony Fernandez	147	143	143	Eligible for VC consideration

PLAYERS IN THE TOP 200 IN ALL THREE CATEGORIES

Player	Rank in Games Played	Rank in At-Bats	Rank in Hits	Status
Graig Nettles	28	68	160	Eligible for VC consideration
Darrell Evans	29	69	161	Eligible for VC consideration
Willie McCovey	39	114	165	BWA
Mike Schmidt	73.5	104	156	BWA
Willie Stargell	86	139.5	157	BWA
Bert Campaneris	91	83	152.5	Eligible for VC consideration
Ted Williams	102.5	159.5	69	BWA
Don Baylor	102.5	113	192	Eligible for VC consideration
Jim Thome	105	159.5	190	Active 2009
Larry Bowa	113	99	171	Eligible for VC consideration
John Olerud	118	177	155	Eligible in 2011
Willie Randolph	125	130	166	Eligible for VC consideration
Willie McGee	126	167.5	145.5	Eligible for VC consideration
Joe Carter	129.5	97	173	Eligible for VC consideration
Ruben Sierra	131	128	183	Eligible in 2012
Pee Wee Reese	138.5	126	176	VC
Tommy Leach	149	136	187	Eligible for VC consideration
Willie Wilson	151	156	167	Eligible for VC consideration
Jeff Bagwell	152	151	132	Eligible in 2011
Harry Heilmann	153.5	153	67.5	BWA
Garret Anderson	153.5	95	89	Active 2009
Derek Jeter	156	87	49	Active 2009
Bid McPhee	157	106	151	VC
Johnny Damon	158	100	108	Active 2009
Stuffy McInnis	159	150	112	Eligible for VC consideration
Joe Cronin	160.5	179	140	BWA
Orlando Cepeda	160.5	139.5	122	VC
Willie Keeler	162	90	32	BWA
Yogi Berra	164	184	184.5	BWA
Joe Kuhel	168	132	164	Eligible for VC consideration
Kenny Lofton	169	121	106	Eligible in 2013
Jim Rice	172.5	111	102	BWA

Player	Rank in Games Played	Rank in At-Bats	Rank in Hits	Status
Keith Hernandez	174	198	174	Eligible for VC consideration
Sherry Magee	175	190	177	Eligible for VC consideration
Ed Konetchy	176	167.5	184.5	Eligible for VC consideration
Bernie Williams	183	146	126	Eligible in 2012
Jesse Burkett	187	98	41	VC
George Sisler	189.5	109	44	BWA
Ken Boyer	196.5	188	187	Eligible for VC consideration

HALL OF FAMERS IN THE TOP 200 IN ONE OR TWO CATEGORIES

	Rank in Hits	Rank in At-Bats	Rank in Games Played
Joe Medwick	94	170	
Kirby Puckett	135.5		
Dan Brouthers	139		
Bill Terry	168.5		
Joe DiMaggio	163		
Hugh Duffy	141		
Jim O'Rourke	135.5	191	
Monte Ward		169	
Ed Delahanty	75	184	
Joe Kelley	162		
Kiki Cuyler	137.5		
Joe Sewell	159		
Billy Herman	123	158	
Pie Traynor	108	182	
Billy Hamilton	180.5		
Bill Mazeroski		155	144
Edd Roush	116	199.5	
Johnny Bench		164	147
Harmon Killebrew		118	65.5
Heinie Manush	85	165	
Roger Connor	96	152	
Lloyd Waner	100	154	
Jim Bottomley	133	187	
Gary Carter		133	100

HALL OF FAMERS NOT IN THE TOP 200 IN ANY OF THE THREE CATEGORIES

Baseball Writers' Association Name	Position	Veterans Committee Name	Position
Roy Campanella	C	Roger Bresnahan	C
Mickey Cochrane	C	Buck Ewing	C
Bill Dickey	C	Rick Ferrell	C
Gabby Hartnett	C	Ernie Lombardi	C

Baseball Writers' Association		Veterans Committee	
Name	*Position*	*Name*	*Position*
Hank Greenberg	1B	Ray Schalk	C
Jackie Robinson	2B	Frank Chance	1B
Lou Boudreau	SS	George Kelly	1B
Ralph Kiner	LF	Johnny Mize	1B
Duke Snider	CF	Johnny Evers	2B
		Tony Lazzeri	2B
		Bobby Doerr	2B
		Frank Baker	3B
		Jimmy Collins	3B
		Freddie Lindstrom	3B
		George Kell	3B
		Joe Gordon	2B
		Travis Jackson	SS
		Hughie Jennings	SS
		Phil Rizzuto	LF
		Joe Tinker	RF
		Dave Bancroft	CF
		Arky Vaughan	CF
		Chick Hafey	RF
		Chuck Klein	RF
		Earl Combs	RF
		Hack Wilson	RF
		Elmer Flick	RF
		King Kelly	CF
		Tommy McCarthy	CF
		Sam Thompson	RF
		Ross Youngs	RF
		Larry Doby	CF
		Earl Averill	CF

GAMES PLAYED

Twenty-one players have played in 2,800 or more games. Of that number:

15	are in the Hall of Fame
1	(Pete Rose) is ineligible for consideration
3	(Barry Bonds, Craig Biggio and Rafael Palmeiro) have not been retired for five years
1	(Rusty Staub) can be considered by the Veterans' Committee
1	(Harold Baines) is currently under consideration on the BWA ballot

Seventy-five players have played in 2,400 or more games. Of that number:

45	are in the Hall of Fame
1	(Rose) is ineligible for consideration
7	(Bonds, Biggio and Palmeiro plus Fred McGriff, Julio Franco, Luis Gonzalez and Steve Finley) have not been retired for five years

4	(Baines plus Dave Parker, Tim Raines and Andre Dawson) are currently under consideration on the BWA ballot
15	(Staub plus Vada Pinson, Dwight Evans, Bill Buckner, Willie Davis, Buddy Bell, Graig Nettles, Darrell Evans, Ted Simmons, Ron Fairly, Bill Dahlen, Chili Davis, Gary Gaetti, Dave Concepcion and Mickey Vernon) can be considered by the Veteran's Committee
3	(Ken Griffey, Jr., Gary Sheffield and Omar Vizquel) were all active during the 2009 season

Eighty-one (57.4 percent) of the Hall of Famers have appeared in 2,000 or more games.

Ninety-two (65.2 percent) of the Hall of Famers have appeared in 1,900 or more games.

One hundred-two (72.3 percent) of the Hall of Famers have appeared in 1,800 or more games.

One hundred-thirteen (80.1 percent) of the Hall of Famers have appeared in 1,700 or more games.

AT-BATS

Twenty-three players have had 10,000 or more at-bats. Of that number:

20	are in the Hall of Fame
1	(Pete Rose) is ineligible
2	(Craig Biggio and Rafael Palmeiro) have not been retired for five years

Fifty-two players have had 9,200 or more at-bats. Of that number:

38	are in the Hall of Fame
1	(Rose) is ineligible
3	(Omar Vizquel, Gary Sheffield and Ken Griffey, Jr.) were active during the 2009 season
4	(Biggio and Palmeiro plus Barry Bonds and Steve Finley) have not been retired for five years
3	(Dave Parker, Harold Baines and Andre Dawson) are currently under consideration on the BWA ballot
3	(Rusty Staub, Vada Pinson and Bill Buckner) are eligible for Veterans' Committee consideration

Sixty-nine (48.9 percent) of the Hall of Famers have 8,000 or more at-bats

Eighty-seven (61.7 percent) of the Hall of Famers have 7,500 or more at-bats

Ninety-eight (69.5 percent) of the Hall of Famers have 7,000 or more at-bats

HITS

Twenty-six players have amassed 3,000 or more base hits. Of that number:

23	are in the Hall of Fame
1	(Pete Rose) is ineligible for consideration
2	(Craig Biggio and Rafael Palmeiro) have not been retired for five years

Forty-four players have 2,800 or more career hits. Of that number:

39	are in the Hall of Fame
1	(Rose) is ineligible for consideration
3	(Biggio, and Palmeiro plus Barry Bonds) have not been retired for five years
1	(Harold Baines) is currently on the BWA ballot

Eighty-nine players have 2,500 or more career hits. Of that number:

59	are in the Hall of Fame
1	(Rose) is ineligible for consideration
11	(Vada Pinson, Al Oliver, Rusty Staub, Bill Buckner, Willie Davis, Steve Garvey, Buddy Bell, Doc Cramer, Lave Cross, George Van Haltern and Jimmy Ryan) are eligible for consideration by the Veterans' Committee
7	(Biggio, Bonds and Palmeiro plus Roberto Alomar, Julio Franco, Steve Finley and Luis Gonzalez) have not been retired for five years
7	(Omar Vizquel, Gary Sheffield, Ivan Rodriguez, Derek Jeter, Alex Rodriguez, Garret Anderson and Ken Griffey, Jr.) were active during the 2009 season
4	(Baines plus Dave Parker, Tim Raines and Andre Dawson) are currently on the BWA ballot

One hundred-seven (75.9 percent) of the 141 Hall of Famers have accumulated at least 2,000 career hits.

PLAYERS WITH 2,000 HITS AND 200 HOME RUNS

Approximately one half of the 26 members of the 3,000-hit club were also well known for their power. We decided to trace this phenomenon farther to see what, if any, correlation exists between career hits and career home runs:

Player	Hits	Rank	Home Runs	Rank	Status
Hank Aaron	3771	3	755	2	BWA
Stan Musial	3630	4	475	28.5	BWA
Carl Yastrzemski	3419	6	452	33	BWA

Player	Hits	Rank	Home Runs	Rank	Status
Paul Molitor	3319	8	234	228	BWA
Willie Mays	3283	10	660	4	BWA
Eddie Murray	3255	11	504	25	BWA
Cal Ripken	3184	13	431	38	BWA
George Brett	3154	14	317	104.5	BWA
Robin Yount	3142	16	251	193.5	BWA
Dave Winfield	3110	18	465	31	BWA
Craig Biggio	3060	19	291	132.5	Eligible in 2013
Rickey Henderson	3055	20	297	127	BWA
Rafael Palmeiro	3020	23	569	11	Eligible in 2011
Al Kaline	3007	25	399	46.5	BWA
Roberto Clemente	3000	26	240	215.5	BWA
Frank Robinson	2943	30	586	7	BWA
Barry Bonds	2935	31	762	1	Eligible in 2013
Rogers Hornsby	2930	33.5	301	124	BWA
Al Simmons	2927	35	307	114	BWA
Mel Ott	2876	38	511	23	BWA
Babe Ruth	2873	39	714	3	BWA
Harold Baines	2866	40	384	54	Currently on BWA ballot
Brooks Robinson	2848	42	268	165	BWA
Andre Dawson	2774	45	438	36	Currently on BWA ballot
Ken Griffey, Jr.	2763	46	630	5	Active 2009
Vada Pinson	2757	47	256	179.5	Eligible for VC consideration
Derek Jeter	2747	49	224	239.5	Active 2009
Al Oliver	2743	50	219	249	Eligible for VC consideration
Goose Goslin	2735	51	248	198.5	VC
Tony Perez	2732	52	379	60.5	BWA
Roberto Alomar	2724	53	210	265.5	Eligible in 2010
Lou Gehrig	2721	54	493	26.5	BWA
Rusty Staub	2716	55	292	131	Eligible for VC consideration
Dave Parker	2712	57	339	84	Currently on BWA ballot
Ivan Rodriguez	2711	58.5	305	120	Active 2009
Billy Williams	2711	58.5	426	40.5	BWA
Gary Sheffield	2689	62	509	24	Active 2009
Ted Williams	2654	69	521	19	BWA
Jimmy Foxx	2646	70	534	17	BWA
Steve Garvey	2599	74	272	160	Eligible for VC consideration
Luis Gonzalez	2591	76	354	75.5	Eligible in 2014
Reggie Jackson	2584	78	563	13	BWA
Ernie Banks	2583	79	512	21.5	BWA
Steve Finley	2548	82	304	122.5	Eligible in 2013
Alex Rodriguez	2531	84	583	8.5	Active 2009
Joe Morgan	2517	86	268	165	BWA
Buddy Bell	2514	87	201	291.5	Eligible for VC consideration
Garret Anderson	2501	89	285	143.5	Active 2009
Manny Ramirez	2494	91	546	15	Active 2009
Fred McGriff	2490	92	493	26.5	Eligible in 2010
Ted Simmons	2472	93	248	198.5	Eligible for VC consideration
Joe Medwick	2471	94	205	279	BWA
Frank E. Thomas	2468	95	521	19	Eligible in 2014

Player	Hits	Rank	Home Runs	Rank	Status
Jeff Kent	2461	98	377	63.5	Eligible in 2014
Jim Rice	2452	102	382	57	BWA
Dwight Evans	2446	104	385	53	Eligible for VC consideration
Johnny Damon	2425	107	207	273.5	Active 2009
Mickey Mantle	2415	109	536	16	BWA
Sammy Sosa	2408	110	609	6	Eligible in 2013
Chipper Jones	2406	111	426	40.5	Active 2009
Ryne Sandberg	2386	113	282	148	BWA
Chili Davis	2380	115	350	79	Eligible for VC consideration
Lou Whitaker	2369	118	244	204.5	Eligible for VC consideration
Carlton Fisk	2356	120	376	65	BWA
Orlando Cepeda	2351	122	379	60.5	VC
Joe Torre	2342	124	252	190	Eligible for VC consideration
Bernie Williams	2336	126	287	139	Eligible in 2012
Andres Galarraga	2333	127	399	46.5	Eligible in 2010
Eddie Mathews	2315	131	512	21.5	BWA
Jeff Bagwell	2314	132	449	34	Eligible in 2011
Jim Bottomley	2313	133	219	249	VC
Kirby Puckett	2304	135.5	207	273.5	BWA
Gary Gaetti	2280	142	360	71	Eligible for VC consideration
Ron Santo	2254	145.5	342	81	Eligible for VC consideration
Marquis Grissom	2251	149.5	227	237	Eligible in 2011
Vladimir Guerrero	2249	152.5	407	44.5	Active 2009
Edgar Martinez	2247	154	309	112	Eligible in 2010
John Olerud	2239	155	255	183	Eligible in 2011
Mike Schmidt	2234	156	548	14	BWA
Willie Stargell	2232	157	475	28.5	BWA
Graig Nettles	2225	160	390	50	Eligible for VC consideration
Darrell Evans	2223	161	414	42	Eligible for VC consideration
Joe DiMaggio	2214	163	361	70	BWA
Willie McCovey	2211	165	521	19	BWA
Cecil Cooper	2192	170	241	213	Eligible for VC consideration
Joe Carter	2184	173	396	49	Eligible for VC consideration
Will Clark	2176	175	284	144.5	Eligible for VC consideration
Larry Walker	2160	179	383	55	Eligible in 2011
Don Mattingly	2153	182	222	243.5	Currently on BWA ballot
Ruben Sierra	2152	183	306	117	Eligible in 2012
Yogi Berra	2150	184.5	358	73	BWA
Ken Boyer	2143	187	282	148	Eligible for VC consideration
Jim Thome	2138	190	564	12	Active 2009
Don Baylor	2135	192	338	86	Eligible for VC consideration
Todd Helton	2134	194	325	96	Active 2009
Moises Alou	2134	194	332	89.5	Eligible in 2014
Mike Piazza	2127	197.5	427	39	Eligible in 2013
Duke Snider	2116	200	407	44.5	BWA
Miguel Tejada	2114	201	285	142.5	Active 2009
Bobby Abreu	2111	202.5	256	179.5	Active 2009
Dale Murphy	2111	202.5	398	48	Currently on BWA ballot
Ellis Burks	2107	205	352	77	Eligible in 2010
Paul O'Neill	2105	206	281	150	Eligible for VC consideration

Player	Hits	Rank	Home Runs	Rank	Status
Felipe Alou	2101	209	206	277	Eligible for VC consideration
Brian Downing	2099	211	275	156	Eligible for VC consideration
Gary Carter	2092	213.5	324	98.5	BWA
Harmon Killebrew	2086	218	573	10	BWA
Tim Wallach	2085	219	260	175.5	Eligible for VC consideration
Chuck Klein	2076	224	300	125	VC
Del Ennis	2063	228.5	288	136	Eligible for VC consideration
Wally Joyner	2060	231	204	281	Eligible for VC consideration
Bob L. Johnson	2051	234	288	136	Eligible for VC consideration
Johnny Bench	2048	235	389	51	BWA
Bobby Doerr	2042	237	223	241.5	VC
Carlos Delgado	2038	239	473	30	Active 2009
Ken Singleton	2029	242	246	201	Eligible for VC consideration
Reggie Smith	2020	244.5	314	109	Eligible for VC consideration
Earl Averill, Sr.	2019	246	238	219.5	VC
Gary Matthews	2011	249.5	234	228	Eligible for VC consideration
Johnny Mize	2011	249.5	359	72	VC
Bobby Bonilla	2010	251.5	287	139	Eligible for VC consideration
Todd Zeile	2004	256.5	253	186.5	Eligible in 2010
Shawn Green	2003	258	328	92.5	Eligible in 2013

Two hundred fifty-eight players have accumulated 2,000 or more hits and two hundred ninety-five have achieved the 200 home run mark. Of the 123 players listed above who have accomplished both milestones:

50	(40.7%) are in the Hall of Fame. Forty-three were elected by the Baseball Writers and seven by the Veterans' Committee
15	were active during the 2009 season
5	are currently on the BWA ballot
23	have not been retired for five years so are not yet eligible
30	are eligible for consideration by the Veterans' Committee

When those who are active, not yet eligible or currently under consideration are factored out the Hall of Famers increases to 62.5 percent.

The Longevity Factor Among Pitchers

When Nolan Ryan was elected to the Hall of Fame he became the twentieth of twenty-four 300-game winners to be included. Roger Clemens, Greg Maddux and Tom Glavine (not yet eligible) and Randy Johnson, active in 2009, are the only non Hall of Famers among this select group.

Of the top 100 pitchers in career victories 47 are in the Hall of Fame. The other 14 can be put into one of three categories:

1. Close to the top 100. Rube Marquard with 201 wins, Jack Chesbro with 198 wins, Dennis Eckersley with 197 wins, Dazzy Vance with 197 wins, Ed Walsh with 195 wins, Rube Waddell with 193 wins and Lefty Gomez with 189 wins fall just short of the 204 minimum victories among the 100 leaders.

2. Injuries and a tragic death. Sandy Koufax compiled brilliant statistics in a relatively brief 12-year career. An arthritic elbow caused his untimely retirement. Dizzy Dean's arm problems also shortened his career to 12 years but like Koufax he compiled some impressive numbers. Addie Joss accumulated 160 wins in only 9 seasons but died at age 31 before the 1911 season started.

3. The recognition of the relief pitcher. Hoyt Wilhelm's election in 1985 broke the drought for relievers. In 1992, Rollie Fingers became the second relief pitcher to achieve Hall of Fame status. His 341 saves ranked third on the all-time list at the time of his election. Bruce Sutter whose split-fingered fastball enabled him to record 300 saves and a 2.83 earned run average was elected in 2006. Rich Gossage joined the ranks in 2008 with his 310 saves and 3.01 earned run average.

ANALYSIS OF PITCHERS RANKING IN THE TOP 100 IN WINS, INNINGS PITCHED AND GAMES STARTED

Category	No. of Pitchers	Hall of Fame [BWA-VC]	Currently on Ballot	No. in Inactive or Not Yet Elig.	Elig. for VC Consid.	% in Hall of Fame
Top 25	16	13 [11–2]	0	2	1	81.3%
Top 50	38	25 [16–9]	2	5	6	67.6%
Top 75	57	34 [22–12]	2	7	14	59.6%
Top 100	78	39 [25–14]	2	11	26	50.0%

PITCHERS IN TOP 25 IN ALL THREE CATEGORIES

Pitcher	Rank in Wins	Rank in Innings Pitched	Rank in Games Started	Status
Cy Young	1	1	1	BWA
Walter Johnson	2	3	13	BWA
Grover Alexander	3.5	10	22	BWA
Pud Galvin	5	2	10	VC
Warren Spahn	6	8	14	BWA
Greg Maddux	8	13	4	Eligible in 2014
Roger Clemens	9	15	7	Eligible in 2013
Tim Keefe	10	12	23.5	VC
Steve Carlton	11	9	6	BWA
Nolan Ryan	14.5	5	2	BWA
Don Sutton	14.5	7	3	BWA

Pitcher	Rank in Wins	Rank in Innings Pitched	Rank in Games Started	Status
Phil Niekro	16	4	5	BWA
Gaylord Perry	17	6	9	BWA
Tom Seaver	18	17	15	BWA
Early Wynn	23.5	21	18	BWA
Tommy John	25	19	8	Eligible for VC consideration

PITCHERS IN TOP 50 IN ALL THREE CATEGORIES

Pitcher	Rank in Wins	Rank in Innings Pitched	Rank in Games Started	Status
Christy Mathewson	3.5	18	28	BWA
Kid Nichols	7	11	26	VC
John Clarkson	12	22	39	VC
Eddie Plank	13	27	33.5	VC
Hoss Radbourn	19	23	42.5	VC
Mickey Welch	20	16	29	VC
Tom Glavine	21	29	12	Eligible in 2014
Randy Johnson	22	37	21	Active 2009
Bert Blyleven	26	14	11	Currently on BWA ballot
Robin Roberts	27	20	19.5	BWA
Tony Mullane	28.5	24	41	Eligible for VC consideration
Ferguson Jenkins	28.5	26	23.5	BWA
Jim Kaat	30	25	16	Eligible for VC consideration
Red Ruffing	31	31	31.5	BWA
Burleigh Grimes	32.5	35	45.5	VC
Jim Palmer	34	41	37	BWA
Eppa Rixey	35.5	28	27	VC
Gus Weyhing	38	32	42.5	Eligible for VC consideration
Jamie Moyer	40	44	19.5	Active 2009
Jack Morris	41.5	49	35.5	Currently on BWA ballot
Dennis Martinez	49	39	25	Eligible for VC consideration
Jack Powell	49	30	40	Eligible for VC consideration

PITCHERS IN TOP 75 IN ALL THREE CATEGORIES

Pitcher	Rank in Wins	Rank in Innings Pitched	Rank in Games Started	Status
Lefty Grove	23.5	42	74.5	BWA
Mike Mussina	32.5	64	31.5	Eligible in 2014
Bob Feller	35.5	48	53	BWA

Pitcher	Rank in Wins	Rank in Innings Pitched	Rank in Games Started	Status
Jim McCormick	37	33	51	Eligible for VC consideration
Ted Lyons	39	36	53	BWA
Red Faber	41.5	38	55.5	VC
Bob Gibson	44	45	57	BWA
Vic Willis	45	40	64	VC
Juan Marichal	51	68	74.5	BWA
Frank Tanana	52.5	34	17	Eligible for VC consideration
David Wells	54.5	76	48	Eligible in 2013
Sad Sam Jones	61.5	46	50	Eligible for VC consideration
Luis Tiant	61.5	70	53	Eligible for VC consideration
Jim Bunning	65.5	53	38	VC
Catfish Hunter	65.5	74	59.5	BWA
Jerry Koosman	69.5	47	35.5	Eligible for VC consideration
Joe Niekro	71	61	44	Eligible for VC consideration
Jerry Reuss	72	56	30	Eligible for VC consideration
Earl Whitehill	75.5	63	62.5	Eligible for VC consideration

PITCHERS IN TOP 100 IN ALL THREE CATEGORIES

Pitcher	Rank in Wins	Rank in Innings Pitched	Rank in Games Started	Status
Carl Hubbell	43	60	86	BWA
Jack Quinn	46	43	78	Eligible for VC consideration
Amos Rusie	49	51	90	VC
Herb Pennock	52.5	62	97.5	BWA
Waite Hoyt	56.5	52	93.5	VC
George Mullin	64	55	88.5	Eligible for VC consideration
Mel Harder	67.5	78	84	Eligible for VC consideration
Paul Derringer	67.5	57	78	Eligible for VC consideration
Kenny Rogers	73.5	89	61	Eligible in 2014
Mickey Lolich	77.5	58	47	Eligible for VC consideration
Freddie Fitzsimmons	77.5	95	91	Eligible for VC consideration
Charlie Hough	80	50	80.5	Eligible for VC consideration

Pitcher	Rank in Wins	Rank in Innings Pitched	Rank in Games Started	Status
Curt Schilling	80	93	83	Eligible in 2013
Jim Perry	82.5	90.5	77	Eligible for VC consideration
Rick Reuschel	84	65	33.5	Eligible for VC consideration
John Smoltz	85	72	58	Active 2009
Kevin Brown	88.5	94	59.5	Eligible in 2011
Bobo Newsom	88.5	54	55.5	Eligible for VC consideration
Billy Pierce	88.5	87.5	85	Eligible for VC consideration
Vida Blue	93	86	62.5	Eligible for VC consideration
Don Drysdale	93	77	67.5	BWA

Ethnic Minorities in the Hall of Fame

Although there were isolated instances of minorities playing briefly in the major leagues, usually under false identities, Jackie Robinson's appearance as a Brooklyn Dodger in 1947 marks the breaking of the color barrier in major league baseball. To see how minorities have fared in Hall of Fame balloting since 1962, the first year of Robinson's eligibility, we reviewed the Baseball Writer's Association Hall of Fame selections from 2009 to 1962.

Year	No. Elected	No. of Minorities Elected	Player(s)	Cumulative % of Minorities Elected
2009	2	2	Rickey Henderson, Jim Rice	100%
2008	1	0		66.7%
2007	2	1	Tony Gwynn	60.0%
2006	1	0		50.0%
2005	2	0		37.5%
2004	2	0		30.0%
2003	2	1	Eddie Murray	33.3%
2002	1	1	Ozzie Smith	38.5%
2001	2	2	Dave Winfield, Kirby Puckett	46.7%
2000	2	1	Tony Perez	47.1%
1999	3	0		40.0%
1998	1	0		38.1%
1997	1	0		36.4%
1996	0	0		36.4%
1995	1	0		34.8%
1994	1	0		33.3%
1993	1	1	Reggie Jackson	36.0%

Year	No. Elected	No. of Minorities Elected	Player(s)	Cumulative % of Minorities Elected
1992	2	0		33.3%
1991	3	2	Rod Carew, Ferguson Jenkins	36.7%
1990	2	1	Joe Morgan	37.5%
1989	2	0		35.3%
1988	1	1	Wilver Stargell	37.1%
1987	2	1	Billy Williams	37.8%
1986	1	1	Willie McCovey	39.5%
1985	2	1	Lou Brock	40.0%
1984	3	1	Luis Aparicio	39.5%
1983	2	1	Juan Marichal	40.0%
1982	2	2	Henry Aaron, Frank Robinson	42.6%
1981	1	1	Bob Gibson	43.8%
1980	2	0		42.0%
1979	1	1	Willie Mays	43.1%
1978	1	0		42.3%
1977	1	1	Ernie Banks	43.4%
1976	2	0		41.8%
1975	1	0		41.1%
1974	2	0		39.7%
1973SE	1	1	Roberto Clemente	40.7%
1973	1	0		40.0%
1972	3	0		38.1%
1971	0	0		38.1%
1970	1	0		37.5%
1969	2	1	Roy Campanella	37.9%
1968	1	0		37.3%
1967RO	1	0		36.8%
1967	0	0		36.8%
1966	1	0		36.2%
1965			No Election	
1964RO	1	0		35.7%
1964	0	0		35.7%
1963			No Election	
1962	2	1	Jackie Robinson	36.1%
Totals	72	26		

Between 1975 and 1983 minority representation in the Hall of Fame was 40 percent or more and since 1962 stands at 36.1 percent. There are two possible interpretations to this phenomenon. One would be that the writers have gone out of their way to consider minority candidates. The other would be that once given the opportunity to compete, the minority player has set such a high standard that recognition cannot be ignored. Considering the 26 names that appear on the list, it would seem that the latter interpretation comes closer to reality. As rosters continue to be stocked with minority talent it can be safely assumed that the number of Hall of Famers of ethnic minority background will increase.

PART III: ANALYSIS OF HALL OF FAME PLAYERS BY POSITION

Introduction

In Part III the Hall of Fame voting is broken down by position in an effort to determine the overlooked players and perhaps expose questionable inclusions. The tables and analyses in this part of the study are organized by position, with the following six segments to the coverage of each position.

1. Listing of every player who has received a vote in a Baseball Writers' Association of America election, in order of the highest percentage of votes received in an election.
2. Yearly list of the players receiving the highest percentage of votes.
3. General analysis of the voting.
4. Rank in voting by year which includes only those who achieved at least 10 percent of the vote.
5. Yearly list of the number of players who received at least 10 percent of the vote and the number each year who ultimately were elected to the Hall of Fame via the Baseball Writers' Association (BWA) or the Veterans Committee (VC). In addition the year that each non Hall of Famer received at least 10 percent of the vote is indicated.
6. Brief conclusions about the 10 percent vote in the preceding table.

Pitchers

Name	Years Pitched First–Last	Highest %-age	%-age Range	Number of Elections*	HOF	Year Elected	Years Pitched
Tom Seaver	1967–1986	98.8%		1	BWA	1992	20
Nolan Ryan	1966–1993	98.8%		1	BWA	1999	27
Steve Carlton	1965–1988	95.8%		1	BWA	1994	24
Bob Feller	1936–1956	93.8%		1	BWA	1962	18
Jim Palmer	1965–1984	92.6%		1	BWA	1990	19

*Number of elections in which any votes were received; ( ) indicates a run-off election.

163

Name	Years Pitched First–Last	Highest %-age	%-age Range	Number of Elections*	HOF	Year Elected	Years Pitched
Christy Mathewson	1900–1916	90.7%		1	BWA	1936	17
Carl Hubbell	1928–1943	87.0%	9.7%–87.0%	3(1)	BWA	1947	16
Red Ruffing	1924–1947	86.9%	(2.1%)–86.9%	15(3)	BWA	1967	22
Robin Roberts	1948–1966	86.9%	56.1%–86.9%	4	BWA	1976	19
Sandy Koufax	1955–1966	86.9%		1	BWA	1972	12
Ted Lyons	1923–1946	86.5%	1.5%–86.5%	10(1)	BWA	1955	21
Rich Gossage	1972–1994	85.8%	33.3%–85.8%	9	BWA	2008	22
Bob Gibson	1959–1975	84.0%		1	BWA	1981	17
Hoyt Wilhelm	1952–1972	83.8%	38.9%–83.8%	8	BWA	1985	21
Juan Marichal	1960–1975	83.7%	58.1%–83.7%	3	BWA	1983	16
Walter Johnson	1907–1927	83.6%		1	BWA	1936	21
Warren Spahn	1942–1965	83.2%		1	BWA	1973	21
Dennis Eckersley	1975–1998	83.2%		1	BWA	2004	24
Rollie Fingers	1968–1985	82.1%	65.7%–82.1%	2	BWA	1992	17
Dazzy Vance	1915–1935	81.7%	0.4%–81.7%	16(1)	BWA	1955	16
Don Sutton	1966–1988	81.6%	56.9%–81.6%	5	BWA	1998	23
Grover Alexander	1911–1930	80.9%	24.3%–80.9%	3	BWA	1938	20
Phil Niekro	1964–1987	80.3%	60.0%–80.3%	5	BWA	1997	24
Dizzy Dean	1930–1947	79.2%	6.9%–79.2%	9(2)	BWA	1953	12
Bob Lemon	1941–1958	78.6%	(1.3%)–78.6%	12(2)	BWA	1976	15
Don Drysdale	1956–1969	78.4%	21.0%–78.4%	10	BWA	1984	14
Whitey Ford	1950–1967	77.8%	67.1%–77.8%	2	BWA	1974	16
Herb Pennock	1912–1934	77.7%	(6.1%)–77.7%	8(1)	BWA	1948	22
Gaylord Perry	1962–1983	77.2%	68.0%–77.2%	3	BWA	1991	22
Bruce Sutter	1976–1988	76.9%	24.0%–76.9%	13	BWA	2006	12
Lefty Grove	1925–1941	76.4%	5.3%–76.4%	4(1)	BWA	1947	17
Jim Hunter	1965–1979	76.3%	53.7%–76.3%	3	BWA	1987	15
Cy Young	1890–1911	76.1%	49.1%–76.1%	2	BWA	1937	22
Early Wynn	1939–1963	76.0%	27.9%–76.0%	4	BWA	1972	23
Ferguson Jenkins	1965–1983	75.4%	52.3%–75.4%	3	BWA	1991	19
Jim Bunning	1955–1971	74.2%	33.3%–74.2%	15	VC	1996	17
Rube Waddell	1897–1910	65.3%	14.6%–65.3%	7(1)	VC	1946	13
Bert Blyleven	1970–1992	62.7%	14.1%–62.7%	12			22
Ed Walsh	1904–1917	56.9%	8.8%–56.9%	7(1)	VC	1946	14
Eppa Rixey	1912–1933	52.8%	0.4%–52.8%	16	VC	1963	21
Lefty Gomez	1930–1943	46.1%	0.6%–46.1%	15	VC	1972	14
Lee Smith	1980–1997	45.0%	36.6%–45.0%	7			18
Chief Bender	1903–1925	44.7%	0.9%–44.7%	14(1)	VC	1953	16
Jack Morris	1977–1994	44.0%	19.6%–44.0%	10			18
Clark Griffith	1891–1914	43.7%	2.0%–43.7%	6(1)	VC	1946†	21
Hal Newhouser	1939–1955	42.8%	(1.3%)–42.8%	12(2)	VC	1992	17
Burleigh Grimes	1916–1934	34.2%	0.4%–34.2%	14	VC	1964	19
Johnny Sain	1942–1955	34.0%	0.6%–34.0%	10			11
Allie Reynolds	1942–1954	33.6%	0.5%–33.6%	13(2)			13
Tommy John	1963–1989	31.7%	18.7%–31.7%	15			26
Luis Tiant	1964–1982	30.9%	7.2%–30.9%	15			19
Red Faber	1914–1933	30.9%	0.4%–30.9%	16	VC	1964	20
Johnny Vander Meer	1937–1951	29.8%	0.4%–29.8%	12(2)			13
Jim Kaat	1959–1983	29.6%	14.0%–29.6%	15			25

*Number of elections in which any votes were received; ( ) indicates a run-off election.
†Elected as an executive.

Name	Years Pitched First–Last	Highest %-age	%-age Range	Number of Elections*	HOF	Year Elected	Years Pitched
Mordecai Brown	1903–1916	27.7%	2.7%–27.7%	7(1)	VC	1949	14
Eddie Plank	1901–1917	27.0%	10.2%–27.0%	6	VC	1946	17
Joe McGinnity	1899–1908	26.2%	6.0%–26.2%	6(1)	VC	1946	10
Mickey Lolich	1963–1979	25.5%	5.1%–25.5%	15			16
Mel Harder	1928–1947	25.4%	0.4%–25.4%	11(2)			20
Lew Burdette	1950–1967	24.1%	1.9%–24.1%	15			18
Bucky Walters	1931–1950	23.7%	1.3%–23.7%	13(2)			19
Waite Hoyt	1918–1938	19.2%	0.4%–19.2%	15	VC	1969	21
Roy Face	1953–1969	18.9%	5.5%–18.9%	15			16
Joe Wood	1908–1920	18.0%	0.4%–18.0%	9			11
Don Newcombe	1949–1960	15.3%	(0.7%)–15.3%	15(1)			10
Addie Joss	1902–1910	14.2%	5.5%–14.2%	6	VC	1978	9
Rube Marquard	1908–1925	13.9%	0.4%–13.9%	13	VC	1971	18
Babe Adams	1906–1926	13.7%	2.8%–13.7%	15			19
Sparky Lyle	1967–1982	13.1%	3.4%–13.1%	4			16
Stan Coveleski	1912–1928	12.8%	0.4%–12.8%	5	VC	1969	14
Don Larsen	1953–1967	12.3%	5.9%–12.3%	15			14
Orel Hershiser	1983–2000	11.2%	4.4%–11.2%	2			18
Vic Raschi	1946–1955	10.2%	0.4%–10.2%	9			10
Dickie Kerr	1919–1925	10.0%	0.4%–10.0%	11			4
Bobo Newsom	1929–1953	9.4%	(0.4%)–9.4%	11(2)			20
Ron Guidry	1975–1988	8.8%	4.9%–8.8%	9			14
Vida Blue	1969–1986	8.7%	3.1%–8.7%	4			17
Jesse Haines	1918–1937	8.3%	0.4%–8.3%	12	VC	1970	19
Tommy Bridges	1930–1946	7.5%	(0.4%)–7.5%	6(1)			16
Nick Altrock	1898–1924	7.5%	0.4%–7.5%	7			16
Dave Stewart	1978–1995	7.4%	4.9%–7.4%	2			16
Wilbur Wood	1961–1978	7.0%	3.1%–7.0%	6			17
Lon Warneke	1930–1945	6.5%	0.8%–6.5%	5			15
Sal Maglie	1945–1958	6.5%	3.9%–6.5%	2			10
Nap Rucker	1907–1916	6.4%	0.4%–6.4%	7			10
Fernando Valenzuela	1980–1997	6.3%	3.8%–6.3%	2			17
Paul Derringer	1931–1945	6.2%	0.4%–6.2%	7			15
Freddie Fitzsimmons	1925–1943	6.0%	0.6%–6.0%	7			19
Dolf Luque	1914–1935	5.6%	0.4%–5.6%	9			20
Hal Schumacher	1931–1946	5.0%	0.4%–5.0%	7			13
Schoolboy Rowe	1933–1949	5.0%	1.1%–5.0%	4			15
Fred Hutchinson	1939–1953	5.0%	0.6%–5.0%	2			11
Art Nehf	1915–1929	4.9%	0.4%–4.9%	11			15
Jeff Reardon	1979–1994	4.8%		1			16
Ewell Blackwell	1942–1955	4.7%	1.8%–4.7%	3			10
Howard Ehmke	1915–1930	4.5%	0.4%–4.5%	10			15
Eddie Rommel	1920–1932	4.5%	0.4%–4.5%	8			13
Wilbur Cooper	1912–1926	4.4%	0.4%–4.4%	9			15
David Cone	1986–2003	3.9%		1			17
Dan Quisenberry	1979–1990	3.8%		1			12
Harvey Haddix	1952–1965	3.8%	0.3%–3.8%	10			14
Wes Ferrell	1927–1941	3.6%	0.6%–3.6%	5			15
Jack Quinn	1909–1933	3.4%	0.7%–3.4%	3			23

*Number of elections in which any votes were received; ( ) indicates a run-off election.

Name	Years Pitched First–Last	Highest %-age	%-age Range	Number of Elections*	HOF	Year Elected	Years Pitched
Dwight Gooden	1984–2000	3.3%		1			16
Carl Erskine	1948–1959	3.2%	0.7%–3.2%	8			12
Dennis Martinez	1976–1998	3.2%		1			23
Amos Rusie	1889–1901	3.1%	0.4%–3.1%	5	VC	1977	10
Spud Chandler	1937–1947	3.0%	0.4%–3.0%	5			11
Dave McNally	1962–1975	2.8%	1.2%–2.8%	4			14
John Hiller	1965–1980	2.6%		1			15
Bill Dineen	1898–1909	2.6%	0.4%–2.6%	5			12
Orval Grove	1940–1949	2.6%	1.9%–2.6%	2			10
Harry Brecheen	1940–1953	2.6%	0.6%–2.6%	7			12
Kid Nichols	1890–1906	2.6%	0.5%–2.6%	5	VC	1949	15
George Earnshaw	1928–1936	2.5%	0.8%–2.5%	5			9
Charlie Root	1923–1941	2.5%	0.4%–2.5%	6			17
Jim Abbott	1989–1999	2.5%		1			10
Vernon Law	1950–1967	2.4%	1.3%–2.4%	7			16
Bobby Shantz	1949–1964	2.3%	0.8%–2.3%	5			16
Carl Mays	1915–1929	2.3%		1			15
Jack Chesbro	1899–1909	2.2%	0.5%–2.2%	4	VC	1946	11
Wild Bill Donovan	1898–1918	2.0%	0.4%–2.0%	5			18
Virgil Trucks	1941–1958	2.0%		1			17
Jim Perry	1959–1975	1.9%	1.5%–1.9%	2			17
Billy Pierce	1945–1964	1.9%	1.0%–1.9%	5			18
Firpo Marberry	1923–1936	1.9%	0.4%–1.9%	5			14
Joe Bush	1912–1928	1.9%		1			17
Rick Sutcliffe	1976–1994	1.8%		1			18
Al Schacht	1919–1921	1.8%	0.4%–1.8%	3			3
Emil J. Leonard	1933–1953	1.8%	0.7%–1.8%	7			20
Jack Coombs	1906–1920	1.7%	0.4%–1.7%	5			14
J. R. Richard	1971–1980	1.6%		1			10
Ellis Kinder	1946–1957	1.5%		1			12
Mike Marshall	1967–1981	1.5%		1			14
Urban Shocker	1916–1928	1.5%	0.4%–1.5%	5			13
George Uhle	1919–1936	1.5%	0.5%–1.5%	3			17
Tug McGraw	1965–1984	1.4%		1			19
Ron Perranoski	1961–1973	1.4%		1			13
Darryl Kile	1991–2002	1.4%		1			12
Dave Stieb	1979–1998	1.4%		1			16
Kent Tekulve	1974–1989	1.3%		1			16
Curt Simmons	1947–1967	1.3%	0.8%–1.3%	2			20
Red Lucas	1923–1938	1.3%	0.4%–1.3%	3			15
Joe Niekro	1967–1988	1.3%		1			22
Brett Saberhagen	1984–2001	1.3%		1			16
Ken Holtzman	1965–1979	1.2%	1.0%–1.2%	2			15
Milt Pappas	1957–1973	1.2%		1			17
Tom Henke	1982–1995	1.2%		1			14
Bill Doak	1912–1929	1.1%		1			16
Eddie Lopat	1944–1955	1.1%	0.3%–1.1%	5			12
Mort Cooper	1938–1949	1.1%	0.4%–1.1%	4			11
Earl Whitehill	1923–1939	1.1%	0.5%–1.1%	3			17

*Number of elections in which any votes were received; ( ) indicates a run-off election.

Name	Years Pitched First–Last	Highest %-age	%-age Range	Number of Elections*	HOF	Year Elected	Years Pitched
Guy Bush	1923–1945	1.0%		1			17
Art Houtteman	1945–1957	1.0%		1			12
Jim Tobin	1937–1945	1.0%		1			9
Jerry Koosman	1967–1985	0.9%		1			19
Charlie Hough	1970–1994	0.8%		1			25
Deacon Phillippe	1899–1911	0.8%	0.4%–0.8%	4			13
Van Mungo	1931–1945	0.8%	0.4%–0.8%	4			14
Joe Oescheger	1914–1925	0.8%		1			12
Hugh Mulcahy	1935–1947	0.8%		1			9
Ray Kremer	1924–1933	0.8%	0.8%–0.8%	2			10
Jake Miller	1924–1933	0.8%		1			9
Leon Cadore	1915–1924	0.8%		1			10
Bill Hallahan	1925–1938	0.8%	0.4%–0.8%	4			12
Bill Sherdel	1918–1932	0.8%	0.4%–0.8%	9			15
Mel Stottlemyre	1964–1974	0.8%		1			11
Camilo Pascual	1954–1971	0.8%	0.3%–0.8%	2			18
Andy Messersmith	1968–1979	0.8%	0.7%–0.8%	2			12
Jim Lonberg	1965–1979	0.8%	0.7%–0.8%	2			15
Lee Meadows	1915–1929	0.8%		1			15
Sherry Smith	1911–1927	0.8%		1			14
Johnny Podres	1953–1969	0.8%	0.5%–0.8%	3			15
Preacher Roe	1938–1954	0.8%	0.3%–0.8%	6			12
John Wetteland	1989–2000	0.8%		1			12
Jack McDowell	1987–1999	0.8%		1			12
Hub Pruett	1922–1932	0.7%	0.4%–0.7%	5			7
Lindy McDaniel	1955–1975	0.7%	0.2%–0.7%	2			21
Fred Toney	1911–1923	0.7%		1			12
Jimmy Ring	1917–1928	0.7%		1			12
Denny McLain	1963–1972	0.7%	0.3%–0.7%	3			10
Jim Bouton	1962–1978	0.7%		1			10
Bill F. Lee	1969–1982	0.7%		1			14
Morrie Martin	1949–1959	0.7%		1			10
Marv Grissom	1946–1959	0.7%		1			10
Rip Sewell	1932–1949	0.6%	0.4%–0.6%	3			13
Eddie Dyer	1922–1927	0.6%		1			6
Jimmy Key	1984–1998	0.6%		1			15
Rick Aguilera	1985–2000	0.6%		1			16
Jesse Tannehill	1894–1911	0.5%		1			15
Jim Turner	1937–1945	0.5%		1			9
John Clarkson	1882–1894	0.5%		1	VC	1963	12
Tully Sparks	1897–1910	0.5%		1			12
Steve Gromek	1941–1957	0.5%		1			17
Jim Brewer	1960–1976	0.5%		1			17
Steve Blass	1964–1974	0.5%		1			10
Bob Kuzava	1946–1957	0.5%		1			10
Claude Osteen	1957–1975	0.5%		1			18
Jack Dunn	1897–1904	0.5%	0.4%–0.5%	3			7
Ted Breitenstein	1891–1901	0.5%		1			11
Cy Falkenberg	1903–1917	0.5%		1			12

*Number of elections in which any votes were received; ( ) indicates a run-off election.

Name	Years Pitched First–Last	Highest %-age	%-age Range	Number of Elections*	HOF	Year Elected	Years Pitched
Jim Maloney	1960–1971	0.5%	0.5%–0.5%	2			12
Dizzy Trout	1939–1957	0.5%		1			15
Sam Leever	1898–1910	0.5%		1			13
Dick Rudolph	1910–1927	0.5%	0.4%–0.5%	2			13
Sam P. Jones	1914–1935	0.5%	0.4%–0.5%	3			22
Bugs Raymond	1904–1911	0.5%		1			6
Ray Sadecki	1960–1977	0.5%		1			18
John Tudor	1979–1990	0.4%		1			12
Jerry Reuss	1969–1990	0.4%		1			22
Mike Scott	1979–1991	0.4%		1			13
Rick Reuschel	1972–1991	0.4%		1			19
Mike Flanagan	1975–1992	0.4%		1			18
Jumbo Elliott	1923–1934	0.4%		1			10
Monte Pearson	1932–1941	0.4%		1			10
Alvin Crowder	1926–1936	0.4%	0.4%–0.4%	2			11
Curt Davis	1934–1946	0.4%		1			13
Whitlow Wyatt	1929–1945	0.4%		1			16
Tom Zachary	1918–1936	0.4%	0.4%–0.4%	2			19
Jack Scott	1916–1929	0.4%		1			12
Rube Walberg	1923–1937	0.4%	0.4%–0.4%	2			15
Watty Clark	1924–1937	0.4%		1			12
Chick Fraser	1896–1909	0.4%		1			14
Noodles Hahn	1899–1906	0.4%		1			8
Andy Coakley	1902–1911	0.4%		1			9
Hub Perdue	1911–1915	0.4%	0.4%–0.4%	2			5
Johnny Allen	1932–1944	0.4%		1			13
Larry Benton	1923–1935	0.4%		1			13
Howie Camnitz	1904–1915	0.4%		1			11
Satchel Paige	1948–1965	0.4%		1	VC	1971‡	6
Bob Forsch	1974–1989	0.4%		1			16
Willie Hernandez	1977–1989	0.4%		1			13
Dave Righetti	1979–1995	0.4%		1			16
Frank Viola	1982–1996	0.4%		1			15
Sid Fernandez	1983–1997	0.4%		1			15
Rick Honeycutt	1977–1997	0.4%		1			21
Doug Drabek	1986–1998	0.4%		1			13
Tom Candiotti	1983–1999	0.4%		1			16
Jeff Montgomery	1987–1999	0.4%		1			13
Doug Jones	1982–2000	0.4%		1			16
Rod Beck	1991–2004	0.4%		1			13
Robb Nen	1993–2002	0.4%		1			10
Don McMahon	1957–1974	0.3%		1			18
Dave Giusti	1962–1977	0.3%		1			15
Dock Ellis	1968–1979	0.3%		1			12
Jim Hearn	1947–1959	0.3%	0.3%–0.3%	2			13
Bob Porterfield	1948–1959	0.3%		1			12
Ned Garver	1948–1961	0.3%		1			14
John Candelaria	1975–1993	0.2%		1			19

*Number of elections in which any votes were received; ( ) indicates a run-off election.
‡Elected for his career in the Negro Leagues.

Name	Years Pitched First–Last	Highest %-age	%-age Range	Number of Elections*	HOF	Year Elected	Years Pitched
Bill Gullickson	1979–1994	0.2%		1			14
Bruce Hurst	1980–1994	0.2%		1			15
Bob Welch	1978–1994	0.2%		1			17
Jim Bibby	1972–1984	0.2%		1			12
Mike Torrez	1967–1984	0.2%		1			18
Burt Hooton	1971–1985	0.2%		1			15
Bill Campbell	1973–1987	0.2%		1			15
Dennis Leonard	1974–1986	0.2%		1			12
Sonny Siebert	1964–1975	0.2%		1			12
Chris Short	1959–1973	0.2%		1			15
Clay Carroll	1964–1978	0.2%		1			15
Al Hrabosky	1970–1982	0.2%		1			13
Jack Billingham	1968–1980	0.2%		1			13
Mike Krukow	1976–1989	0.2%		1			14
Steve Bedrosian	1981–1995	0.2%		1			14
Tom Browning	1984–1995	0.2%		1			12
Ron Darling	1983–1995	0.2%		1			13
Jim DeShaies	1984–1995	0.2%		1			12
Jose Rijo	1984–1995	0.2%		1			12
Mark Davis	1980–1997	0.2%		1			15
Randy Myers	1985–1998	0.2%		1			14
Chuck Finley	1986–2002	0.2%		1			17
Todd Stottlemyre	1988–2002	0.2%		1			14
Jesse Orosco	1979–2003	0.2%		1			24
Mickey Welch	1880–1892				VC	1973	13
Hoss Radbourn	1880–1891				VC	1939	12
Pud Galvin	1879–1892				VC	1965	14
Tim Keefe	1880–1893				VC	1964	14
Vic Willis	1898–1910				VC	1995	13

*Number of elections in which any votes were received; ( ) indicates a run-off election.

Includes only those who achieved 10% of the vote in any year

1936		1937		1938	
Christy Mathewson	90.7% BWA	Young	76.1% BWA	Alexander	80.9% BWA
Walter Johnson	86.3% BWA	Alexander	62.2%	Waddell	56.5%
Cy Young	49.1%	Waddell	33.3%	Walsh	42.0%
Grover Alexander	24.3%	Ed Walsh	27.9%	Brown	20.6%
Rube Waddell	14.6%	Mordecai Brown	15.4%	Eddie Plank	14.5%
				Herb Pennock	14.1%
				Joe McGinnity	13.7%

1939				1942			
Waddell	65.3%	McGinnity	11.7%	Waddell	54.1%	Plank	27.0%
Walsh	48.2%	Plank	10.2%	Walsh	48.5%	McGinnity	25.3%
Brown	19.7%	Addie Joss	10.2%	Pennock	30.9%	Bender	23.6%
Pennock	14.6%			Clark Griffith	30.5%	Dazzy Vance	15.9%
Chief Bender	14.6%			Brown	27.0%	Joss	14.2% VC-1978

1945	
Waddell	62.3%
Walsh	55.5%
Griffith	43.7%
Brown	18.6%
Pennock	18.2%
McGinnity	17.8%
Bender	16.2%
Plank	13.4%
Lefty Grove	11.3%

1946	
Waddell	60.4%
Walsh	56.9%
Carl Hubbell	50.0%
Griffith	36.1%
Grove	35.1%
Brown	27.7%
McGinnity	26.2%
Pennock	20.3%
Dizzy Dean	19.8%
Bender	19.3%
Plank	16.8%
Vance	15.3%

1946 Run Off		
Waddell	33.1%	VC-1946
Walsh	40.3%	VC-1946
Hubbell	28.5%	
Griffith	31.2%	VC-Exec. 1946
Grove	23.2%	
Brown	18.3%	VC-1949
McGinnity	17.9%	VC-1946
Pennock	6.1%	
Dizzy Dean	17.1%	
Bender	13.3%	
Plank	0	VC-1946
Vance	0.0%	

1947	
Hubbell	87.0% BWA
Grove	76.4% BWA
Dean	54.7%
Pennock	53.4%
Bender	44.7%
Vance	31.1%
Joe Wood	18.0%
Babe Adams	13.7%
Rube Marquard	11.2%

1948	
Pennock	77.7% BWA
Dean	33.1%
Vance	19.0%
Lefty Gomez	13.2%
Ted Lyons	12.4%

1949	
Dean	57.5%
Vance	21.6%
Lyons	19.0%
Red Ruffing	14.4%
Gomez	11.1%

1949 Run Off	
Dean	43.3%
Vance	8.0%
Lyons	7.5%
Ruffing	2.1%
Gomez	0.0%

1950	
Dean	50.9%
Vance	31.1%
Lyons	25.1%
Gomez	10.8%

1951	
Dean	64.2%
Lyons	31.4%
Vance	31.0%
Bender	15.5%
Gomez	10.2%

1952	
Dean	65.0%
Vance	44.9%
Lyons	43.2%
Bender	29.9%
Gomez	12.4%

1953	
Dean	79.2% BWA
Vance	56.8%
Lyons	52.7%
Bender	39.4% VC
Gomez	13.3%

1954	
Lyons	67.5%
Vance	62.7%
Gomez	15.1%
Ruffing	11.5%

1955	
Lyons	86.5% BWA
Vance	81.7% BWA
Gomez	28.3%
Ruffing	23.9%
Marquard	13.9% VC-1971
Waite Hoyt	13.1%
Red Faber	10.8%
Dickie Kerr	10.0%

1956	
Ruffing	50.3%
Gomez	46.1%
Hoyt	19.2%
Faber	17.6%
Eppa Rixey	14.0%
Burleigh Grimes	13.0%

1958	
Ruffing	37.2%
Gomez	28.6%
Grimes	26.7%
Faber	25.6%
Hoyt	13.9%
Johnny Vandermeer	13.2%
Stan Coveleski	12.8% VC-1969
Bucky Walters	12.4%
Rixey	12.0%

1960

Rixey	52.8%
Grimes	34.2%
Ruffing	32.0%
Faber	30.9%
Gomez	19.0%
Vander Meer	11.5%
Hoyt	10.8%

1962

Bob Feller	93.8% BWA
Ruffing	45.0%
Rixey	30.6% VC-1963
Grimes	26.9% VC-1964
Faber	18.8% VC-1964
Gomez	12.5% VC-1972
Hoyt	11.3% VC-1969

1964

Ruffing	70.1%
Mel Harder	25.4%
Vander Meer	25.4%
Walters	17.4%
Allie Reynolds	17.4%
Hal Newhouser	12.9%
Bob Lemon	11.9%

1964 Run Off

Ruffing	81.4%*
Vander Meer	8.8%
Harder	6.2%
Walters	3.5%
Reynolds	2.7%
Newhouser	1.3%
Lemon	1.3%

1966

Ruffing	68.9%
Vander Meer	23.8%
Reynolds	19.9%
Walters	18.5%
Harder	11.3%

1967

Ruffing	72.6%
Vander Meer	29.8%
Reynolds	26.4%
Walters	22.3%
Newhouser	21.3%
Harder	17.8%
Lemon	12.0%

1967 Run Off

Ruffing	86.9% BWA
Vander Meer	11.4%
Walters	7.8%
Reynolds	6.7%
Harder	4.6%
Newhouser	4.2%
Lemon	2.3%

1968

Reynolds	33.6%
Vander Meer	27.9%
Walters	23.7%
Newhouser	23.7%
Lemon	16.6%

1969

Reynolds	28.8%
Vander Meer	27.9%
Early Wynn	27.9%
Newhouser	24.1%
Lemon	16.5%

1970

Wynn	46.7%
Reynolds	29.7%
Vander Meer	29.3%
Newhouser	26.7%
Lemon	23.3%

1971

Wynn	66.7%
Reynolds	30.6%
Vander Meer	27.2%
Newhouser	26.1%
Lemon	25.0%

1972

Sandy Koufax	86.9% BWA
Wynn	76.0% BWA
Lemon	29.5%
Reynolds	26.5%
Newhouser	23.2%

1973

Warren Spahn	83.2% BWA
Whitey Ford	67.1%
Robin Roberts	56.1%
Lemon	46.6%
Reynolds	24.5%
Newhouser	20.8%
Johnny Sain	12.4%

1974

Ford	77.8% BWA
Roberts	61.4%
Lemon	52.1%
Reynolds	27.7%
Sain	14.0%

1975

Roberts	72.7%
Lemon	64.4%
Newhouser	42.8% VC-1992
Sain	34.0%
Don Drysdale	21.0%
Vic Raschi	10.2%

1976

Roberts	86.9% BWA
Lemon	78.6% BWA
Drysdale	29.4%
Don Larsen	12.1%

1977

Drysdale	51.4%
Jim Bunning	38.1%
Lew Burdette	22.2%
Don Newcombe	11.2%
Larsen	10.2%

1978

Drysdale	57.8%
Bunning	47.8%
Hoyt Wilhelm	41.7%
Burdette	20.1%
Newcombe	12.7%

*In 1964 Run Off only one player was elected. Luke Appling received 83.6% of the vote besting Ruffing's 81.4%

1979			*1980*			*1981*	
Drysdale	53.9%		Drysdale	61.8%		Bob Gibson	84.0% BWA
Wilhelm	38.9%		Wilhelm	54.3%		Drysdale	60.6%
Bunning	34.0%		Bunning	46.0%		Wilhelm	59.4%
Larsen	12.3%		Burdette	17.1%		Juan Marichal	58.1%
Burdette	12.3%		Newcombe	15.3%		Bunning	40.9%
Newcombe	12.0%					Burdette	12.0%

1982			*1983*			*1984*	
Marichal	73.5%		Marichal	83.7% BWA		Drysdale	78.4% BWA
Wilhelm	56.9%		Wilhelm	65.0%		Wilhelm	72.0%
Drysdale	56.1%		Drysdale	64.7%		Bunning	49.9%
Bunning	33.3%		Bunning	36.9%		Burdette	24.1%
Burdette	10.4%		Burdette	11.5%		Roy Face	16.1%

1985			*1986*			*1987*	
Wilhelm	83.8% BWA		Hunter	68.0%		Hunter	76.3% BWA
Bunning	54.2%		Bunning	65.6%		Bunning	70.0%
Jim Hunter	53.7%		Burdette	22.6%		Burdette	23.2%
Burdette	20.8%		Lolich	20.2%		Lolich	20.3%
Mickey Lolich	19.7%		Face	17.4%		Face	18.9%
Face	15.7%						

1988			*1989*			*1990*	
Bunning	74.2%		Gaylord Perry	68.0%		Jim Palmer	92.6% BWA
Luis Tiant	30.9%		Bunning	63.3%		Perry	72.1%
Lolich	25.5%		Ferguson Jenkins	52.3%		Jenkins	66.7%
Sparky Lyle	13.1%		Jim Kaat	19.5%		Bunning	57.9%
			Tiant	10.5%		Kaat	17.8%
			Lolich	10.5%		Face	11.3%
			Face	10.5%			

1991			*1992*			*1993*	
Perry	77.2% BWA		Tom Seaver	98.8% BWA		Phil Niekro	65.7%
Jenkins	75.4% BWA		Fingers	81.2% BWA		Kaat	29.6%
Rollie Fingers	65.7%		Kaat	26.5%		Tiant	14.7%
Bunning	63.7%		Tiant	11.6%		Lolich	10.2%
Kaat	14.0%		Lolich	10.5%			

1994			*1995*			*1996*	
Steve Carlton	95.8% BWA		P. Niekro	62.2%		P. Niekro	68.3%
P. Niekro	60.0%		Sutton	57.4%		Sutton	63.8%
Don Sutton	56.9%		Sutter	29.8%		Sutter	29.1%
Bruce Sutter	24.0%		Kaat	21.7%		John	21.7%
Kaat	21.5%		Tommy John	21.3%		Kaat	19.4%
						Tiant	13.6%

1997				*1998*			
P. Niekro	80.3% BWA	John	20.5%	Sutton	81.6% BWA	Bert Blyleven	17.5%
Sutton	73.2%	Tiant	11.2%	Sutter	31.1%	Tiant	11.0%
Sutter	27.5%			John	27.3%		
Kaat	22.6%			Kaat	27.3%		

1999		
Nolan Ryan	98.8%	BWA
Sutter	24.3%	
Kaat	20.1%	
John	18.7%	
Blyleven	14.1%	
Tiant	10.7%	

2000	
Sutter	38.5%
Rich Gossage	33.3%
John	27.1%
Kaat	25.1%
Jack Morris	22.2%
Blyleven	17.4%
Tiant	17.2%

2001	
Sutter	47.6%
Gossage	44.3%
John	28.3%
Kaat	27.0%
Blyleven	23.5%
Morris	19.6%
Tiant	12.2%

2002	
Sutter	50.4%
Gossage	43.0%
John	26.9%
Blyleven	26.3%
Kaat	23.1%
Morris	20.6%
Tiant	18.0%

2003	
Sutter	53.6%
Lee Smith	42.3%
Gossage	42.1%
Blyleven	29.2%
Kaat	26.2%
John	23.4%
Morris	22.8%

2004		
Dennis Eckersley	83.2%	BWA
Sutter	59.5%	
Gossage	40.7%	
Smith	36.6%	
Blyleven	35.4%	
Morris	26.3%	
John	21.9%	

2005	
Sutter	66.7%
Gossage	55.2%
Blyleven	40.9%
Smith	38.8%
Morris	33.3%
John	23.8%

2006		
Sutter	76.9%	BWA
Gossage	64.6%	
Blyleven	53.3%	
Smith	45.0%	
Morris	41.2%	
John	29.6%	
Orel Hershiser	11.2%	

2007	
Gossage	71.2%
Blyleven	47.7%
Smith	39.8%
Morris	37.1%
John	22.9%

2008		
Gossage	85.8%	BWA
Blyleven	61.9%	
Smith	43.3%	
Morris	42.9%	
John	29.1%	

2009	
Blyleven	62.7%
Smith	44.5%
Morris	44.0%
John	31.7%

Analysis of Voting for Pitchers

The first three ballots saw the election of four of the all-time greats, Christy Mathewson and Walter Johnson in 1936, Cy Young in 1937, and Grover Alexander in 1938. The next four elections saw between eight to twelve pitchers receiving over 10 percent of the vote but none able to gain election. The log jam was broken in 1946 with four pitchers and one executive (Clark Griffith) selected by the Veterans Committee.

In 1947, Hubbell and Grove, two great southpaws, were elected by the Baseball Writers. Dizzy Dean, the top-ranked pitcher for five consecutive years, reached the pinnacle in 1953. From 1972 through 1976, six pitchers were elected by the BWA, three in their first year of eligibility. A long period of waiting for Veterans Committee selections occurred between the election of Addie Joss in 1978 and Hal Newhouser in 1992.

Allie Reynolds is the only pitcher who has ranked first in voting (1968 and 1969) and not been elected to the Hall of Fame. Don Sutton after a near miss in the 1997 balloting was elected with 81.6 percent of the vote in 1998. Three-hundred-game winners have yet to be denied admission to the Hall of Fame. This was again borne out in 1999 when Nolan Ryan in his first year of eligibility became the twentieth and last of the 300-win fraternity at that time to be enshrined.

From 2000 through 2003 the same six pitchers (Sutter, Gossage, John, Kaat, Blyleven and Morris) received more than 10 percent of the votes. However, none were close to achieving the requisite 75 percent. In 2003, Lee Smith was added to this group in his first year on the ballot while Jim Kaat dropped off after 15 years. 2004 saw Dennis Eckersley elected in his initial try with the revised group of six following. Again in 2005 the same six received enough support to remain on the ballot. The 2006 ballot saw Bruce Sutter elected with the same five (Gossage, Blyleven, Smith, Morris and John) following. Orel Hershiser replaced Sutter which saw six pitchers with over 10 percent of the vote. In 2007 Hershiser was dropped while the previous five received votes in the same order as 2006. Gossage was recognized by the voters in 2008 while Blyleven, Smith, Morris and John again trailed in the same order. In the 2009 voting the same four finished in the fourth through seventh slots.

Rank in Voting by Years (10% or more of the votes)

	Last Year	1936	1937	1938	1939	1942	1945	1946	1946 RO	1947
Christy Mathewson	1916	1B								
Walter Johnson	1927	2B								
Cy Young	1911	3	1B							
Grover Alexander	1930	4	2	1B						
Rube Waddell	1910	5	3	2	1	1	1	1	2V	
Ed Walsh	1917		4	3	2	2	2	2	1V	
Mordecai Brown	1916		5	4	3	5T	4	6	6V-1949	
Eddie Plank	1917			5	4T	5T	8	11	V	
Herb Pennock	1934			6	7T	3	5	8		4
Joe McGinnity	1908			7	6	7	6	7	7V	
Chief Bender	1925				4T	8	7	10	9	5
Addie Joss	1910				7T	10				

B—Baseball Writers' Association of America
V—Veterans Committee
T—Tie in voting

	Last Year	1936	1937	1938	1939	1942	1945	1946	1946 RO	1947
Clark Griffith	1914					4	3	4	3V-Exec	
Dazzy Vance	1935					9		12		6
Lefty Grove	1941						9	5	5	2B
Carl Hubbell	1943							3	4	1B
Dizzy Dean	1947							9	8	3
Joe Wood	1920									7
Babe Adams	1926									8
Rube Marquard	1925									9

	Last Year	1948	1949	1949 RO	1950	1951	1952	1953	1954	1955
Herb Pennock		1B								
Joe McGinnity										
Chief Bender						4	4	4V		
Addie Joss										
Clark Griffith										
Dazzy Vance		3	2		2	3	2	2	2	2B
Dizzy Dean		2	1	1	1	1	1	1B		
Rube Marquard										5V-1971
Lefty Gomez	1943	4	5		4	5	5	5	3	3
Ted Lyons	1946	5	3		3	2	3	3	1	1B
Red Ruffing	1947		4						4	4
Waite Hoyt	1938									6
Red Faber	1933									7
Dickie Kerr	1925									8

	Last Year	1956	1958	1960	1962	1964	1964 RO	1966	1967	1967 RO
Lefty Gomez		2	2	5	6V-1972					
Red Ruffing		1	1	3	2	1	1	1	1	1B
Waite Hoyt		3	5	7	7V-1969					
Red Faber		4	4	4	5V-1964					
Eppa Rixey	1933	5	9	1	3V-1963					
Burleigh Grimes	1934	6	3	2	4V-1964					
Johnny Vandermeer	1951		6	6		2T		2	2	2
Stan Coveleski	1928		7V-1969							
Bucky Walters	1950		8			4T		4	4	
Bob Feller	1956				1B					
Allie Reynolds	1954					4T		3	3	
Hal Newhouser	1955					6			5	
Mel Harder	1947					2T		5	6	
Bob Lemon	1958					7			7	

B—Baseball Writers' Association of America
V—Veterans Committee
T—Tie in voting

	Last Year	1968	1969	1970	1971	1972	1973	1974	1975	1976
Johnny Vandermeer		2	2T	3	3					
Bucky Walters		3T								
Allie Reynolds		1	1	2	2	4	5	4		
Hal Newhouser		3T	4	4	4	5	6		3V-1992	
Bob Lemon		5	5	5	5	3	4	3	2	2B
Early Wynn	1963		2T	1	1	2B				
Sandy Koufax	1966					1B				
Warren Spahn	1965						1B			
Whitey Ford	1967						2	1B		
Robin Roberts	1966						3	2	1	1B
Johnny Sain	1955						7	5	4	
Don Drysdale	1969								5	3
Don Larsen	1967									4
Vic Raschi	1955								6	

	Last Year	1977	1978	1979	1980	1981	1982	1983	1984	1985
Drysdale		1	1	1	1	2	3	3	1B	
Larsen		5		4T						
Jim Bunning	1971	2	2	3	3	5	4	4	3	2
Lew Burdette	1967	3	4	4T	4	6	5	5	4	4
Don Newcombe	1960	4	5	6	5					
Hoyt Wilhelm	1972		3	2	2	3	2	2	2	1B
Bob Gibson	1975					1B				
Juan Marichal	1975					4	1	1B		
Roy Face	1969								5	6
Jim Hunter	1979									3
Mickey Lolich	1979									5

	Last Year	1986	1987	1988	1989	1990	1991	1992	1993	1994
Bunning		2	2	1	2	4	4	V-1996		
Burdette		3	3							
Face		5	5		7	6				
Hunter		1	1B							
Lolich		4	4	3	6			5	4	
Luis Tiant	1982			2	5			4	3	
Sparky Lyle	1982			4						
Gaylord Perry	1983				1	2	1B			
Ferguson Jenkins	1983				3	3	2B			
Jim Kaat	1983				4	5	5	3	2	5
Jim Palmer	1984				1B					
Rollie Fingers	1985					3	2B			
Tom Seaver	1986						1B			
Phil Niekro	1987								1	2
Steve Carlton	1988									1B

B—Baseball Writers' Association of America
V—Veterans Committee
T—Tie in voting

	Last Year	1986	1987	1988	1989	1990	1991	1992	1993	1994
Don Sutton	1988									3
Bruce Sutter	1988									4

	Last Year	1995	1996	1997	1998	1999	2000	2001	2002	2003
Tiant			6	6	6	6	7	7	7	
Kaat		4	5	4	3T	3	4	4	5	5
Niekro		1	1	1B						
Sutton		2	2	2	1B					
Sutter		3	3	3	2	2	1	1	1	1
Tommy John	1989	5	4	5	3T	4	3	3	3	6
Bert Blyleven	1992				5	5	6	5	4	4
Nolan Ryan	1993					1B				
Rich Gossage	1994						2	2	2	3
Jack Morris	1994						5	6	6	7
Lee Smith	1997									2

	Last Year	2004	2005	2006	2007	2008	2009
Dennis Eckersley	1998	1B					
Sutter		2	1	1B			
Gossage		3	2	2	1	1B	
Smith		4	4	4	3	3	2
Blyleven		5	3	3	2	2	1
Morris		6	5	5	4	4	3
John		7	6	6	5	5	4
Orel Hershiser	2000			7			

B—Baseball Writers' Association of America
V—Veterans Committee
T—Tie in voting

Year	No. with 10% or More of Votes	No. in Hall of Fame BWA	VC	Cumulative Total (Different Individuals)	Non–Hall of Famers
1936	5	4	1	5	
1937	5	2	3	7	
1938	7	2	5	10	
1939	8	1	7	12	
1942	10	2	8	14	
1945	9	2	7	15	
1946	12	5	7	17	
1947	9	5	2	20	Babe Adams, Joe Wood
1948	5	4	1	22	
1949	5	4	1	23	
1950	4	3	1	23	
1951	5	3	2	23	
1952	5	3	2	23	
1953	5	3	2	23	

Year	No. with 10% or More of Votes	No. in Hall of Fame BWA	VC	Cumulative Total (Different Individuals)	Non–Hall of Famers
1954	4	3	1	23	
1955	8	3	4	26	Dickie Kerr
1956	6	1	5	28	
1958	9	1	6	31	Johnny Vander Meer, Bucky Walters
1960	7	1	5	31	
1962	7	2	5	32	
1964	7	2	1	36	Mel Harder, Allie Reynolds
1966	5	1	0	36	
1967	7	2	1	36	
1968	5	1	1	36	
1969	5	2	1	37	
1970	5	2	1	37	
1971	5	2	1	37	
1972	5	3	1	38	
1973	7	4	1	42	Johnny Sain
1974	5	3	0	42	
1975	6	3	1	44	Vic Raschi
1976	4	3	0	45	Don Larsen
1977	5	1	1	48	Don Newcombe, Lew Burdette
1978	5	2	1	49	
1979	6	2	1	49	
1980	5	2	1	49	
1981	6	4	1	51	
1982	5	3	1	51	
1983	5	3	1	51	
1984	5	2	1	52	Roy Face
1985	6	2	1	54	Mickey Lolich
1986	5	1	1	54	
1987	5	1	1	54	
1988	4	0	1	56	Luis Tiant, Sparky Lyle
1989	7	2	1	59	Jim Kaat
1990	6	3	1	60	
1991	5	3	1	61	
1992	5	2	0	62	
1993	4	1	0	63	
1994	5	2	0	66	
1995	5	1	0	67	Tommy John
1996	6	1	0	67	
1997	6	1	0	67	
1998	6	1	0	68	Bert Blyleven
1999	6	1	0	69	
2000	7	0	0	71	Jack Morris
2001	7	0	0	71	
2002	7	0	0	71	
2003	7	0	0	72	Lee Smith
2004	7	1	0	73	
2005	6	0	0	73	
2006	7	1	0	74	Orel Hershiser
2007	5	0	0	74	
2008	5	1	0	74	
2009	4	0	0	74	

Conclusions (Pitchers)

Every pitcher who received 10 percent of the vote from 1936 through 1946 was eventually selected to the Hall of Fame.

Every pitcher who received 10 percent of the vote from 1936 through 1956 with the exception of three (Babe Adams, Joe Wood and Dickie Kerr) was eventually elected to the Hall of Fame.

Of 74 individuals who received 10 percent of the vote in at least one election through 2009, 51 are in the Hall of Fame (35 elected by the Baseball Writers Association and 16 by the Veterans Committee).

Three pitchers are still under consideration by the BWA: Lee Smith (2009; seventh year of eligibility), Bert Blyleven (2009; twelfth year of eligibility) and Jack Morris (2009; tenth year of eligibility). The remaining 20 pitchers are all eligible for future consideration by the Veterans Committee.

Catchers

Name	Years Played First–Last	Highest %-age	%-age Range	Number of Elections*	HOF	Year Elected	Years Played
Johnny Bench	1967–1983	96.4%		1	BWA	1989	17
Yogi Berra	1946–1965	85.6%	67.2%–85.6%	2	BWA	1972	19
Bill Dickey	1928–1946	80.2%	6.9%–80.2%	9(2)	BWA	1954	17
Carlton Fisk	1969–1993	79.6%	66.4%–79.6%	2	BWA	2000	24
Mickey Cochrane	1925–1937	79.5%	10.2%–79.5%	6(1)	BWA	1947	13
Roy Campanella	1948–1957	79.4%	(55.6%)–79.4%	5(2)	BWA	1969	10
Gary Carter	1974–1992	78.0%	33.8%–78.0%	6	BWA	2003	19
Gabby Hartnett	1922–1941	77.7%	0.8%–77.7%	11(1)	BWA	1955	20
Roger Bresnahan	1897–1915	53.8%	20.8%–53.8%	6	VC	1945	17
Ray Schalk	1912–1929	45.0%	1.8%–45.0%	16(1)	VC	1955	18
Al Lopez	1928–1947	39.0%	0.5%–39.0%	10(2)	VC	1977*	19
Wilbert Robinson	1886–1902	38.2%	2.5%–38.2%	5	VC	1945*	17
Hank Gowdy	1910–1930	35.9%	0.6%–35.9%	17			17
Joe Torre	1960–1977	22.2%	5.3%–22.2%	15			18
Elston Howard	1955–1968	20.7%	5.2%–20.7%	15			14
Ernie Lombardi	1931–1947	16.4%	1.3%–16.4%	9(2)	VC	1986	17
Thurman Munson	1969–1979	15.5%	4.8%–15.5%	15			11
Walker Cooper	1940–1957	14.4%	1.5%–14.4%	10			18
Johnny Kling	1900–1913	10.0%	0.4%–10.0%	9			13
Jimmie Wilson	1923–1940	8.8%	0.9%–8.8%	13			18
Muddy Ruel	1915–1934	8.3%	0.4%–8.3%	10			19
Lou Criger	1896–1912	8.0%	0.7%–8.0%	5			16
Bob Boone	1972–1990	7.7%	4.2%–7.7%	5			19
Steve O'Neill	1911–1928	4.9%	0.6%–4.9%	6			17
Wally Schang	1913–1931	4.1%	0.5%–4.1%	5			19
Del Crandall	1949–1966	3.9%	1.6%–3.9%	4			16
Tim McCarver	1959–1980	3.8%		1			21

*Elected as a Manager

Name	Years Played First–Last	Highest %-age	%-age Range	Number of Elections*	HOF	Year Elected	Years Played
Ted Simmons	1968–1988	3.7%		1			21
Jimmy Archer	1904–1918	3.0%	1.1%–3.0%	3			12
Birdie Tebbetts	1936–1952	3.0%	0.4%–3.0%	2			14
Bill Carrigan	1906–1916	2.5%	0.7%–2.5%	4			10
Bob O'Farrell	1915–1935	2.4%	1.1%–2.4%	3			21
Moe Berg	1923–1939	1.9%	1.1%–1.9%	2			15
Jim Hegan	1941–1960	1.7%	0.7%–1.7%	2			17
Lance Parrish	1977-1995	1.7%		1			19
Branch Rickey	1905–1914	1.3%	0.8%–1.3%	2	VC	1967†	4
Luke Sewell	1921–1942	1.1%	0.6%–1.1%	3			20
Mike Gonzalez	1912–1932	1.1%	0.4%–1.1%	5			17
Charlie Berry	1925–1938	1.1%	0.4%–1.1%	2			11
Marty Bergen	1896–1899	1.0%	0.4%–1.0%	3			4
Ossee Schreck	1897–1908	1.0%	0.7%–1.0%	3			11
Wes Westrum	1947–1957	1.0%		1			11
Spud Davis	1928–1945	0.8%	0.7%–0.8%	2			16
Hank Severeid	1911–1926	0.8%		1			15
Earl Smith	1919–1930	0.8%	0.5%–0.8%	2			12
Cy Perkins	1915–1934	0.8%		1			17
Del Rice	1945–1961	0.7%		1			17
Buck Ewing	1880–1897	0.7%		1	VC	1939	18
Bubbles Hargrave	1913–1930	0.6%	0.4%–0.6%	3			12
Red Dooin	1902–1916	0.5%	0.4%–0.5%	2			15
Larry McLean	1901–1915	0.5%		1			13
Otto Miller	1910–1922	0.5%		1			13
Pat Moran	1901–1914	0.5%	0.4%–0.5%	4			14
Gabby Street	1904–1931	0.5%	0.4%–0.5%	3			8
Billy Sullivan, Sr.	1899–1916	0.5%	0.5%–0.5%	2			16
Bill Killefer	1909–1921	0.5%		1			13
Rick Ferrell	1929–1947	0.5%	0.4%–0.5%	3	VC	1984	18
Smokey Burgess	1949–1967	0.5%	0.3%–0.5%	2			18
Bill Freehan	1961–1976	0.5%		1			15
Manny Sanguillen	1967–1980	0.5%		1			13
Steve Yeager	1972–1986	0.5%		1			15
Ira Thomas	1906–1915	0.4%		1			10
Chief Zimmer	1884–1903	0.4%		1			19
Heine Peitz	1892–1913	0.4%		1			16
Harry Danning	1933–1942	0.4%	0.4%–0.4%	2			10
Gus Mancuso	1928–1945	0.4%		1			17
Clyde Sukeforth	1926–1945	0.4%		1			10
Tony Pena	1980–1997	0.4%		1			18
Clint Courtney	1951–1961	0.3%		1			11
Terry Kennedy	1978–1991	0.2%		1			14
Rick Dempsey	1969–1992	0.2%		1			24
Gene Tenace	1969–1983	0.2%		1			15
Jim Sundberg	1974–1989	0.2%		1			16
Darren Daulton	1983–1997	0.2%		1			14
Terry Steinbach	1986–1999	0.2%		1			14

*Elected as a Manager
†Elected as an Executive

(Includes all those receiving 5% or more of the vote or the top two.)

1936	
Mickey Cochrane	35.4%
Roger Bresnahan	20.8%

1937	
Bresnahan	21.4%
Ray Schalk	11.9%
Johnny Kling	10.0%
Lou Criger	8.0%

1938	
Bresnahan	25.6%
Schalk	17.2%
Kling	9.9%
Wilbert Robinson	6.5%

1939	
Bresnahan	24.5%
Robinson	16.8%
Schalk	12.8%
Cochrane	10.2%
Kling	5.1%

1942	
Robinson	38.2%
Cochrane	37.8%
Bresnahan	24.5%
Schalk	22.7%
Kling	6.4%

1945	
Bresnahan	53.8% VC
Cochrane	50.6%
Robinson	32.8% VC Mgr
Schalk	13.4%
Bill Dickey	6.9%

1946	
Cochrane	39.6%
Dickey	19.8%
Schalk	17.8%
Kling	9.9%

1946 Run Off	
Cochrane	24.7%
Dickey	12.1%
Schalk	0
Kling	0

1947	
Cochrane	79.5% BWA
Schalk	31.1%

1948	
Dickey	32.2%
Gabby Hartnett	27.3%
Schalk	18.2%
Jimmie Wilson	6.6%

1949	
Dickey	42.5%
Hartnett	22.9%
Schalk	15.7%
Hank Gowdy	6.5%

1949 Run Off	
Dickey	20.9%
Hartnett	3.7%
Schalk	9.1%
Gowdy	0

1950	
Dickey	46.7%
Hartnett	32.3%
Schalk	9.6%

1951	
Dickey	52.2%
Hartnett	25.2%
Schalk	16.4%
Gowdy	11.5%

1952	
Dickey	59.4%
Hartnett	32.9%
Schalk	18.8%
Gowdy	14.5%

1953	
Dickey	67.8%
Hartnett	39.4%
Schalk	22.0%
Gowdy	19.7%

1954	
Dickey	80.2% BWA
Hartnett	59.9%
Schalk	21.4%
Gowdy	20.2%

1955	
Hartnett	77.7% BWA
Schalk	45.0% VC
Gowdy	35.9%
Wilson	5.2%

1956	
Gowdy	25.4%
Wilson	8.8%
Muddy Ruel	8.3%

1958	
Gowdy	16.9%
Al Lopez	12.6%

1960	
Gowdy	14.1%
Lopez	9.7%

1962	
Lopez	6.9%
Ernie Lombardi	3.1%

1964	
Roy Campanella	57.2%
Lopez	28.4%
Lombardi	16.4%

1964 Run Off	
Campanella	61.1%
Lopez	15.0%
Lombardi	4.0%

1966	
Campanella	65.2%
Lopez	36.1%
Lombardi	11.3%

1967	
Campanella	69.9%
Lopez	39.0%
Lombardi	14.7%

1967 Run Off	
Campanella	55.6%
Lopez	16.3% VC-1977 Mgr
Lombardi	8.2% VC-1986

1968

| Campanella | 72.4% |
| Walker Cooper | 2.8% |

1969

| Campanella | 79.4% BWA |
| Cooper | 1.5% |

1970

| Cooper | 3.0% |

1971

| Yogi Berra | 67.2% |
| Cooper | 1.9% |

1972

| Yogi Berra | 85.6% BWA |
| Cooper | 2.0% |

1973

| Cooper | 2.1% |
| Smokey Burgess | 0.3% |

1974

| Elston Howard | 5.2% |
| Cooper | 2.5% |

1975

| Howard | 6.4% |
| Cooper | 3.6% |

1976

| Cooper | 14.4% |
| Howard | 14.2% |

1977

| Cooper | 11.7% |
| Howard | 11.2% |

1978

| Howard | 10.8% |
| Del Crandall | 1.6% |

1979

| Howard | 6.9% |
| Crandall | 2.1% |

1980

| Howard | 7.5% |

1981

| Howard | 20.7% |
| Thurman Munson | 15.5% |

1982

| Howard | 9.6% |
| Munson | 6.3% |

1983

| Howard | 8.6% |
| Joe Torre | 5.3% |

1984

Howard	11.2%
Torre	11.2%
Munson	7.2%

1985

Howard	13.7%
Torre	11.1%
Munson	8.1%

1986

Torre	14.1%
Howard	12.0%
Munson	8.2%

1987

Torre	11.4%
Howard	10.7%
Munson	6.8%

1988

Torre	14.1%
Howard	12.4%
Munson	7.5%

1989

Johnny Bench	96.4% BWA
Torre	8.9%
Munson	6.9%

1990

| Torre | 12.4% |
| Munson | 7.4% |

1991

| Torre | 9.3% |
| Munson | 6.3% |

1992

| Torre | 14.4% |
| Munson | 7.4% |

1993

| Torre | 14.9% |
| Munson | 9.5% |

1994

| Torre | 11.6% |
| Munson | 6.8% |

1995

| Torre | 10.9% |
| Munson | 6.5% |

1996

| Torre | 10.6% |
| Boone | 7.7% |

1997

| Torre | 22.2% |
| Boone | 5.9% |

1998

| Gary Carter | 42.3% |
| Boone | 5.5% |

1999

Carlton Fisk	66.4%
Carter	33.8%
Boone	5.4%

2000

| Fisk | 79.6% BWA |
| Carter | 49.7% |

2001	2002	2003
Carter 64.9%	Carter 72.7%	Carter 78.0% BWA
Lance Parrish 1.7%		Tony Pena 0.4%

2004	2005	2006
No catchers received votes	Terry Steinbach 0.2%	No catchers received votes

2007	2008	2009
No catchers received votes	No catchers received votes	No catchers received votes

Analysis of Voting for Catchers

In the balloting of the late '30s to the middle '40s, Cochrane, Bresnahan, Schalk and Robinson vied for voter recognition. At that time, the rules were fuzzy. Cochrane led the voting at his position in 1936, while he was still active. Robinson's votes were undoubtedly for his managerial prowess. Bresnahan led the vote-getting among catchers for four of six years until his induction in 1945.

Bill Dickey and Gabby Hartnett finished one-two in the voting for seven consecutive years until their election in 1954 and 1955, respectively. Ray Schalk, after finishing second, third or fourth for fourteen years, was similarly rewarded by the Veteran's Committee in 1955. Hank Gowdy became the favorite for the next three elections but his support was minimal (14.1 percent to 25.4 percent).

Roy Campanella led for five consecutive elections receiving 79.4 percent in 1969. His competitors Al Lopez and Ernie Lombardi were both later tapped by the Veteran's Committee, Lopez as a manager. Lombardi's support in the BWA elections was never very strong. His best year netted 16.4 percent of the vote.

In 1972, Yogi Berra was elected in his second year on the ballot. The quartet of Walker Cooper, Elston Howard, Thurman Munson and Joe Torre from 1976 through 1997 only on two occasions got over 20 percent of the vote (Howard 20.7 percent in 1981 and Torre 22.2 percent in 1997). Torre's eligibility ran out in 1997. The only carryover to 1998 was Bob Boone who garnered 5.5 percent of the vote, barely enough to stay on the ballot.

Rick Ferrell was never a factor in Baseball Writers' Association balloting but was selected by the Veteran's Committee in 1984.

In 1989, Johnny Bench became the only catcher to be elected in his first year on the ballot.

Carlton Fisk was elected in 2000, his second year, and Gary Carter, after being overshadowed by Fisk, received recognition in 2003. Since that time catchers have rarely appeared on the Hall of Fame ballot.

Gary Carter made an excellent showing in his first year of eligibility (1998) getting 42.3 percent of the votes. However, Carlton Fisk moved ahead of Carter on the 1999 ballot and was elected in 2000. Meanwhile, Carter increased his position with 72.7 percent of the votes in 2002 and in 2003 met the Hall of Fame standard with 78.0 percent of the votes.

No Catcher received a vote in the 2004, 2006, 2007 and 2008 elections and Terry Steinbach garnered but one vote in 2005.

Buck Ewing, who tied for the top spot in the Veterans Election of 1936 with 51.3 percent of the vote, was elected in 1939 by a triumvirate composed of Commissioner Landis and League Presidents Frick and Harridge.

Rank in Voting by Years (10% or more of votes)

	Last Year	1936	1937	1938	1939	1942	1945	1946	1946 RO	1947
Mickey Cochrane	1937	1			4	2	2	1	1	1B
Roger Bresnahan	1915	2	1	1	1	3	1V			
Ray Schalk	1929		2	2	3	4	4	3		2
Johnny Kling	1913		3							
Wilbert Robinson	1902					2	1	3V-Mgr		
Bill Dickey	1946							2	2	

	Last Year	1948	1949	1949 RO	1950	1951	1952	1953	1954	1955
Schalk		3	3			3	3	4	3	2V
Dickey		1	1	1	1	1	1	1	1B	
Gabby Hartnett	1941	2	2		2	2	2	2	2	1B
Hank Gowdy	1930					4	4	3	4	3

	Last Year	1956	1958	1960	1962	1964	1964 RO	1966	1967	1967 RO
Gowdy		1	1	1						
Al Lopez	1947		2			2	2	2	2	2
Roy Campanella	1957					1	1	1	1	1
Ernie Lombardi	1947					3		3	3	

	Last Year	1968	1969	1970	1971	1972	1973	1974	1975	1976
Lopez										
Campanella		1	1B							
Lombardi										
Yogi Berra	1965				1	1B				
Walker Cooper	1957									1
Elston Howard	1968									2

B—Baseball Writers Association of America
V—Veterans Committee
T—Tie in voting

	Last Year	1977	1978	1979	1980	1981	1982	1983	1984	1985
Lopez		V-Mgr.								
Lombardi										
Cooper		1								
Howard		2	1			1			1T	1
Thurman Munson	1979						2		1T	
Joe Torre	1977									2

	Last Year	1986	1987	1988	1989	1990	1991	1992	1993	1994
Lombardi		V								
Howard		2	2	2						
Torre		1	1	1		1		1	1	1
Johnny Bench	1983				1B					

	Last Year	1995	1996	1997	1998	1999	2000	2001	2002	2003
Torre		1	1	1						
Gary Carter	1992					1	2	2	1	1	1B
Carlton Fisk	1993					1	1B			

B—Baseball Writers Association of America
V—Veterans Committee
T—Tie in voting

Year	No. with 10% or More of Votes	No. in Hall of Fame BWA	VC	Cumulative Total (Different Individuals)	Non–Hall of Famers
1936	2	1	1	2	
1937	3	0	2	4	Johnny Kling
1938	2	0	2	4	
1939	4	1	3	5	
1942	4	1	3	5	
1945	4	1	3	5	
1946	3	2	1	6	
1947	2	1	1	6	
1948	3	2	1	7	
1949	3	2	1	7	
1950	2	2	0	7	
1951	4	2	1	8	Hank Gowdy
1952	4	2	1	8	
1953	4	2	1	8	
1954	4	2	1	8	
1955	3	1	1	8	
1956	1	0	0	8	
1958	2	0	1	9	

Year	No. with 10% or More of Votes	No. in Hall of Fame		Cumulative Total (Different Individuals)	Non–Hall of Famers
		BWA	VC		
1960	1	0	0	9	
1962	0	0	0	9	
1964	3	1	2	11	
1966	3	1	2	11	
1967	3	1	2	11	
1968	1	1	0	11	
1969	1	1	0	11	
1970	0	0	0	11	
1971	1	1	0	12	
1972	1	1	0	12	
1973	0	0	0	12	
1974	0	0	0	12	
1975	0	0	0	12	
1976	2	0	0	14	Walker Cooper, Elston Howard
1977	2	0	0	14	
1978	1	0	0	14	
1979	0	0	0	14	
1980	0	0	0	14	
1981	2	0	0	15	Thurman Munson
1982	0	0	0	15	
1983	0	0	0	15	
1984	2	0	0	16	Joe Torre
1985	2	0	0	16	
1986	2	0	0	16	
1987	2	0	0	16	
1988	2	0	0	16	
1989	1	1	0	17	
1990	1	0	0	17	
1991	0	0	0	17	
1992	1	0	0	17	
1993	1	0	0	17	
1994	1	0	0	17	
1995	1	0	0	17	
1996	1	0	0	17	
1997	1	0	0	17	
1998	1	0	0	18	
1999	2	0	0	19	
2000	2	1	0	19	
2001	1	0	0	19	
2002	1	0	0	19	
2003	1	1	0	19	
2004	0	0	0	19	
2005	0	0	0	19	
2006	0	0	0	19	
2007	0	0	0	19	
2008	0	0	0	19	
2009	0	0	0	19	

Conclusions (Catchers)

From 1936 through 1975, twelve catchers received 10 percent of the vote. Of that number, ten were eventually elected to the Hall of Fame.

Through 2009, nineteen catchers have received 10 percent of the vote. Of that number, thirteen have been elected to the Hall of Fame. With the exception of Hank Gowdy, every catcher who has received 25 percent of the vote is in the Hall of Fame. The six non–Hall of Fame catchers are all eligible for consideration by the Veteran's Committee.

First Basemen

Name	Years Played First–Last	Highest %-age	%-age Range	Number of Elections*	HOF	Year Elected	Years Played
Lou Gehrig	1923–1939	100.0%	22.6%–100%	2	BWA	1939	17
George Sisler	1915–1930	85.8%	34.1%–85.8%	4	BWA	1939	15
Eddie Murray	1977–1997	85.3%		1	BWA	2003	21
Hank Greenberg	1930–1947	85.0%	1.2%–85.0%	9(1)	BWA	1956	13
Harmon Killebrew	1954–1975	83.1%	59.3%–83.1%	4	BWA	1984	22
Willie McCovey	1959–1980	81.4%		1	BWA	1986	22
Jimmy Foxx	1925–1945	79.2%	9.3%–79.2%	8	BWA	1951	20
Bill Terry	1923–1936	77.4%	2.7%–77.4%	14(1)	BWA	1954	14
Tony Perez	1964–1986	77.2%	50.1%–77.2%	9	BWA	2000	23
Orlando Cepeda	1958–1974	73.6%	10.1%–73.6%	15	VC	1999	17
Frank Chance	1898–1914	72.5%	2.2%–72.5%	7(1)	VC	1946	17
Gil Hodges	1943–1963	63.4%	24.1%–63.4%	15			18
Johnny Mize	1936–1953	43.6%	(4.6%)–43.6%	12(1)	VC	1981	15
Steve Garvey	1969–1987	42.6%	20.5%–42.6%	15			19
Phil Cavaretta	1934–1955	35.6%	0.4%–35.6%	12(2)			22
Jim Bottomley	1922–1937	33.1%	2.7%–33.1%	12	VC	1974	16
Don Mattingly	1982–1995	28.2%	9.9%–28.2%	9			14
Mickey Vernon	1939–1960	24.9%	(0.7%)–24.9%	15(1)			20
Mark McGwire	1986–2001	23.6%	21.9%–23.6%	3			16
Dick Allen	1963–1977	18.9%	3.7%–18.9%	14			15
Ted Kluszewski	1947–1961	14.4%	2.5%–14.4%	15			15
Keith Hernandez	1974–1990	10.8%	4.3%–10.8%	9			17
Charlie Grimm	1916–1936	9.8%	0.4%–9.8%	12			20
Hal Chase	1905–1919	9.0%	4.9%–9.0%	2			15
Joe Judge	1915–1934	5.6%	0.5%–5.6%	7			20
Stuffy McInnis	1909–1927	5.2%	0.5%–5.2%	7			19
Rudy York	1934–1948	5.0%	0.6%–5.0%	2			13
Will Clark	1986–2000	4.4%		1			15
Mark Grace	1988–2003	4.1%		1			16
Fred Tenney	1894–1911	3.1%	0.4%–3.1%	5			17
Frank McCormick	1934–1948	3.0%	0.6%–3.0%	4			13
Bill Buckner	1969–1990	2.1%			1		22
George Kelly	1915–1932	1.9%	0.6%–1.9%	7	VC	1973	16
Bill White	1956–1969	1.9%	1.0%–1.9%	3			13

*Number of elections in which votes were received ( ) indicates run off election.

Name	Years Played First–Last	Highest %-age	%-age Range	Number of Elections*	HOF	Year Elected	Years Played
Norm Cash	1958–1974	1.6%		1			17
Dolph Camilli	1933–1945	1.5%	0.5%–1.5%	4			12
Pedro Guerrero	1978–1992	1.3%		1			15
Whitey Lockman	1945–1960	1.3%		1			15
Boog Powell	1961–1977	1.3%		1			17
Lew Fonseca	1921–1933	1.2%	0.8%–1.2%	5			12
Roy Sievers	1949–1965	1.1%	0.8%–1.1%	2			17
Mo Vaughn	1991–2003	1.1%		1			12
Kent Hrbek	1981–1994	1.0%		1			14
Jake Daubert	1910–1924	1.0%	0.4%–1.0%	5			15
Harry Davis	1895–1917	1.0%	0.4%–1.0%	2			22
Del Ennis	1946–1959	1.0%	0.7%–1.0%	2			14
Hal Morris	1988–2000	1.0%		1			13
Ron Fairly	1958–1978	0.8%		1			21
Vic Power	1954–1965	0.8%	0.6%–0.8%	2			12
Earl Torgeson	1947–1961	0.7%		1			15
Bob Watson	1966–1984	0.7%		1			19
Lee May	1965–1982	0.5%		1			18
Gus Suhr	1930–1940	0.5%	0.4%–0.5%	3			11
Andre Thornton	1973–1987	0.5%		1			14
Joe Kuhel	1930–1947	0.5%		1			18
Jake Stahl	1903–1913	0.4%	0.4%–0.4%	2			9
Jake Beckley	1881–1907	0.4%		1	VC	1971	20
Buck Jordan	1927–1938	0.4%		1			10
Lu Blue	1921–1933	0.4%		1			13
Wally Pipp	1913–1928	0.4%		1			15
Gregg Jefferies	1987–2000	0.4%		1			14
Walt Dropo	1949–1961	0.3%		1			13
George Scott	1966–1979	0.2%		1			14
Mike Hargrove	1974–1985	0.2%		1			12
Mike Jorgensen	1968–1985	0.2%		1			17
John Kruk	1986–1995	0.2%		1			10
Cecil Fielder	1985–1998	0.2%		1			13
Cap Anson	1876–1897				VC	1939	22
Dan Brouthers	1879–1904				VC	1945	19
Roger Connor	1880–1897				VC	1976	18

*Number of elections in which votes were received ( ) indicates run off election.

(Includes all those receiving 5% or more of the votes)

1936		1937		1938	
George Sisler	34.1%	Sisler	52.7%	Sisler	63.3%
Lou Gehrig	22.6%	Frank Chance	24.4%	Chance	50.8%
Jimmy Foxx	9.3%	Hal Chase	9.0%		

1939		1942		1945	
Gehrig	100% BWA*	Chance	57.7%	Chance	58.4%	Chance	72.5%
Sisler	85.8% BWA	Bill Terry	5.8%	Terry	15.5%	Terry	13.0%

*Elected by acclamation of Baseball Writers' Association.

1946

Chance	71.3%
Terry	15.3%
Foxx	12.9%

1946 Run Off

Chance	57.0% VC
Terry	0
Foxx	0

1947

Terry	28.6%
Foxx	6.2%

1948

Terry	43.0%
Foxx	41.3%
Charlie Grimm	5.0%

1949

Foxx	55.6%
Terry	52.9%
Greenberg	43.8%
Grimm	6.5%
Jim Bottomley	5.2%
Stuffy McInnis	5.2%

1949 Run Off

Foxx	47.6%
Terry	25.7%
Greenberg	23.5%
Grimm	0
Bottomley	0
McInnis	0

1950

Terry	62.9%
Foxx	61.7%
Greenberg	38.3%
Grimm	7.8%

1951

Foxx	79.2% BWA
Terry	65.5%
Greenberg	29.6%

1952

Terry	66.2%
Greenberg	32.1%

1953

Terry	72.3%
Greenberg	30.3%

1954

Terry	77.4% BWA
Greenberg	38.5%
Bottomley	6.3%

1955

Greenberg	62.5%
Bottomley	10.4%

1956

Greenberg	85.0% BWA
Bottomley	21.8%

1958

Bottomley	21.4%
Grimm	9.8%

1960

Bottomley	33.1%
Johnny Mize	16.7%
Joe Judge	5.6%

1962

Bottomley	12.5% VC-1974
Mize	8.8%

1964

Mize	26.9%
Phil Cavaretta	10.9%
Rudy York	5.0%

1964 Run Off

Mize	5.3%
Cavaretta	0.4%
York	0

1966

Mize	26.8%
Mickey Vernon	6.6%

1967

Mize	30.5%
Cavaretta	5.1%

1967 Run Off

Mize	4.6%
Cavaretta	1.3%

1968

Mize	36.4%
Cavaretta	8.1%
Vernon	7.8%

1969

Mize	34.1%
Gil Hodges	24.1%
Cavaretta	10.9%
Vernon	6.2%

1970

Hodges	48.3%
Mize	42.0%
Cavaretta	17.0%

1971

Hodges	50.0%
Mize	43.6%
Cavaretta	23.1%

1972

Hodges	40.7%
Mize	39.6%
Cavaretta	15.4%

1973

Hodges	57.4%
Mize	41.3% VC-1981
Cavaretta	19.2%
Vernon	6.1%

1974

Hodges	54.2%
Cavaretta	16.7%
Ted Kluszewski	7.7%
Vernon	7.4%

1975

Hodges	51.9%
Cavaretta	35.6%
Kluszewski	9.1%
Vernon	6.1%

1976

Hodges	60.1%
Vernon	13.4%
Kluszewski	12.9%

1977

Hodges	58.5%
Kluszewski	14.4%
Vernon	13.6%

1978

Hodges	59.6%
Vernon	17.4%
Kluszewski	13.5%

1979

Hodges	56.0%
Vernon	20.4%
Kluszewski	13.4%

1980

Hodges	59.7%
Vernon	24.9%
Kluszewski	13.0%
Orlando Cepeda	12.5%

1981

Hodges	60.1%
Harmon Killebrew	59.6%
Cepeda	19.2%
Kluszewski	14.0%

1982

Killebrew	59.3%
Hodges	49.4%
Cepeda	10.1%

1983

Killebrew	71.9%
Hodges	63.4%
Cepeda	15.8%

1984

Killebrew	83.1% BWA
Cepeda	30.8%

1985

Cepeda	28.9%
Dick Allen	7.1%

1986

Willie McCovey	81.4% BWA
Cepeda	35.8%
Allen	9.6%

1987

Cepeda	43.3%
Allen	13.3%

1988

Cepeda	46.6%
Allen	12.2%

1989

Cepeda	39.4%
Allen	7.8%

1990

Cepeda	47.5%
Allen	13.1%

1991

Cepeda	43.3%
Allen	13.3%

1992

Cepeda	57.2%
Tony Perez	50.0%
Allen	16.0%

1993

Cepeda	59.6%
Perez	55.1%
Steve Garvey	41.6%
Allen	16.5%

1994

Cepeda	73.6%
Perez	57.8%
Garvey	36.5%
Allen	14.5%

1995

Perez	56.3%
Garvey	42.6%
Allen	15.7%

1996

Perez	65.7%
Garvey	37.2%
Allen	18.9%
Keith Hernandez	5.1%

1997

Perez	66.0%
Garvey	35.3%
Allen	16.7%
Hernandez	9.5%

1998		1999		2000	
Perez	67.9%	Perez	60.8%	Perez	77.2% BWA
Garvey	41.2%	Garvey	30.2%	Garvey	32.1%
Hernandez	10.8%	Hernandez	6.8%	Hernandez	10.4%

2001		2002		2003	
Garvey	34.2%	Garvey	28.4%	Eddie Murray	85.3% BWA
Don Mattingly	28.2%	Mattingly	20.3%	Garvey	27.8%
Hernandez	8.0%	Hernandez	6.1%	Mattingly	13.7%
				Hernandez	6.0%

2004		2005		2006	
Garvey	24.3%	Garvey	20.5%	Garvey	26.0%
Mattingly	12.8%	Mattingly	11.4%	Mattingly	12.3%

2007		2008		2009	
Mark McGwire	23.5%	McGwire	23.6%	McGwire	21.9%
Garvey	21.1%	Mattingly	15.8%	Mattingly	11.9%
Mattingly	9.9%				

Analysis of Voting for First Basemen

The top vote-getters from 1936 through 1956 were all elected to the Hall of Fame; five by the Baseball Writers and one by the Veterans Committee. Then in sequence Jim Bottomley, Johnny Mize, Phil Cavaretta, Mickey Vernon, Ted Kluszewski, Gil Hodges and Orlando Cepeda ran out the string on the BWA ballot. Hodges led the voting in 12 of his 15 years and Cepeda, who achieved 73.6 percent in his last year, was recognized by the Veterans Committee in 1999.

Bottomley in 1974 and Mize in 1981 broke the drought but the prospects for Cavaretta and Vernon appear less optimistic with the Veteran's Committee.

Harmon Killebrew was then elected in 1984, his fourth year on the ballot. Willie McCovey was elected two years later in his first appearance on the ballot.

Since Orlando Cepeda completed his eligibility in 1994, Tony Perez, Steve Garvey and Dick Allen have finished one, two, three in 1995, 1996 and 1997. Allen completed his 15 years on the Writers' ballot and must now be considered by the Veteran's Committee. Perez, in his ninth year on the ballot was elected in 2000. He was the leading vote-getter among first basemen for six consecutive years.

In 2001 and 2002, Garvey, Mattingly and Hernandez finished one, two, three but with minimal support. In 2003 Eddie Murray made an auspicious debut by gaining election in his first year. After the 2004 election only Garvey and Mattingly remained on the ballot. In 2007 Garvey completed his 15 years and was replaced by Mark McGwire. The 2008 election saw only McGwire and Mattingly receiving votes. The same duo received enough support in 2009 to remain on the 2010 ballot.

Rank in Voting by Years (10% or more of the votes)

	Last Year	1936	1937	1938	1939	1942	1945	1946	1946 RO	1947
George Sisler	1930	1	1	1	2B					
Lou Gehrig	1939	2			1B					
Frank Chance	1914		2	2	3	1	1	1	1V	
Bill Terry	1936					2	2	2		1
Jimmy Foxx	1945							3		

	Last Year	1948	1949	1949 RO	1950	1951	1952	1953	1954	1955
Terry		1	2	2	1	2	1	1	1B	
Foxx		2	1	1	2	1B				
Hank Greenberg	1947		3	3	3	3	2	2	2	1
Jim Bottomley	1937									2

	Last Year	1956	1958	1960	1962	1964	1964 RO	1966	1967	1967 RO
Greenberg		1B								
Bottomley		2	1	1	1V–1974					
Johnny Mize	1953			2		1		1	1	
Phil Cavaretta	1955					2				

	Last Year	1968	1969	1970	1971	1972	1973	1974	1975	1976
Mize		1	1	2	2	2	2(V–1981)			
Cavaretta			3	3	3	3	3	2	2	
Gil Hodges	1963		2	1	1	1	1	1	1	1
Mickey Vernon	1960									2
Ted Kluszewski	1961									3

	Last Year	1977	1978	1979	1980	1981	1982	1983	1984	1985
Hodges		1	1	1	1	1	2	2		
Vernon		3	2	2	2					
Kluszewski		2	3	3	3	4				
Orlando Cepeda	1974				4	3	3	3	2	1
Harmon Killebrew	1975					2	1	1	1B	

	Last Year	1986	1987	1988	1989	1990	1991	1992	1993	1994
Cepeda		2	1	1	1	1	1	1	1	1(V–1999)

B—Baseball Writers Association of America
V—Veterans Committee
T—Tie in Voting

	Last Year	1986	1987	1988	1989	1990	1991	1992	1993	1994
Willie McCovey	1980	1B								
Dick Allen	1977		2	2		2	2	3	4	4
Tony Perez	1986							2	2	2
Steve Garvey	1987								3	3

	Last Year	1995	1996	1997	1998	1999	2000	2001	2002	2003
Allen		3	3	3						
Perez		1	1	1	1	1	1B			
Garvey		2	2	2	2	2	2	1	1	2
Keith Hernandez	1990				3		3			
Don Mattingly	1995							2	2	3
Eddie Murray	1997									1B

	Last Year	2004	2005	2006	2007	2008	2009
Garvey		1	1	1	2		
Mattingly		2	2	2	3	2	2
Mark McGwire	2001				1	1	1

B—Baseball Writers Association of America
V—Veterans Committee
T—Tie in Voting

Year	No. with 10% or More of Votes	No. in Hall of Fame BWA	VC	Cumulative Total (Different Individuals)	Non–Hall of Famers
1936	2	2	0	2	
1937	2	1	1	3	
1938	2	1	1	3	
1939	3	2	1	3	
1942	2	1	1	4	
1945	2	1	1	4	
1946	3	2	1	5	
1947	1	1	0	5	
1948	2	2	0	5	
1949	3	3	0	6	
1950	3	3	0	6	
1951	3	3	0	6	
1952	2	2	0	6	
1953	2	2	0	6	
1954	2	2	0	6	
1955	2	1	1	7	
1956	2	1	1	7	
1958	1	0	1	7	
1960	2	0	2	8	
1962	1	0	1	8	
1964	2	0	1	9	Phil Cavaretta
1966	1	0	1	9	
1967	1	0	1	9	

Year	No. with 10% or More of Votes	No. in Hall of Fame BWA	VC	Cumulative Total (Different Individuals)	Non–Hall of Famers
1968	1	0	1	9	
1969	3	0	1	10	Gil Hodges
1970	3	0	1	10	
1971	3	0	1	10	
1972	3	0	1	10	
1973	3	0	1	10	
1974	2	0	0	10	
1975	2	0	0	10	
1976	3	0	0	12	Ted Kluszewski, Mickey Vernon
1977	3	0	0	12	
1978	3	0	0	12	
1979	3	0	0	12	
1980	4	0	1	13	
1981	4	1	1	14	
1882	3	1	1	14	
1983	3	1	1	14	
1984	2	1	1	14	
1985	1	0	1	14	
1986	2	1	1	15	
1987	2	0	1	16	Dick Allen
1988	2	0	1	16	
1989	1	0	1	16	
1990	2	0	1	16	
1991	2	0	1	16	
1992	3	1	1	17	
1993	4	1	1	18	Steve Garvey
1994	4	1	1	18	
1995	3	1	0	18	
1996	3	1	0	18	
1997	3	1	0	18	
1998	3	1	0	19	Keith Hernandez
1999	2	1	0	19	
2000	3	1	0	19	
2001	2	0	0	20	Don Mattingly
2002	2	0	0	20	
2003	3	1	0	21	
2004	2	0	0	21	
2005	2	0	0	21	
2006	2	0	0	21	
2007	3	0	0	22	Mark McGwire
2008	2	0	0	22	
2009	2	0	0	22	

Conclusions (First Basemen)

Every first baseman who received 10 percent of the vote from 1936 through 1962 was eventually elected to the Hall of Fame.

Every first baseman who received 10 percent of the vote from 1936 through 1975 with the exception of Phil Cavaretta and Gil Hodges was eventually elected to the Hall of Fame.

Of the twenty-two individuals who received 10 percent of the vote in at least one election through 2009, thirteen are in the Hall of Fame (9 elected by the Baseball Writer's Association and 4 by the Veterans' Committee).

Two first basemen are still under consideration by the Baseball Writer's Association: Mark McGwire (2009; third year of eligibility) and Don Mattingly (2009; ninth year of eligibility).

The remaining seven are eligible for consideration by the Veterans' Committee.

Second Basemen

Name	Years Played First–Last	Highest %-age	%-age Range	Number of Elections	HOF	Year Elected	Years Played
Rod Carew	1967–1985	90.5%		1	BWA	1991	19
Charlie Gehringer	1924–1942	85.0%	4.0%–85.0%	5(2)	BWA	1949	19
Frankie Frisch	1919–1937	84.5%	6.2%–84.5%	6(1)	BWA	1947	19
Nap Lajoie	1896–1916	83.6%	64.6%–83.6%	2	BWA	1937	21
Joe Morgan	1963–1984	81.8%		1	BWA	1990	22
Rogers Hornsby	1915–1937	78.1%	17.6%–78.1%	5	BWA	1942	23
Eddie Collins	1906–1930	77.7%	26.5%–77.7%	4	BWA	1939	25
Jackie Robinson	1947–1956	77.5%		1	BWA	1962	10
Ryne Sandberg	1981–1997	76.2%	49.2%–76.2%	3	BWA	2005	16
Nelson Fox	1947–1965	74.7%	10.8%–74.7%	15	VC	1997	19
Johnny Evers	1902–1929	64.4%	2.7%–64.4%	7(1)	VC	1946	18
Miller Huggins	1904–1916	63.9%	1.2%–63.9%	8(1)	VC	1964*	13
Red Schoendienst	1945–1963	42.6%	19.1%–42.6%	15	VC	1989	19
Bill Mazeroski	1956–1972	42.3%	6.1%–42.3%	15	VC	2001	17
Tony Lazzeri	1926–1939	33.2%	0.4%–33.2%	14(1)	VC	1991	14
Joe Gordon	1938–1950	28.5%	0.4%–28.5%	14	VC	2008	11
Bobby Doerr	1937–1951	25.0%	0.8%–25.0%	13(1)	VC	1986	14
Billy Herman	1931–1947	20.2%	0.8%–20.2%	8(1)	VC	1975	15
Bucky Harris	1919–1931	16.9%	0.4%–16.9%	10	VC	1975*	12
Frank White	1973–1990	3.8%		1			18
Lou Whitaker	1977–1995	2.9%		1			19
Bobby Grich	1970–1986	2.6%		1			17
Bobby Richardson	1955–1966	2.0%	0.5%–2.0%	3			12
Bill Wambsganns	1914–1926	2.0%	0.4%–2.0%	6			13
Max Bishop	1924–1935	1.9%	0.4%–1.9%	4			12
Gil McDougald	1951–1960	1.7%	0.3%–1.7%	9			10
Larry Doyle	1907–1920	1.5%	0.4%–1.5%	3			14
Tony Cuccinello	1930–1945	1.1%	0.5%–1.1%	2			15
Frankie Gustine	1939–1950	1.1%		1			12
Eddie Stanky	1943–1953	1.1%		1			11
Willie Randolph	1975–1992	1.1%		1			18
Hughie Critz	1924–1935	1.0%		1			12

*Elected as a manager.

Name	Years Played First–Last	Highest %-age	%-age Range	Number of Elections	HOF	Year Elected	Years Played
Marty McManus	1920–1934	0.8%	0.7%–0.8%	2			15
Davey Johnson	1965–1978	0.7%		1			13
Jerry Remy	1975–1984	0.7%		1			10
Buddy Myer	1925–1941	0.7%		1			17
Jewel Ens	1922–1925	0.6%		1			4
Dave Cash	1969–1980	0.5%		1			12
Eddie Miksis	1944–1958	0.5%		1			14
Burgess Whitehead	1933–1946	0.5%		1			9
Danny Murphy	1900–1915	0.5%	0.4%–0.5%	2			16
Otto Knabe	1905–1916	0.5%	0.4%–0.5%	2			11
Kid Gleason	1888–1912	0.5%	0.4%–0.5%	4			22
Davey Lopes	1972–1987	0.5%		1			16
Bill Cissell	1928–1938	0.5%		1			9
Buck Herzog	1908–1920	0.4%		1			13
Bobby Lowe	1890–1907	0.4%		1			18
Germany Schaefer	1901–1918	0.4%		1			15
Claude Ritchey	1897–1909	0.4%		1			13
Bill Sweeney	1907–1914	0.4%		1			8
Steve Yerkes	1909–1916	0.4%		1			7
Sparky Adams	1922–1934	0.4%	0.4%–0.4%	2			13
Phil Garner	1973–1988	0.4%		1			16
Pep Young	1933–1945	0.4%		1			10
Sibby Sisti	1939–1954	0.4%		1			13
George Grantham	1922–1934	0.4%		1			13
Steve Sax	1981–1994	0.4%		1			14
Billy Martin	1950–1961	0.3%		1			11
Tommy Helms	1964–1977	0.3%		1			14
Felix Millan	1966–1977	0.3%		1			12
Glenn Beckert	1965–1975	0.2%		1			11
Juan Samuel	1983–1998	0.2%		1			16
Chuck Knoblauch	1991–2002	0.2%		1			12
Bid McPhee	1882–1899				VC	2000	18

(Includes all those receiving 5% or more of the vote or top two

1936	
Nap LaJoie	64.6%
Rogers Hornsby	46.5%
Eddie Collins	26.5%
Frankie Frisch	6.2%

1937	
La Joie	83.6% BWA
Collins	57.2%
Hornsby	26.4%
Johnny Evers	21.9%

1938	
Collins	66.8%
Evers	34.7%
Miller Huggins	18.3%
Hornsby	17.6%

1939	
Collins	77.7% BWA
Hornsby	64.2%
Evers	39.1%
Huggins	35.4%
Frisch	9.5%

1942	
Hornsby	78.1% BWA
Huggins	47.6%
Evers	39.1%
Frisch	36.1%

1945	
Evers	54.3%
Huggins	53.8%
Frisch	40.9%

1946

Evers	64.4%
Huggins	63.9%
Frisch	51.5%
Charlie Gehringer	21.3%

1946 Run Off

Evers	41.8% VC
Huggins	40.3% VC Mgr 1954
Frisch	25.5%
Gehringer	8.7%

1947

Frisch	84.5% BWA
Gehringer	65.2%

1948

Gehringer	43.0%
Tony Lazzeri	17.4%

1949

Gehringer	66.7%
Lazzeri	13.1%
Bucky Harris	7.2%

1949 Run Off

Gehringer	85.0% BWA
Lazzeri	3.2%

1950

Lazzeri	12.6%
Harris	2.4%

1951

Lazzeri	11.9%
Harris	4.0%

1952

Lazzeri	12.4%
Harris	5.1%

1953

Lazzeri	10.6%
Harris	8.0%

1954

Lazzeri	11.9%
Bill Wambsganns	1.6%

1955

Lazzeri	26.3%
Wambsganns	2.0%

1956

Lazzeri	33.2%
Bobby Doerr	2.6%

1958

Lazzeri	30.1%
Harris	16.9%
Doerr	9.4%

1960

Lazzeri	21.9%
Harris	11.5% VC Mgr 1975
Doerr	5.6%

1962

Jackie Robinson	77.5% BWA
Doerr	6.3%
Lazzeri	5.0% VC 1991

1964

Joe Gordon	14.9%
Billy Herman	12.9%
Doerr	11.9%

1964 Run Off

Gordon	0.4%
Herman	4.0%
Doerr	2.2%

1966

Gordon	10.3%
Doerr	9.9%
Herman	9.3%

1967

Gordon	22.6%
Herman	20.2%
Doerr	12.2%

1967 Run Off

Gordon	4.2%
Herman	4.6% VC 1978
Doerr	4.9%

1968

Gordon	27.2%
Doerr	17.0%

1969

Gordon	28.5%
Red Schoendienst	19.1%
Doerr	18.2%

1970

Schoendienst	32.3%
Gordon	26.3% VC 2008
Doerr	25.0%

1971

Schoendienst	34.2%
Doerr	21.7% VC 1986
Nelson Fox	10.8%

1972

Schoendienst	26.3%
Fox	16.2%

1973

Schoendienst	25.3%
Fox	19.2%

1974

Schoendienst	30.1%
Fox	21.6%

1975

Schoendienst	26.0%
Fox	21.0%

1976

Fox	44.8%
Schoendienst	33.2%

1977

Fox	39.7%
Schoendienst	27.4%

1978

Fox	39.3%
Schoendienst	34.3%
Bill Mazeroski	6.1%

1979

Fox	40.3%
Schoendienst	36.8%
Mazeroski	8.3%

1980

Schoendienst	42.6%
Fox	41.8%
Mazeroski	8.6%

1981

Fox	41.9%
Schoendienst	41.4%
Mazeroski	9.5%

1982

Schoendienst	32.5%
Fox	30.6%
Mazeroski	6.7%

1983

Fox	46.3%
Schoendienst	39.0% VC 1989
Mazeroski	12.8%

1984

Fox	61.0%
Mazeroski	18.4%

1985

Fox	74.7% VC 1997
Mazeroski	22.0%

1986

Mazeroski	23.5%
Dave Cash	0.5%

1987

Mazeroski	30.3%

1988

Mazeroski	33.5%

1989

Mazeroski	30.0%

1990

Joe Morgan	81.8% BWA
Mazeroski	29.5%

1991

Rod Carew	90.5% BWA
Mazeroski	32.1%

1992

Mazeroski	42.3% VC 2001

1993

Davey Lopes	0.5%

1994

Phil Garner	0.4%

1995

No Players
Received Votes

1996

Frank White 3.8%

1997

No Players
Received Votes

1998

Willie Randolph 1.1%

1999

No Players
Received Votes

2000

Steve Sax 0.4%

2001

Lou Whitaker 2.9%

2002

No Players
Received Votes

2003

Ryne Sandberg 49.2%

2004

Sandberg	61.1%
Juan Samuel	0.2%

2005

Sandberg 76.2% BWA

2006

No Players
Received Votes

2007

No Players
Received Votes

2008

Chuck Knoblauch 0.2%

2009

No Players
Received Votes

Analysis of Voting for Second Basemen

Lajoie, Hornsby and Collins waged a three-man battle for supremacy among the first candidates. Then Evers, Huggins and Frisch finished one, two, three for three consecutive years before election.

Tony Lazzeri led his position in voting for nine years with over 10 percent of the vote but was not recognized by the Veteran's Committee until 1991. Jackie Robinson became the first second baseman to be elected in his first year on the ballot. Joe Morgan in 1990 and Rod Carew in 1991 are the only others to merit this distinction.

The trio of Gordon, Herman and Doerr competed for several years with interesting results. While Gordon received a greater percentage of the votes than the other two, he was still not recognized by the Veteran's Committee until 2008.

The head-to-head battle between Red Schoendienst and Nelson Fox had them trading the top two positions six times in twelve years. Since their duel ended, the only consistent vote-getter has been Bill Mazeroski who led the balloting five years and was displaced twice in that streak by the eligibility of Morgan and then Carew. Since 1992, no second baseman had been able to get 10 percent of the vote until Ryne Sandberg accumulated 49.2 percent in the 2003 election, 61.1 percent in 2004 and was subsequently enshrined in 2005. No second baseman received votes in the 2006, 2007 and 2009 elections. In 2008 the only vote-getter was Chuck Knoblauch with 0.2 percent.

The voting among second basemen has been very clear cut. All those who have obtained 20 percent or more are in the Hall of Fame, with Gordon (28.5 percent) finally gaining recognition in 2008. The next in line, Frank White, achieved only 3.8 percent of the vote in 1996 and was dropped from the ballot.

Rank in Voting by Years (10% or more of the votes)

	Last Year	1936	1937	1938	1939	1942	1945	1946	1946 RO	1947
Nap LaJoie	1916	1	1B							
Rogers Hornsby	1937	2	3	4	2	1B				
Eddie Collins	1930	3	2	1	1B					
Johnny Evers	1929		4	2	3	3	1	1	1V	
Miller Huggins	1916			3	4	2	2	2	2V-Mgr 1954	

B—Baseball Writers Association of America
V—Veterans Committee

	Last Year	1936	1937	1938	1939	1942	1945	1946	1946 RO	1947
Frankie Frisch	1937					4	3	3	3	1B
Charlie Gehringer	1942							4		2

	Last Year	1948	1949	1949 RO	1950	1951	1952	1953	1954	1955
Gehringer		1	1	1B						
Tony Lazzeri	1939	2	2		1	1	1	1	1	1

	Last Year	1956	1958	1960	1962	1964	1964 RO	1966	1967	1967 RO
Lazzeri		1	1	1V-1991						
Bucky Harris	1931		2	2V-Mgr 1975						
Jackie Robinson	1956				1B					
Joe Gordon	1950					1		1	1	
Billy Herman	1947					2			2	V-1978
Bobby Doerr	1951					3			3	

	Last Year	1968	1969	1970	1971	1972	1973	1974	1975	1976
Gordon		1	1	2V-2008						
Doerr		2	3	3	2V-1986					
Red Schoendienst	1963		2	1	1	1	1	1	1	2
Nelson Fox	1965				3	2	2	2	2	1

	Last Year	1977	1978	1979	1980	1981	1982	1983	1984	1985
Schoendienst		2	2	2	1	2	1	2V-1989		
Fox		1	1	1	2	1	2	1	1	1V-1997
Bill Mazeroski	1972							3	2	2

	Last Year	1986	1987	1988	1989	1990	1991	1992	1993	1994
Mazeroski	1984	1	1	1	1	2	2	1V-2001		
Joe Morgan	1984					1B				
Rod Carew	1985						1B			

	1995	1996	1997	1998	1999	2000	2001	2002	2003
Ryne Sandberg	1997								1

	2004	2005	2006	2007	2008	2009
Sandberg	1	1B				

B—Baseball Writers Association of America
V—Veterans Committee

Year	No. with 10% or More of Votes	No. in Hall of Fame BWA	VC	Cumulative Total (Different Individuals)	Non–Hall of Famers
1936	3	3	0	3	
1937	4	3	1	4	
1938	4	2	2	5	
1939	4	2	2	5	
1942	4	2	2	6	
1945	3	1	2	6	
1946	4	2	2	7	
1947	2	2	0	7	
1948	2	1	1	8	
1949	2	1	1	8	
1950	1	0	1	8	
1951	1	0	1	8	
1952	1	0	1	8	
1953	1	0	1	8	
1954	1	0	1	8	
1955	1	0	1	8	
1956	1	0	1	8	
1958	2	0	2	9	
1960	2	0	2	9	
1962	1	1	0	10	
1964	3	0	3	13	
1966	1	0	1	13	
1967	3	0	3	13	
1968	2	0	2	13	
1969	3	0	3	14	
1970	3	0	3	14	
1971	3	0	3	15	
1972	2	0	2	15	
1973	2	0	2	15	
1974	2	0	2	15	
1975	2	0	2	15	
1976	2	0	2	15	
1977	2	0	2	15	
1978	2	0	2	15	
1979	2	0	2	15	
1980	2	0	2	15	
1981	2	0	2	15	
1982	2	0	2	15	
1983	3	0	3	16	
1984	2	0	2	16	
1985	2	0	2	16	
1986	1	0	1	16	
1987	1	0	1	16	
1988	1	0	1	16	
1989	1	0	1	16	
1990	2	1	1	17	
1991	2	1	1	18	
1992	1	0	1	18	
1993	0	0	0	18	
1994	0	0	0	18	
1995	0	0	0	18	

Year	No. with 10% or More of Votes	No. in Hall of Fame BWA	VC	Cumulative Total (Different Individuals)	Non–Hall of Famers
1996	0	0	0	18	
1997	0	0	0	18	
1998	0	0	0	18	
1999	0	0	0	18	
2000	0	0	0	18	
2001	0	0	0	18	
2002	0	0	0	18	
2003	1	0	0	19	
2004	1	0	0	19	
2005	1	1	0	19	
2006	0	0	0	19	
2007	0	0	0	19	
2008	0	0	0	19	
2009	0	0	0	19	

Conclusions (Second Basemen)

Every second baseman who received 10 percent of the vote from 1936 through 2009 was eventually elected to the Hall of Fame.

Of the 19 individuals who received 10 percent of the vote in at least one election through 2009, nine were elected by the Baseball Writer's Association and ten by the Veterans' Committee.

Third Basemen

Name	Years Played First–Last	Highest %–age	%–age Range	Number of Elections	HOF	Year Elected	Years Played
George Brett	1973–1993	98.2%		1	BWA	1999	21
Mike Schmidt	1972–1989	96.5%		1	BWA	1995	18
Brooks Robinson	1955–1977	92.0%		1	BWA	1983	23
Wade Boggs	1982–1999	91.9%		1	BWA	2005	18
Paul Molitor	1978–1998	85.2%		1	BWA	2004	21
Eddie Mathews	1952–1968	79.4%	32.3%–79.4%	5	BWA	1978	17
Pie Traynor	1920–1937	76.9%	1.1%–76.9%	8(1)	BWA	1948	17
Jimmy Collins	1895–1908	49.0%	25.7%–49.0%	6	VC	1945	14
Ron Santo	1960–1974	43.1%	3.9%–43.1%	15			15
George Kell	1943–1957	36.8%	3.5%–36.8%	15	VC	1983	15
Frank Baker	1908–1922	30.4%	0.4%–30.4%	11(1)	VC	1955	13
Ken Boyer	1955–1969	25.5%	2.5%–25.5%	15			15
John McGraw	1891–1906	17.4%	1.8%–17.4%	2	VC	1937*	16
Jimmie Dykes	1918–1939	10.0%	0.5%–10.0%	11			22
Graig Nettles	1967–1988	8.4%	4.7%–8.4%	4			22
Red Rolfe	1931–1942	4.9%	0.6%–4.9%	8			10
Stan Hack	1932–1947	4.8%	0.5%–4.8%	7			16

*Elected as manager

Name	Years Played First–Last	Highest %–age	%–age Range	Number of Elections	HOF	Year Elected	Years Played
Bill Madlock	1973–1987	4.5%		1			15
Freddie Lindstrom	1924–1936	4.4%	0.7%–4.4%	5	VC	1976	13
Bill McKechnie	1907–1920	3.5%	0.6%–3.5%	4	VC	1962*	11
Joe Dugan	1917–1931	3.0%	0.4%–3.0%	7			14
Bill Bradley	1899–1915	2.5%	0.4%–2.5%	6			14
Mike Higgins	1930–1946	2.3%	0.4%–2.3%	4			14
Bob Elliott	1939–1953	2.0%	0.6%–2.0%	3			15
Heinie Groh	1912–1927	2.0%	0.4%–2.0%	8			16
Ron Cey	1971–1987	1.9%		1			17
Ossie Bluege	1922–1939	1.7%	0.4%–1.7%	6			18
Buddy Bell	1972–1989	1.7%		1			18
Darrell Evans	1969–1989	1.7%		1			21
Cookie Lavagetto	1934–1947	1.5%	0.7%–1.5%	2			10
Eddie Grant	1905–1915	1.3%	0.4%–1.3%	5			10
Grady Hatton	1946–1960	1.3%	0.3%–1.3%	2			12
Matt Williams	1987–2003	1.3%		1			17
Willie Kamm	1923–1935	1.1%	0.4%–1.1%	2			13
Billy Werber	1930–1942	1.1%	0.4%–1.1%	4			11
Hans Lobert	1903–1917	1.0%	0.4%–1.0%	4			14
Eddie Foster	1910–1923	0.8%		1			13
Gary Gaetti	1981–2000	0.8%		1			20
Sal Bando	1966–1981	0.7%		1			16
Clete Boyer	1955–1971	0.7%	0.3%–0.7%	2			16
Carney Lansford	1978–1992	0.6%		1			15
Billy Cox	1941–1955	0.6%		1			11
Doug DeCinces	1973–1987	0.5%		1			15
Harry Steinfeldt	1898–1911	0.5%	0.4%–0.5%	3			14
Charlie Irwin	1893–1902	0.4%	0.4%–0.4%	2			10
Arlie Latham	1880–1909	0.4%	0.4%–0.4%	2			17
Lave Cross	1887–1907	0.4%	0.4%–0.4%	2			21
Wid Conroy	1901–1911	0.4%		1			11
Larry Parrish	1974–1988	0.4%		1			15
Jimmy Austin	1909–1929	0.4%		1			18
Ken Keltner	1937–1950	0.4%	0.4%–0.4%	2			13
Bobby Bonilla	1986–2001	0.4%		1			16
Ken Caminiti	1987–2001	0.4%		1			15
Travis Fryman	1990–2002	0.4%		1			13
Bobby Adams	1946–1959	0.3%		1			14
Bob Bailey	1962–1978	0.2%		1			17
Don Money	1968–1983	0.2%		1			16
Richie Hebner	1968–1985	0.2%		1			18
Ray Knight	1974–1988	0.2%		1			13
Tim Wallach	1980–1996	0.2%		1			17
Terry Pendleton	1984–1998	0.2%		1			15

*Elected as manager

(Includes all those receiving 5% or more of the vote or the top 2)

1936		1937		1938	
Jimmy Collins	25.7%	Collins	32.8%	Collins	30.2%
Pie Traynor	7.1%	John McGraw	17.4% VC Mgr	Baker	12.2%
		Frank Baker	6.5%		

1939	1942	1945
Collins 26.3%	Collins 29.2%	Collins 49.0% VC
Baker 10.9%	Traynor 19.3%	Traynor 32.8%
	Baker 16.7%	Baker 10.5%

1946	1946 Run Off	1947
Traynor 32.2%	Traynor 20.2%	Traynor 73.9%
Baker 19.3%	Baker 13.7%	Baker 30.4%

1948	1949	1949 Run Off
Traynor 76.9% BWA	Jimmie Dykes 4.6%	Dykes 0
	Stan Hack 2.6%	Hack 0

1950	1951	1952
Hack 4.8%	Baker 3.5% VC 1955	Dykes 2.1%
Red Rolfe 4.2%	Bill McKechnie 3.5% VC 1962 Mgr	Rolfe 1.7%

1953	1954	1955
Dykes 1.9%	Heinie Groh 0.4%	Groh 2.0%
Rolfe 1.9%	Ossie Bluege 0.4%	Dykes 0.4%

1956	1958	1960
Freddie Lindstrom 1.6%	Dykes 9.8%	Dykes 10.0%
Rolfe 1.6%	Rolfe 4.9%	Rolfe 3.7%

1962	1964	1964 Run Off
Lindstrom 4.4% VC	George Kell 16.4%	Kell 3.5%
Dykes 3.8%	Bob Elliott 2.0%	Elliott 0

1966	1967	1967 Run Off
Kell 9.6%	Kell 13.7%	Kell 3.6%
Grady Hatton 1.3%	Hatton 0.3%	Hatton 0

1968	1969	1970
Kell 16.6%	Kell 17.6%	Kell 30.0%

1971	1972	1973
Kell 29.2%	Kell 29.0%	Kell 30.0%

1974	1975	1976
Eddie Mathews 32.3%	Mathews 40.9%	Mathews 48.7%
Kell 25.8%	Kell 31.5%	Kell 33.2%

1977	1978	1979
Mathews 62.4%	Mathews 79.4% BWA	K. Boyer 4.6%
Kell 36.8% VC	Ken Boyer 4.7%	Clete Boyer 0.7%

1980	1981	1982
Ron Santo 3.9%	No 3B received votes	No 3B received votes

1983	1984	1985
Brooks Robinson 92.0% BWA	Bob Bailey 0.2%	Ken Boyer 17.2%
		Santo 13.4%

1986	1987	1988
K. Boyer 22.4%	K. Boyer 23.2%	K. Boyer 25.5%
Santo 15.1%	Santo 18.9%	Santo 25.3%

1989	1990	1991
Santo 16.8%	Santo 21.6%	Santo 26.2%
K. Boyer 13.9%	K. Boyer 17.6%	K. Boyer 13.1%

1992	1993	1994
Santo 31.6%	Santo 36.6%	Santo 33.0%
K. Boyer 16.5%	K. Boyer 16.3%	K. Boyer 11.9%
		Graig Nettles 8.4%

1995	1996	1997
Mike Schmidt 96.5% BWA	Santo 37.0%	Santo 39.3%
Santo 30.2%	Nettles 7.9%	Nettles 4.7%
Nettles 6.1%		

1998	1999	2000
Santo 43.1%	George Brett 98.2% BWA	No 3B Received
Carney Lansford 0.6%		Votes

2001	2002	2003
No 3B Received Votes	Tim Wallach 0.2%	No 3B Received Votes

2004	2005	2006
Paul Molitor 85.2% BWA	Wade Boggs 91.9% BWA	Gary Gaetti 0.8%
Terry Pendleton 0.2%		

2007	2008	2009
Bobby Bonilla 0.4%	Travis Fryman 0.4%	Matt Williams 1.3%
Ken Caminiti 0.4%		

Analysis of Voting for Third Basemen

Jimmy Collins led the voting at his position for the first six elections (1936–1945) at which time he was selected by the Veteran's Committee.

After trailing Collins in the 1937 voting, John McGraw was selected by the Executive Committee in 1937 as a manager.

Following Collins' selection, Pie Traynor and Frank Baker finished first and second in 1946 and 1947. In 1948 Traynor gained election by the BWA and it wasn't until 1960 that Jimmy Dykes was able to garner 10 percent of the vote. Meanwhile, Baker, who had finished second five times and third twice among third basemen in the balloting, was tapped by the Veteran's Committee in 1955.

The third baseman of the '60s and '70s was George Kell who was the top vote-getter from 1964 through 1973 until Eddie Mathews became eligible in 1974. Mathews took over the top spot for five years until his election in 1978. Relegated to the second position behind Mathews for four years, Kell was recognized by the Veteran's Committee in 1983. That same year, Brooks Robinson became the first at his position to be elected in his first year of eligibility.

From 1985 through 1994, Ken Boyer and Ron Santo shared the first and second spots in the voting, but neither could muster the 75 percent necessary for election.

In the 1995 election, Mike Schmidt became the second third baseman to be recognized in his first year on the ballot. In 1999, George Brett received 98.2 percent of the vote in his first year of eligibility. Again in 2004, Paul Molitor was a first year inductee although he spent more time as a designated hitter. The next year Wade Boggs became the fourth consecutive third baseman to achieve election in his first year on the ballot. Since 2005 no third baseman has received notable voter support.

From a historical perspective, the Veteran's Committee selection of Collins, Baker and Kell appear completely defensible. The inclusion of Freddie Lindstrom raises some questions, however. Several third baseman have received greater voter support than Lindstrom's high of 4.4 percent.

Rank in Voting by Years (10% or more of the votes)

	Last Year	1936	1937	1938	1939	1942	1945	1946	1946 RO	1947
Jimmy Collins	1908	1	1	1	1	1	1V			
John McGraw	1906		2V-Mgr.							
Frank Baker	1922			2	2	3	3	2	2	2V–1955
Pie Traynor	1937					2	2	1	1	1

	Last Year	1948	1949	1949 RO	1950	1951	1952	1953	1954	1955
Traynor		1B								

	Last Year	1956	1958	1960	1962	1964	1964 RO	1966	1967	1967 RO
Jimmy Dykes	1939			1						
George Kell	1957					1			1	

	Last Year	1968	1969	1970	1971	1972	1973	1974	1975	1976
Kell		1	1	1	1	1	1	2	2	2
Eddie Matthews	1968							1	1	1

	Last Year	1977	1978	1979	1980	1981	1982	1983	1984	1985
Kell		2V-1983								
Matthews		1	1B							
Brooks Robinson	1977							1B		
Ken Boyer	1969									1
Ron Santo	1974									2

	Last Year	1986	1987	1988	1989	1990	1991	1992	1993	1994
Boyer		1	1	1	2	1	2	2	2	2
Santo		2	2	2	1	2	1	1	1	1

	Last Year	1995	1996	1997	1998	1999	2000	2001	2002	2003
Santo		2	1	1	1					
Mike Schmidt	1989	1B								
George Brett	1993					1B				

	Last Year	2004	2005	2006	2007	2008	2009
Paul Molitor	1998	1B					
Wade Boggs	1999		1B				

Year	No. with 10% or More of Votes	No. in Hall of Fame BWA	VC	Cumulative Total (Different Individuals)	Non–Hall of Famers
1936	1	0	1	1	
1937	2	0	2	2	
1938	2	0	2	3	
1939	2	0	2	3	
1942	3	1	2	4	
1945	3	1	2	4	
1946	2	1	1	4	
1947	2	1	1	4	
1948	1	1	0	4	
1949	0	0	0	4	
1950	0	0	0	4	
1951	0	0	0	4	
1952	0	0	0	4	
1953	0	0	0	4	
1954	0	0	0	4	
1955	0	0	0	4	

Year	No. with 10% or More of Votes	No. in Hall of Fame BWA	VC	Cumulative Total (Different Individuals)	Non–Hall of Famers
1956	0	0	0	4	
1958	0	0	0	4	
1960	1	0	0	5	Jimmy Dykes
1962	0	0	0	5	
1964	1	0	1	6	
1966	0	0	0	6	
1967	1	0	1	6	
1968	1	0	1	6	
1969	1	0	1	6	
1970	1	0	1	6	
1971	1	0	1	6	
1972	1	0	1	6	
1973	1	0	1	6	
1974	2	1	1	7	
1975	2	1	1	7	
1976	2	1	1	7	
1977	2	1	1	7	
1978	1	1	0	7	
1979	0	0	0	7	
1980	0	0	0	7	
1981	0	0	0	7	
1982	0	0	0	7	
1983	1	1	0	8	
1984	0	0	0	8	
1985	2	0	0	10	Ken Boyer, Ron Santo
1986	2	0	0	10	
1987	2	0	0	10	
1988	2	0	0	10	
1989	2	0	0	10	
1990	2	0	0	10	
1991	2	0	0	10	
1992	2	0	0	10	
1993	2	0	0	10	
1994	2	0	0	10	
1995	2	1	0	11	
1996	1	0	0	11	
1997	1	0	0	11	
1998	1	0	0	11	
1999	1	1	0	12	
2000	0	0	0	12	
2001	0	0	0	12	
2002	0	0	0	12	
2003	0	0	0	12	
2004	1	1	0	13	
2005	1	1	0	14	
2006	0	0	0	14	
2007	0	0	0	14	
2008	0	0	0	14	
2009	0	0	0	14	

Conclusions (Third Basemen)

Every third baseman who received 10 percent of the vote from 1936 through 1958 was eventually elected to the Hall of Fame.

Every third baseman who received 10 percent of the vote from 1936 through 1984 with the exception of Jimmy Dykes was eventually elected to the Hall of Fame.

Of 14 individuals who have received 10 percent of the vote in at least one election through 2009, eleven are in the Hall of Fame (7 elected by the Baseball Writer's Association and 4 by the Veterans' Committee).

Ron Santo, Ken Boyer and Jimmy Dykes are eligibile for consideration by the Veterans' Committee.

Shortstops

Name	Years Played First-Last	Highest %-age	%-age Range	Number of Elections	HOF	Year Elected	Years Played
Cal Ripken	1981–2001	98.5%		1	BWA	2007	21
Honus Wagner	1897–1917	95.1%		1	BWA	1936	21
Ozzie Smith	1978–1996	91.7%		1	BWA	2002	19
Luis Aparacio	1956–1973	84.6%	12.0%–84.6%	6	BWA	1984	18
Ernie Banks	1953–1971	83.8%		1	BWA	1977	19
Luke Appling	1930–1950	83.6%	0.8%–83.6%	7(1)	BWA	1964	20
Rabbit Maranville	1912–1935	82.9%	(11.0%)–82.9%	14(2)	BWA	1954	23
Joe Cronin	1926–1945	78.8%	3.7%–78.8%	10(1)	BWA	1956	20
Robin Yount	1974–1993	77.5%		1	BWA	1999	20
Lou Boudreau	1938–1952	77.3%	1.0%–77.3%	10(2)	BWA	1970	15
Pee Wee Reese	1940–1958	47.9%	(5.2%)–47.9%	14(2)	VC	1984	16
Maury Wills	1959–1972	40.6%	13.8%–40.6%	15			14
Marty Marion	1940–1953	40.0%	0.5%–40.0%	12(2)			13
Phil Rizzuto	1941–1956	38.4%	0.5%–38.4%	14(2)	VC	1994	13
Hughie Jennings	1891–1918	37.2%	2.0%–37.2%	5	VC	1945	17
Arky Vaughan	1932–1948	29.0%	0.4%–29.0%	11(2)	VC	1985	14
Joe Tinker	1902–1916	27.2%	4.4%–27.2%	6(1)	VC	1946	15
Alvin Dark	1946–1960	21.3%	(2.3%)–21.3%	15(1)			14
Alan Trammell	1977–1996	18.2%	13.4%–18.2%	8			20
Dave Bancroft	1915–1930	16.2%	0.4%–16.2%	15	VC	1971	16
Dave Concepcion	1970–1988	16.2%	6.8%–16.2%	15			19
Joe Sewell	1920–1933	8.6%	0.4%–8.6%	7	VC	1977	14
Leo Durocher	1925–1945	7.5%	0.4%–7.5%	8(1)	VC	1994*	17
Travis Jackson	1922–1936	7.3%	0.4%–7.3%	12	VC	1982	15
Glenn Wright	1924–1935	6.7%	0.4%–6.7%	12			11
Frankie Crosetti	1932–1948	5.3%	0.4%–5.3%	6			17
Mark Belanger	1965–1982	3.7%		1			18
Everett Scott	1914–1926	3.2%	0.4%–3.2%	14			13

*Elected as a Manager

Name	Years Played First-Last	Highest %-age	%-age Range	Number of Elections	HOF	Year Elected	Years Played
Bert Campaneris	1964–1983	3.1%		1			19
Bobby Wallace	1894–1918	2.7%	0.5%–2.7%	5	VC	1953	25
Larry Bowa	1970–1985	2.5%		1			16
Art Fletcher	1909–1922	2.5%	0.4%–2.5%	8(1)			13
Roy McMillan	1951–1966	2.3%	1.1%–2.3%	3			16
Dick Groat	1952–1967	1.8%	0.8%–1.8%	6			14
Roger Peckinpaugh	1910–1927	1.5%	0.4%–1.5%	9			17
Charlie Gelbert	1929–1940	1.3%	0.4%–1.3%	4			9
Billy Jurges	1931–1947	1.3%	0.4%–1.3%	2			17
Tommy Thevenow	1924–1938	1.2%		1			15
Terry Turner	1901–1919	1.2%		1			17
Red Kress	1927–1946	1.1%	0.4%–1.1%	2			14
Jack Barry	1908–1919	1.1%	0.4%–1.1%	2			11
Ozzie Guillen	1985–2000	1.0%		1			16
Jim Fregosi	1961–1978	1.0%		1			18
Donie Bush	1908–1923	1.0%	0.4%–1.0%	6			16
Kid Elberfeld	1898–1914	0.8%	0.4%–0.8%	5			14
Dick Bartell	1927–1946	0.8%	0.4%–0.8%	4			18
Tony Fernandez	1983–2001	0.7%		1			17
Rico Petrocelli	1963–1976	0.7%		1			13
Bucky Dent	1973–1984	0.7%		1			12
Bill Russell	1969–1986	0.7%		1			18
Roy Smalley, Sr.	1948–1958	0.5%		1			11
Herman Long	1889–1904	0.5%	0.4%–0.5%	5			16
Don Kessinger	1964–1979	0.5%		1			16
Ray Chapman	1912–1920	0.4%		1			9
Johnny Pesky	1942–1954	0.4%		1			10
Joe Boley	1927–1932	0.4%		1			6
Charley O'Leary	1904–1914	0.4%	0.4%–0.4%	3			11
Bill Dahlen	1891–1911	0.4%		1			21
Garry Templeton	1976 –1991	0.4%		1			16
Jay Bell	1986–2003	0.4%		1			18
Sonny Jackson	1963–1974	0.3%		1			12
Solly Hemus	1949–1959	0.3%		1			11
Chico Carrasquel	1950–1959	0.3%		1			10
Walt Weiss	1987–2000	0.2%		1			14
Leo Cardenas	1960–1975	0.2%	0.2%–0.2%	2			16
Hal Lanier	1964–1973	0.2%		1			10
Bud Harrelson	1965–1980	0.2%		1			16
Chris Speier	1971–1989	0.2%		1			19
Shawon Dunston	1985–2002	0.2%		1			18
Monte Ward	1878–1894				VC	1964	17
George Davis	1890–1909				VC	1998	20

*Elected as a Manager

1936	1937		1938	
Honus Wagner 95.1% BWA	Rabbit Maranville	12.4%	Maranville	27.9%
	Joe Tinker	7.5%	Hughie Jennings	8.8%
			Tinker	6.1%

1939

Maranville	29.9%
Jennings	12.0%

1942

Maranville	28.3%
Jennings	27.5%
Tinker	15.5%

1945

Jennings	37.2% VC
Maranville	20.6%
Tinker	19.8%

1946

Tinker	27.2%
Maranville	24.8%

1946 Run Off

Tinker	17.1% VC
Maranville	11.0%

1947

Maranville	56.5%
Joe Cronin	3.7%

1948

Maranville	31.4%
Cronin	20.7%

1949

Maranville	37.9%
Cronin	21.6%

1949 Run Off

Maranville	20.9%
Cronin	8.6%

1950

Maranville	39.5%
Cronin	19.8%
Dave Bancroft	5.4%

1951

Maranville	48.7%
Cronin	19.5%

1952

Maranville	56.8%
Cronin	20.5%

1953

Maranville	62.1%
Cronin	26.1%

1954

Maranville	82.9% BWA
Cronin	33.7%

1955

Cronin	53.8%
Bancroft	7.6%

1956

Cronin	78.8% BWA
Bancroft	7.8%
Travis Jackson	7.3% VC 1982
Luke Appling	7.3%

1958

Appling	28.9%
Lou Boudreau	24.1%
Bancroft	16.2%
Leo Durocher	5.6%

1960

Appling	26.8%
Marty Marion	13.8%
Boudreau	13.0%
Bancroft	11.2% VC 1971
Joe Sewell	8.6% VC 1977
Glenn Wright	6.7%

1962

Appling	30.0%
Phil Rizzuto	27.5%
Marion	10.0%
Boudreau	7.5%

1964

Appling	70.6%
Pee Wee Reese	36.3%
Boudreau	33.8%
Marion	24.9%
Rizzuto	22.4%
Arky Vaughan	8.5%
Durocher	7.5%

1964 Run Off

Appling	83.6% BWA
Reese	20.8%
Boudreau	19.0%
Marion	7.5%
Rizzuto	4.9%
Vaughan	2.7%
Durocher	0.9%

1966

Boudreau	38.1%
Reese	31.5%
Marion	28.5%
Rizzuto	17.9%
Vaughan	11.9%
Alvin Dark	5.6%

1967

Boudreau	49.0%
Marion	30.8%
Reese	30.5%
Rizzuto	24.3%
Vaughan	15.8%
Dark	13.0%

1967 Run Off

Boudreau	22.2%
Marion	7.2%
Vaughan	6.2%
Reese	5.2%
Rizzuto	4.6%
Dark	2.3%

1968

Boudreau	51.6%	Reese	28.6%
Marion	31.4%	Rizzuto	26.1%
Vaughan	29.0% VC 1985	Dark	12.7%

Frank Crosetti 5.3%

1969
Boudreau	64.1%
Marion	32.9%
Reese	26.2%
Rizzuto	22.9%
Dark	14.1%

1970
Boudreau	77.3% BWA
Marion	40.0%
Reese	32.3%
Rizzuto	26.3%
Dark	18.3%

1971
Reese	35.3%
Marion	34.2%
Rizzuto	25.6%
Dark	15.0%

1972
Reese	32.6%
Marion	30.3%
Rizzuto	26.0%
Dark	13.9%

1973
Marion	33.4%
Reese	33.2%
Rizzuto	29.2%
Dark	13.9%

1974
Reese	38.6%
Rizzuto	30.4%
Dark	14.8%

1975
Reese	42.5%
Rizzuto	32.3%
Dark	13.3%

1976
Reese	47.9%
Rizzuto	38.4% VC 1994
Dark	21.3%

1977
Ernie Banks	83.8% BWA
Reese	42.6%
Dark	17.2%

1978
Reese	44.6% VC 1984
Maury Wills	30.3%
Dark	15.8%

1979
Wills	38.4%
Luis Aparicio	27.8%
Dark	18.5%

1980
Wills	37.9%
Aparicio	32.2%
Dark	11.2%

1981
Wills	40.6%
Aparicio	12.0%

1982
Aparicio	41.9%
Wills	21.9%

1983
Aparicio	67.4%
Wills	20.6%

1984
Aparicio	84.6% BWA
Wills	25.8%

1985
Wills	23.5%
Don Kessinger	0.5%

1986
Wills	29.2%
Bud Harrelson	0.2%

1987
Wills	27.4%

1988
Wills	29.7%
Mark Belanger	3.7%

1989
Wills	21.3%
Bert Campaneris	3.1%

1990
Wills	21.4%
Bucky Dent	0.7%

1991
Wills	13.8%
Larry Bowa	2.5%

1992
Wills	25.6%
Bill Russell	0.7%

1993
No Players Received Votes

1994
Dave Concepcion	6.8%

1995
Concepcion	9.3%
Chris Speier	0.2%

1996
Concepcion	13.4%

1997
Concepcion	12.7%
Garry Templeton	0.4%

1998
Concepcion	14.8%

1999
Robin Yount	77.5% BWA
Concepcion	11.9%

2000
Concepcion	13.4%

2001		2002		2003	
Concepcion	14.4%	Ozzie Smith	91.7% BWA	Trammell	14.1%
		Alan Trammell	15.7%	Concepcion	11.1%
		Concepcion	11.9%		

2004		2005		2006	
Trammell	13.8%	Trammell	16.9%	Trammell	17.7%
Concepcion	11.3%	Concepcion	10.7%	Concepcion	12.5%

2007		2008		2009	
Cal Ripken	98.5% BWA	Trammell	18.2%	Trammell	17.4%
Concepcion	13.6%	Concepcion	16.2%	Jay Bell	0.4%
Trammell	13.4%				

Analysis of Voting for Shortstops

The voting at shortstop has followed an interesting pattern from orderly progression to logjam back to orderly progression. The immortal Honus Wagner was inducted on the initial ballot. Then Jennings and Tinker were selected by the Veteran's in 1945 and 1946.

From 1948 through 1954, Maranville and Cronin ranked one and two until their election by the Baseball Writers.

Then began the era of the shortstop. Between 1958 and 1976, from three to six players vied for recognition. All but Marty Marion and Alvin Dark were eventually elected to the Hall of Fame. Marion received greater voter support than Reese and Rizzuto on five occasions, but is still awaiting selection.

Ernie Banks became the second shortstop to be selected in his first year of eligibility in 1977. Since then, the field has dwindled. For six years Wills and Aparicio were the sole contenders. After Aparicio's election in 1984, Wills was the only shortstop in the running for the next eight years until he completed his 15 years on the ballot in 1992.

Robin Yount became the third shortstop to be elected on his first attempt in 1999.

After fifteen years on the ballot, Dave Concepcion completed his unsuccessful run in 2008. Only Alan Trammell remains on the ballot.

Ozzie Smith received a resounding 91.7 percent of the votes cast in his first year of eligibility in 2002. Alan Trammell also on his first try moved ahead of Concepcion. In 2003, 2004, 2005 and 2006 Trammell again finished ahead of Concepcion. Cal Ripken was another first ballot success in 2007 with Concepcion and Trammell far in arrears in a virtual deadlock.

Rank in Voting by Years (10% or more of the votes)

	Last Year	1936	1937	1938	1939	1942	1945	1946	1946 RO	1947
Honus Wagner	1917	1B								
Rabbit Maranville	1935		1	1	1	1	2	2	2	1
Hughie Jennings	1918			2	2	1V				
Joe Tinker	1916					3	3	1	1V	

	Last Year	1948	1949	1949 RO	1950	1951	1952	1953	1954	1955
Maranville		1	1	1	1	1	1	1	1B	
Joe Cronin	1945	2	2		2	2	2	2	2	1

	Last Year	1956	1958	1960	1962	1964	1964 RO	1966	1967	1967 RO
Cronin		1B								
Luke Appling	1950		1	1	1	1	1B			
Lou Boudreau	1952		2	3		3	3	1	1	1
Dave Bancroft	1930		3	4V 1971						
Marty Marion	1953			2	3	4		3	2	
Phil Rizzuto	1956				2	5		4	4	
Pee Wee Reese	1958					2	2	2	3	
Arky Vaughan	1948							5	5	
Alvin Dark	1960								6	

	Last Year	1968	1969	1970	1971	1972	1973	1974	1975	1976
Boudreau		1	1	1B						
Marion		2	2	2	2	2	1			
Rizzuto		5	4	4	3	3	3	2	2	2V 1994
Reese		4	3	3	1	1	2	1	1	1
Vaughan		3V 1985								
Dark		6	5	5	4	4	4	3	3	3

	Last Year	1977	1978	1979	1980	1981	1982	1983	1984	1985
Reese		2	1V 1984							
Dark		3	3	3	3					
Ernie Banks	1971	1B								
Maury Wills	1972		2	1	1	1	2	2	2	1
Luis Aparicio	1973			2	2	2	1	1	1B	

B—Baseball Writers Association of America
V—Veterans Committee

	Last Year	1986	1987	1988	1989	1990	1991	1992	1993	1994
Wills		1	1	1	1	1	1	1		

	Last Year	1995	1996	1997	1998	1999	2000	2001	2002	2003
Dave Concepcion	1988		1	1	1	2	1	1	3	2
Robin Yount	1993					1B				
Ozzie Smith	1996								1B	
Alan Trammell	1996								2	1

	Last Year	2004	2005	2006	2007	2008	2009
Trammell		1	1	1	3	1	1
Concepcion		2	2	2	2	2	
Cal Ripken	2001				1B		

B—Baseball Writers Association of America
V—Veterans Committee

Year	No. with 10% or More of Votes	No. in Hall of Fame BWA	VC	Cumulative Total (Different Individuals)	Non–Hall of Famers
1936	1	1	0	1	
1937	1	1	0	2	
1938	1	1	0	2	
1939	2	1	1	3	
1942	3	1	2	4	
1945	3	1	2	4	
1946	2	1	1	4	
1947	1	1	0	4	
1948	2	2	0	5	
1949	2	2	0	5	
1950	2	2	0	5	
1951	2	2	0	5	
1952	2	2	0	5	
1953	2	2	0	5	
1954	2	2	0	5	
1955	1	1	0	5	
1956	1	1	0	5	
1958	3	2	1	8	
1960	4	2	1	9	Marty Marion
1962	3	1	1	10	
1964	5	2	2	11	
1966	5	1	3	12	
1967	6	1	3	13	Alvin Dark
1968	6	1	3	13	
1969	5	1	2	13	
1970	5	1	2	13	
1971	4	0	2	13	
1972	4	0	2	13	

Year	No. with 10% or More of Votes	No. in Hall of Fame		Cumulative Total (Different Individuals)	Non–Hall of Famers
		BWA	VC		
1973	4	0	2	13	
1974	3	0	2	13	
1975	3	0	2	13	
1976	3	0	2	13	
1977	3	1	1	14	
1978	3	0	1	15	Maury Wills
1979	3	1	0	16	
1980	3	1	0	16	
1981	2	1	0	16	
1982	2	1	0	16	
1983	2	1	0	16	
1984	2	1	0	16	
1985	1	0	0	16	
1986	1	0	0	16	
1987	1	0	0	16	
1988	1	0	0	16	
1989	1	0	0	16	
1990	1	0	0	16	
1991	1	0	0	16	
1992	1	0	0	16	
1993	0	0	0	16	
1994	0	0	0	16	
1995	0	0	0	16	
1996	1	0	0	17	Dave Concepcion
1997	1	0	0	17	
1998	1	0	0	17	
1999	2	1	0	18	
2000	1	0	0	18	
2001	1	0	0	18	
2002	3	1	0	20	Alan Trammell
2003	2	0	0	20	
2004	2	0	0	20	
2005	2	0	0	20	
2006	2	0	0	20	
2007	3	1	0	21	
2008	2	0	0	21	
2009	1	0	0	21	

Conclusions (Shortstops)

Every shortstop who received 10 percent of the vote from 1936 through 1958 was eventually elected to the Hall of Fame.

Twenty-one individuals have received 10 percent of the vote in at least one election through 2009. Sixteen are in the Hall of Fame (10 elected by the Baseball Writers and 6 by the Veterans Committee). Marty Marion, Maury Wills, Alvin Dark and Dave Concepcion are eligible for consideration by the Veterans Committee. Alan Trammell is on the Baseball Writers' ballot.

Outfielders

Name	Years Played First-Last	Highest %-age	%-age Range	Number of Elections	HOF	Year Elected	Years Played
Ty Cobb	1905–1928	98.2%		1	BWA	1936	24
Henry Aaron	1954–1976	97.8%		1	BWA	1982	23
Tony Gwynn	1982–2001	97.6%		1	BWA	2007	20
Babe Ruth	1914–1935	95.1%		1	BWA	1936	22
Rickey Henderson	1979–2003	94.8%		1	BWA	2009	25
Willie Mays	1951–1973	94.7%		1	BWA	1979	22
Carl Yastrzemski	1961–1983	94.6%		1	BWA	1989	23
Reggie Jackson	1967–1987	93.6%		1	BWA	1993	21
Ted Williams	1939–1960	93.4%		1	BWA	1966	19
Stan Musial	1941–1963	93.2%		1	BWA	1969	22
Roberto Clemente	1955–1972	92.7%		1	BWA	1973*	18
Frank Robinson	1956–1976	89.2%		1	BWA	1982	21
Joe Di Maggio	1936–1951	88.8%	0.4%–88.8%	4	BWA	1955	13
Al Kaline	1953–1974	88.3%		1	BWA	1980	22
Mickey Mantle	1951–1968	88.2%		1	BWA	1974	18
Mel Ott	1926–1947	87.2%	61.4%–87.2%	4	BWA	1951	22
Harry Heilmann	1914–1932	86.8%	1.7%–86.8%	12(1)	BWA	1952	17
Duke Snider	1947–1964	86.5%	17.0%–86.5%	11	BWA	1980	18
Billy Williams	1959–1976	85.7%	23.4%–85.7%	6	BWA	1987	18
Joe Medwick	1932–1948	84.8%	0.8%–84.8%	10(1)	BWA	1968	17
Dave Winfield	1973–1995	84.5%		1	BWA	2001	22
Paul Waner	1926–1945	83.3%	2.0%–83.3%	6(1)	BWA	1952	20
Wilver Stargell	1962–1982	82.4%		1	BWA	1988	21
Tris Speaker	1907–1928	82.1%	58.8%–82.1%	2	BWA	1937	22
Kirby Puckett	1984–1995	82.1%		1	BWA	2001	12
Lou Brock	1961–1979	79.7%		1	BWA	1985	19
Jim Rice	1974–1989	76.4%	29.4%–76.4%	15	BWA	2009	16
Willie Keeler	1892–1910	75.5%	17.7%–75.5%	4	BWA	1939	19
Ralph Kiner	1946–1955	75.4%	(1.3%)–75.4%	12(2)	BWA	1975	10
Al Simmons	1924–1944	75.4%	0.5%–75.4%	8(1)	BWA	1953	20
Enos Slaughter	1938–1959	68.9%	(15.7%)–68.9%	14(1)	VC	1985	19
Andre Dawson	1976–1996	67.0%	45.3%–67.0%	8			21
Edd Roush	1913–1931	54.3%	0.9%–54.3%	19	VC	1962	18
Sam Rice	1915–1934	53.2%	0.4%–53.2%	13	VC	1963	20
Ed Delahanty	1888–1903	52.9%	7.1%–52.9%	6	VC	1945	16
Max Carey	1910–1929	51.1%	0.4%–51.1%	14	VC	1961	20
Tony Oliva	1962–1976	47.3%	15.2%–47.3%	15			15
Roger Maris	1957–1968	43.1%	16.6%–43.1%	15			12
Richie Ashburn	1948–1962	41.7%	2.1%–41.7%	15	VC	1995	15
Harvey Kuenn	1952–1966	39.3%	14.6%–39.3%	15			15
Hack Wilson	1923–1934	38.3%	0.4%–38.3%	15(1)	VC	1979	12
Kiki Cuyler	1921–1938	33.8%	2.5%–33.8%	12	VC	1968	18
Hugh Duffy	1888–1906	33.1%	3.5%–33.1%	5	VC	1945	17
Chuck Klein	1928–1944	27.9%	2.5%–27.9%	12(1)	VC	1980	17

*Special election in 1973

Name	Years Played First-Last	Highest %-age	%-age Range	Number of Elections	HOF	Year Elected	Years Played
Fred Clarke	1894–1915	24.9%	0.4%–24.9%	6	VC	1945	21
Tim Raines	1979–2002	24.3%	22.6%–24.3%	2			23
Lloyd Waner	1927–1945	23.4%	0.4%–23.4%	9(1)	VC	1967	18
Dale Murphy	1976–1993	23.2%	8.5%–23.2%	11			18
Casey Stengel	1912–1925	23.1%	0.8%–23.1%	9	VC	1966*	14
Zack Wheat	1909–1927	23.0%	0.8%–23.0%	16	VC	1959	19
Dave Parker	1973–1991	22.4%	10.3%–22.4%	13			19
Ross Youngs	1917–1926	22.4%	4.4%–22.4%	17(1)	VC	1972	10
Orestes Minoso	1949–1980	21.1%	1.8%–21.1%	15			17
Tommy Henrich	1937–1950	20.7%	1.0%–20.7%	10			11
Pepper Martin	1928–1944	17.3%	0.4%–17.3%	14(1)			13
Lefty O'Doul	1919–1934	16.7%	0.8%–16.7%	10			11
Earl Combs	1924–1935	16.0%	0.4%–16.0%	14	VC	1970	12
Vada Pinson	1958–1975	15.7%	1.4%–15.7%	15			18
Curt Flood	1956–1971	15.1%	2.1%–15.1%	15			15
Goose Goslin	1921–1938	13.5%	0.4%–13.5%	9	VC	1968	18
Duffy Lewis	1910–1921	13.5%	0.4%–13.5%	9			11
Terry Moore	1935–1948	11.7%	0.4%–11.7%	8			11
Dom Di Maggio	1940–1953	11.3%	1.3%–11.3%	9			11
Chick Hafey	1924–1937	10.8%	0.4%–10.8%	12	VC	1971	13
Bobby Bonds	1968–1981	10.6%	4.2%–10.6%	11			14
Heinie Manush	1923–1939	9.4%	0.7%–9.4%	6	VC	1964	17
Dwight Evans	1972–1991	8.2%	3.6%–8.2%	3			20
Rusty Staub	1963–1985	7.9%	3.8%–7.9%	7			23
Hank Bauer	1948–1961	7.9%	2.9%–7.9%	2			14
Albert Belle	1989–2000	7.7%	3.5%–7.7%	2			12
George Foster	1969–1986	6.9%	3.5%–6.9%	4			18
Billy Southworth	1913–1929	6.8%	0.4%–6.8%	8	VC	2008*	13
Charlie Keller	1939–1952	6.1%	0.4%–6.1%	11			13
Doc Cramer	1929–1948	6.0%	0.6%–6.0%	5			20
Harold Baines	1980–2001	5.9%	5.2%–5.9%	3			22
Babe Herman	1926–1945	5.7%	0.4%–5.7%	12			13
Cy Williams	1912–1930	5.7%	0.4%–5.7%	13			19
Fred Lynn	1974–1990	5.5%	4.7%–5.5%	2			17
Earl Averill	1929–1941	5.3%	0.7%–5.3%	7	VC	1975	13
Bob Meusel	1920–1930	5.0%	0.4%–5.0%	11			11
Willie McGee	1982–1999	5.0%	2.3%–5.0%	2			18
Ken Griffey, Sr.	1973–1991	4.7%		1			19
Bobby Thomson	1946–1960	4.6%	(0.3%)–4.6%	14(1)			15
Sam Crawford	1899–1917	4.5%	0.4%–4.5%	7	VC	1957	19
Al Oliver	1968–1985	4.3%		1			18
Manny Mota	1962–1982	4.2%	2.0%–4.2%	2			20
Joe Carter	1983–1998	3.8%		1			16
Larry Doby	1947–1959	3.4%	(0.3%)–3.4%	2(1)	VC	1998	13
Dixie Walker	1931–1949	3.0%	0.6%–3.0%	4			18
Pete Reiser	1940–1952	3.0%	2.3%–3.0%	2			10
Mike Donlin	1899–1914	3.0%	0.4%–3.0%	4			12
Harry Hooper	1909–1925	3.0%	1.2%–3.0%	6	VC	1971	17
Don Baylor	1970–1988	2.6%	2.6%–2.6%	2			19

*Elected as a manager

Name	Years Played First-Last	Highest %-age	%-age Range	Number of Elections	HOF	Year Elected	Years Played
Kirk Gibson	1979–1995	2.5%		1			17
Clyde Milan	1907–1922	2.4%	0.4%–2.4%	7			16
Bing Miller	1921–1936	2.2%	0.4%–2.2%	2			16
Paul O'Neill	1985–2001	2.2%		1			17
Willie Wilson	1976–1994	2.0%		1			19
Wally Moses	1935–1951	1.9%	0.4%–1.9%	6			17
Paul Blair	1964–1980	1.9%		1			17
Jesse Burkett	1890–1905	1.7%	0.5%–1.7%	5	VC	1946	16
Jack Clark	1975–1992	1.5%		1			18
G. J. Burns	1911–1925	1.5%	0.4%–1.5%	5			15
Riggs Stephenson	1921–1934	1.5%	0.4%–1.5%	4			14
Frank Howard	1958–1973	1.4%		1			16
Vic Wertz	1947–1963	1.4%	0.5%–1.4%	9			17
Carl Furillo	1946–1960	1.4%	0.5%–1.4%	5			15
Hank Sauer	1941–1959	1.3%		1			15
Matty Alou	1960–1974	1.3%		1			15
George Bell	1981–1993	1.2%		1			12
Gavvy Cravath	1908–1920	1.2%	0.5%–1.2%	5			11
Tommy Davis	1959–1976	1.2%		1			18
Darryl Strawberry	1983–1999	1.2%		1			17
Jackie Jensen	1950–1961	1.1%	0.3%–1.1%	6			11
Jose Canseco	1985–2001	1.1%		1			17
Del Ennis	1946–1959	1.0%	0.7%1.0%	2			14
Joe Jackson	1908–1920	1.0%	0.9%–1.0%	2			13
Ping Bodie	1911–1921	1.0%	0.7%–1.0%	2			9
Sherry Magee	1904–1919	1.0%	0.4%–1.0%	8			16
George Case	1937–1947	1.0%	0.4%–1.0%	4			11
Augie Galan	1934–1949	1.0%	0.7%–1.0%	2			16
Dusty Baker	1968–1986	0.9%		1			19
Willie Horton	1963–1980	0.9%		1			18
George Selkirk	1934–1942	0.9%	0.4%–0.9%	6			9
Tommy Holmes	1942–1952	0.8%	0.7%–0.8%	2			11
Wally Berger	1930–1940	0.8%	0.5%–0.8%	2			11
Carson Bigbee	1916–1926	0.8%		1			11
Bob L. Johnson	1933–1945	0.8%	0.5%–0.8%	2			13
Sammy West	1927–1942	0.8%		1			16
Freddy Leach	1923–1932	0.8%	0.4%–0.8%	2			10
Bill Virdon	1955–1968	0.8%	0.3%–0.8%	2			12
Felipe Alou	1958–1974	0.8%		1			17
Dave Kingman	1971–1986	0.7%		1			16
Ben Chapman	1930–1946	0.7%	0.4%–0.7%	2			15
Whitey Witt	1916–1926	0.7%		1			10
Hank Edwards	1941–1953	0.7%		1			11
Andy Pafko	1943–1959	0.7%	0.3%–0.7%	2			17
Elmer Valo	1940–1961	0.7%		1			20
Reggie Smith	1966–1982	0.7%		1			17
Bobby Murcer	1965–1983	0.7%		1			17
Joe Moore	1930–1941	0.6%		1			12
Wally Moon	1954–1965	0.6%		1			12
Vince Coleman	1985–1997	0.6%		1			13
Jim Eisenreich	1982–1998	0.6%		1			15
Chili Davis	1981–1999	0.6%		1			19

Name	Years Played First-Last	Highest %-age	%-age Range	Number of Elections	HOF	Year Elected	Years Played
Dante Bichette	1988–2001	0.6%		1			14
Eric Davis	1984–2001	0.6%		1			17
Mickey Rivers	1970–1984	0.5%		1			15
Lou Piniella	1964–1984	0.5%		1			18
Rick Monday	1966–1984	0.5%		1			19
Mickey Stanley	1964–1978	0.5%		1			15
Tommy Leach	1898–1918	0.5%	0.4%–0.5%	2			19
Bill Hinchman	1905–1920	0.5%		1			10
Shano Collins	1910–1925	0.5%		1			16
Red Murray	1906–1917	0.5%	0.4%–0.5%	2			11
Dode Paskert	1907–1921	0.5%		1			15
Frank Schulte	1904–1918	0.5%		1			15
Bobby Veach	1912–1925	0.5%		1			14
Ginger Beaumont	1899–1910	0.5%	0.4%–0.5%	4			12
Jimmy Sheckard	1897–1913	0.5%	0.4%–0.5%	3			17
Fielder Jones	1896–1915	0.5%		1			15
Mule Haas	1925–1938	0.5%	0.4%–0.5%	4			12
Johnny Mostil	1918–1929	0.5%	0.4%–0.5%	2			10
Ken Williams	1915–1929	0.5%	0.4%–0.5%	2			14
Ron Northey	1942–1957	0.5%		1			12
Rocky Colavito	1955–1968	0.5%	0.3%–0.5%	2			14
Cesar Cedeno	1970–1986	0.5%		1			17
Brian Downing	1973–1992	0.4%		1			20
Dave Henderson	1981–1994	0.4%		1			14
Harry Walker	1940–1955	0.4%		1			11
Walt Cruise	1914–1924	0.4%		1			10
Elmer Flick	1898–1910	0.4%		1	VC	1963	13
Joe Kelley	1891–1908	0.4%	0.4%–0.4%	2	VC	1971	17
Jose Cruz	1970–1988	0.4%		1			19
Billy Hamilton	1881–1901	0.4%		1	VC	1961	14
Cy Seymour	1896–1913	0.4%		1			16
Bill Lange	1893–1899	0.4%		1			7
Dave Robertson	1912–1922	0.4%		1			9
Ray Blades	1922–1932	0.4%	0.4%–0.4%	2			10
Sam Chapman	1938–1951	0.4%		1			11
Bill Nicholson	1936–1953	0.4%		1			16
Mike Greenwell	1985–1996	0.4%		1			12
Brett Butler	1981–1997	0.4%		1			17
Kevin Mitchell	1984–1998	0.4%		1			13
Jesus Alou	1963–1979	0.3%		1			15
Jim Hickman	1962–1974	0.3%		1			13
Bill Bruton	1953–1964	0.3%		1			12
Rico Carty	1963–1979	0.3%		1			15
Chet Lemon	1975–1990	0.2%		1			16
Terry Puhl	1977–1991	0.2%		1			15
Lonnie Smith	1978–1994	0.2%		1			17
Greg Luzinski	1970–1984	0.2%		1			15
Johnny Callison	1958–1973	0.2%		1			16
Gates Brown	1963–1975	0.2%		1			13
Jim Northrup	1964–1975	0.2%		1			12
Jose Cardenal	1963–1980	0.2%		1			18
Jeff Burroughs	1970–1985	0.2%		1			16

Name	Years Played First-Last	Highest %-age	%-age Range	Number of Elections	HOF	Year Elected	Years Played
John Lowenstein	1970–1985	0.2%		1			16
Ellis Valentine	1975–1985	0.2%		1			10
Lenny Dykstra	1985–1996	0.2%		1			12
Danny Tartabull	1984–1997	0.2%		1			14
Tony Phillips	1982–1999	0.2%		1			18
Jay Buhner	1984–2001	0.2%		1			15
David Justice	1989–2002	0.2%		1			14
James O'Rourke	1876–1904				VC	1945	19
Thomas McCarthy	1884–1896				VC	1946	13
Sam Thompson	1885–1906				VC	1974	15
King Kelly	1878–1893				VC	1945	16

(Includes only those who achieved 10% of the vote in any year)

1936

Ty Cobb	98.2% BWA
Babe Ruth	95.1% BWA
Tris Speaker	58.8%
Willie Keeler	17.7%

1937

Speaker	82.1% BWA
Keeler	57.2%
Ed Delahanty	34.8%
Fred Clarke	10.9%

1938

Keeler	67.6%
Delahanty	50.4%
Clarke	24.0%
Ross Youngs	15.3%

1939

Keeler	75.5% BWA
Delahanty	52.9%
Clarke	21.5%
Youngs	12.4%

1942

Delahanty	44.6%
Hugh Duffy	33.1%
Clarke	24.9%
Youngs	18.9%

1945

Delahanty	44.9% VC
Duffy	25.9% VC
Clarke	21.5% VC

1946

Youngs	12.4%
Harry Heilmann	11.4%

1946 Run Off

Youngs	0
Heilman	0

1947

Heilmann	40.4%
Zack Wheat	23.0%
Youngs	22.4%
Edd Roush	15.5%

1948

Al Simmons	49.6%
Paul Waner	42.1%
Heilmann	33.1%
Youngs	15.7%
Roush	14.0%
Wheat	12.4%

1949

Mel Ott	61.4%
Simmons	58.2%
P. Waner	43.8%
Heilmann	38.6%
Hack Wilson	15.7%
Youngs	13.1%
Pepper Martin	10.5%

1949 Run Off

Ott	68.4%
Simmons	40.6%
P. Waner	33.7%
Heilmann	27.8%
Wilson	6.4%
Youngs	5.9%
Martin	0

1950

Ott	68.9%
P. Waner	56.9%
Simmons	53.9%
Heilmann	52.1%
Wheat	10.2%
Youngs	10.2%

1951

Ott	87.2% BWA
P. Waner	71.7%
Heilmann	67.7%
Simmons	51.3%
Youngs	15.0%
Max Carey	11.9%

1952

Heilmann	86.8% BWA
P. Waner	83.3% BWA
Simmons	60.3%
Carey	15.4%
Youngs	14.5%
Martin	13.2%
Wheat	12.8%
Casey Stengel	11.5%
Roush	10.3%

1953

Simmons	75.4% BWA
Joe DiMaggio	44.3%
Stengel	23.1% VC 1966 Mgr
Carey	20.8%
Martin	16.3%
Wilson	16.3%
Wheat	12.1%
Roush	12.1%
Youngs	11.7%

1954

J. DiMaggio	69.4%
Carey	21.8%
Roush	20.6%
Wilson	19.0%
Youngs	13.5%
Wheat	13.1%

1955

J. DiMaggio	88.8% BWA
Carey	47.4%
Roush	38.6%
Wilson	32.3%
Wheat	20.3%
Youngs	19.1% VC 1972
Kiki Cuyler	13.9%
Duffy Lewis	13.5%
Sam Rice	11.2%
Chuck Klein	10.0%

1956

Roush	47.2%
Wilson	38.3%
Carey	33.7%
Cuyler	28.5%
Rice	23.3%
Klein	22.8%
Joe Medwick	16.1%
Wheat	13.5% VC 1959
Goose Goslin	13.5%

1958

Carey	51.1% VC 1961
Roush	42.1%
Wilson	35.3%
Rice	33.8%
Cuyler	33.8%
Medwick	18.8%
Martin	17.3%
Lloyd Waner	14.7%
Klein	13.5%
Earl Combs	12.8%
Lefty O'Doul	10.2%

1960

Roush	54.3% VC 1962
Rice	53.2%
Wilson	26.8%
Cuyler	26.8%
O'Doul	16.7%
Combs	16.0% VC 1970
Medwick	14.1%
Klein	13.8%
Goslin	11.2% VC 1968
Martin	10.8%
Chick Hafey	10.8% VC 1971

1962

Rice	50.6% VC 1963
Wilson	24.4% VC 1979
Medwick	21.3%
Cuyler	19.4% VC 1962
Klein	11.3%

1964

Medwick	53.7%
Klein	27.9%
L. Waner	23.4%
Ralph Kiner	15.4%

1964 Run Off

Medwick	57.5%
Klein	8.0% VC 1980
L. Waner	5.3% VC 1967
Kiner	1.3%

1966

Ted Williams	93.4% BWA
Medwick	61.9%
Enos Slaughter	33.1%
Kiner	24.5%

1967

Medwick	72.6%
Kiner	42.5%
Slaughter	42.1%

1967 Run Off

Medwick	81.0%*
Kiner	13.4%
Slaughter	15.7%

1968

Medwick	84.8% BWA
Slaughter	45.6%
Kiner	41.7%
Terry Moore	11.7%

1969

Stan Musial	93.2% BWA
Kiner	40.3%
Slaughter	37.6%
Tommy Henrich	14.7%

1970

Kiner	55.7%
Slaughter	44.3%
Henrich	20.7%
Duke Snider	17.0%

1971

Kiner	58.9%
Slaughter	45.8%
Snider	24.7%

1972

Kiner	59.3%
Slaughter	37.6%
Snider	21.2%

1973

Roberto Clemente	92.7% BWA
Special Election	
Kiner	61.8%
Slaughter	38.2%
Snider	26.6%
Dom DiMaggio	11.3%

*In 1967 Run Off only one player was elected. Red Ruffing received 86.9% of the vote besting Medwick's 81.0%.

1974

Mickey Mantle	88.2%	BWA
Kiner	58.9%	
Slaughter	39.7%	
Snider	30.4%	
Roger Maris	21.4%	
Richie Ashburn	15.3%	

1975

Kiner	75.4%	BWA
Slaughter	48.9%	
Snider	35.6%	
Ashburn	21.0%	
Maris	19.3%	

1976

Slaughter	50.8%
Snider	41.0%
Maris	22.4%
Ashburn	21.9%

1977

Slaughter	58.0%
Snider	55.4%
Ashburn	36.3%
Maris	18.8%
Harvey Kuenn	14.9%

1978

Slaughter	68.9%
Snider	67.0%
Ashburn	41.7%
Maris	21.9%
Kuenn	15.3%

1979

Willie Mays	94.7%	BWA
Snider	71.3%	
Slaughter	68.8%	VC 1985
Ashburn	30.1%	
Maris	29.4%	
Kuenn	14.6%	

1980

Al Kaline	88.3%	BWA
Snider	86.5%	BWA
Ashburn	34.8%	
Maris	28.8%	
Kuenn	21.6%	

1981

Ashburn	35.4%
Maris	23.4%
Kuenn	23.2%

1982

Henry Aaron	97.8%	BWA
Frank Robinson	89.2%	BWA
Ashburn	30.4%	VC 1995
Billy Williams	23.4%	
Maris	16.6%	
Tony Oliva	15.2%	
Kuenn	14.9%	

1983

B. Williams	40.9%
Keunn	20.6%
Oliva	20.1%
Maris	18.4%

1984

B. Williams	50.1%
Oliva	30.8%
Maris	26.6%
Kuenn	26.3%

1985

Lou Brock	79.7%	BWA
B. Williams	63.8%	
Maris	32.4%	
Kuenn	31.6%	
Oliva	28.9%	

1986

B. Williams	74.1%
Maris	41.6%
Oliva	36.2%
Kuenn	33.9%
Orestes Minoso	20.9%
Curt Flood	10.6%
Vada Pinson	10.1%

1987

B. Williams	85.7%	BWA
Maris	42.6%	
Oliva	38.7%	
Kuenn	34.9%	
Minoso	19.9%	
Flood	12.1%	
Pinson	11.6%	

1988

Wilver Stargell	82.4%	BWA
Oliva	47.3%	
Maris	43.1%	
Kuenn	39.3%	
Minoso	21.1%	
Pinson	15.7%	
Flood	11.2%	

1989

Carl Yastrzemski	94.6%	BWA
Oliva	30.2%	
Kuenn	25.7%	
Minoso	13.2%	

1990

Oliva	32.0%
Kuenn	24.1%
Minoso	11.5%

1991
Oliva   36.1%
Kuenn   22.6%

1992
Oliva   40.7%
Minoso 16.0%

1993
Reggie Jackson 93.6% BWA
Oliva   37.1%
Minoso   15.8%
Bobby Bonds   10.6%

1994
Oliva   34.7%
Pinson 10.1%

1995
Oliva   32.4%
Jim Rice 29.8%
Minoso   14.3%
Flood   12.8%

1996
Oliva   36.2%
Rice   35.3%
Flood   15.1%
Minoso   13.2%
Pinson   10.9%

1997
Rice   37.6%
Minoso   17.8%
Dave Parker 17.5%

1998
Rice   42.9%
Parker   22.4%
Minoso   14.0%

1999
Rice   29.4%
Dale Murphy 19.3%
Parker   16.1%
Minoso   14.7%

2000
Rice   51.5%
Murphy 23.2%
Parker   20.8%

2001
Dave Winfield 84.5% BWA
Kirby Puckett   82.1% BWA
Rice   57.9%
Murphy   18.1%
Parker   16.3%

2002
Rice   55.1%
Andre Dawson 45.3%
Murphy   14.8%
Parker   14.0%

2003
Rice   52.2%
Dawson 50.0%
Murphy 11.7%
Parker   10.3%

2004
Rice   54.5%
Dawson 50.0%
Parker   10.5%

2005
Rice   59.5%
Dawson 52.3%
Parker   12.6%
Murphy 10.5%

2006
Rice   64.8%
Dawson 61.0%
Parker   14.4%
Murphy 10.8%

2007
Tony Gwynn 97.6% BWA
Rice   63.5%
Dawson   56.7%
Parker   11.4%

2008
Rice   72.2%
Dawson   65.9%
Tim Raines 24.3%
Parker   15.1%
Murphy   13.8%

2009
R. Henderson   94.8% BWA
Rice   76.4% BWA
Dawson   67.0%
Raines   22.6%
Parker   15.0%
Murphy   11.5%

Analysis of Voting for Outfielders

The election of outfielders in the early balloting followed the predicted script. In the first year, Cobb and Ruth, as expected, were elected by over 95 percent. The next year Tris Speaker moved up from third place and in 1939 Keeler received the required votes after his second year as the top outfielder.

In 1945, the Veterans inducted Delahanty, Duffy and Clarke who had finished as the top three for two straight years. From 1946 through 1955, the Baseball Writers tapped Mel Ott (1951), Harry Heilmann and Paul Waner (1952), Al Simmons (1953), and Joe DiMaggio (1955). It wasn't until 1966 that the next BWA inductee was named. Ted Williams, in his first year, received a resounding 93.4 percent. This was a remarkable feat considering his relationship with the writers. During this period, a large number of players (as many as eleven) were getting over 10 percent of the vote but not enough for election.

Since Williams' election in 1966, 15 more outfielders have been elected by the Baseball Writers. Eleven of that number were first ballot selections (including Clemente inducted in a special election following his tragic death).

The plight of Tony Oliva is worth noting. He had the misfortune to come on the ballot amidst formidable competition. In six of his last nine years of eligibility, he was the top vote-getter among outfielders. The other three years, he was bumped by Wilver Stargell (1988), Carl Yastrzemski (1989), and Reggie Jackson (1993), all first-year selections.

Jim Rice might have fallen victim to the same fate as Oliva. Rice led all outfielders in the voting for four consecutive years, but in the 2001 balloting dropped to third when Dave Winfield and Kirby Puckett were elected in their first year of eligibility. Again in 2002, 2003, 2004, 2005 and 2006 Rice was the top outfielder followed by Andre Dawson. In 2007 Tony Gwynn was a first-ballot election with Rice and Dawson ranking second and third among outfielders. Rice and Dawson both received their highest percentage of votes in 2008 but fell short of the required 75 percent. However, in 2009 in his last year on the ballot, Rice was elected although he finished behind Rickey Henderson another first-year selection.

Rank in Voting by Years (10% or more of votes)

	Last Year	1936	1937	1938	1939	1942	1945	1946	1946 RO	1947
Ty Cobb	1928	1B								
Babe Ruth	1935	2B								
Tris Speaker	1928	3	1B							
Willie Keeler	1910	4	2	1	1B					
Ed Delahanty	1903		3	2	2	1	1V			
Fred Clarke	1915		4	3	3	3	3V			
Ross Youngs	1926			4	4	4		1		3
Hugh Duffy	1906					2	2V			

B—Baseball Writers Association of America
V—Veterans Committee

	Last Year	1936	1937	1938	1939	1942	1945	1946	1946 RO	1947
Harry Heilmann	1932							2		1
Zack Wheat	1927									2
Ed Roush	1931									4

	Last Year	1948	1949	1949 RO	1950	1951	1952	1953	1954	1955
Youngs		4	6		5T	5	5	9	5	6V-1972
Heilmann		3	4	4	4	3	1B			
Wheat		6			5T		7	7	6	5
Roush		5					9	8	3	3
Al Simmons	1944	1	2	2	3	4	3	1B		
Paul Waner	1945	2	3	3	2	2	2B			
Mel Ott	1947		1	1	1	1B				
Hack Wilson	1934		5					6	4	4
Pepper Martin	1944		7				6	5		
Max Carey	1929					6	4	4	2	2
Casey Stengel	1925						8	3V	(1966 Mgr)	
Joe DiMaggio	1951							2	1	1B
Kiki Cuyler	1938									7
Duffy Lewis	1921									8
Sam Rice	1934									9
Chuck Klein	1944									10

	Last Year	1956	1958	1960	1962	1964	1964 RO	1966	1967	1967 RO
Wheat		8V-1959								
Roush		1	2	1V-1962						
Wilson		2	3	3T	2V-1979					
Martin			7	10T						
Carey		3	1V-1961							
Cuyler		4	4T	3T	4V-1962					
Rice		5	4T	2	1V-1963					
Klein		6	9	8	5	2V-1980				
Goose Goslin	1938	9		9V-1968						
Lloyd Waner	1945		8			3V-1967				
Earl Combs	1935		10	6V-1970						
Lefty O'Doul	1934		11	5						

B—Baseball Writers Association of America
V—Veterans Committee

	Last Year	1956	1958	1960	1962	1964	1964 RO	1966	1967	1967 RO
Chick Hafey	1937			10T						
Joe Medwick	1948	7	6	7	3	1	1	2	1	1
Ralph Kiner	1955					4		4	2	3
Ted Williams	1960							1B		
Enos Slaughter	1959							3	3	2

	Last Year	1968	1969	1970	1971	1972	1973 Special	1973	1974	1975
Medwick		1B								
Kiner		3	2	1	1	1		1	2	1B
Slaughter		2	3	2	2	2		2	3	2
Terry Moore	1948	4								
Stan Musial	1963		1B							
Tommy Henrich	1950		4	3						
Duke Snider	1964			4	3	3		3	4	3
Roberto Clemente	1972						1B			
Dom DiMaggio	1953							4		
Mickey Mantle	1968								1B	
Roger Maris	1968								5	5
Richie Ashburn	1962								6	4

	Last Year	1976	1977	1978	1979	1980	1981	1982	1983	1984
Slaughter		1	1	1	3V-1985					
Snider		2	2	2	2	2B				
Maris		3	4	4	5	4	2	5	4	3
Ashburn		4	3	3	4	3	1	3V-1995		
Harvey Kuenn	1966		5	5	6	5	3	7	2	4
Willie Mays	1973				1B					
Al Kaline	1974					1B				
Henry Aaron	1976							1B		
Frank Robinson	1976							2B		
Billy Williams	1976							4	1	1
Tony Oliva	1976							6	3	2

	Last Year	1985	1986	1987	1988	1989	1990	1991	1992	1993
Maris		3	2	2	3					
Kuenn		4	4	4	4	3	2	2		
Williams		2	1	1B						
Oliva		5	3	3	2	2	1	1	1	2
Lou Brock	1979	1B								
Orestes Minoso	1980		5	5	5	4	3		2	3
Curt Flood	1971		6	6	7					

B—Baseball Writers Association of America
V—Veterans Committee

	Last Year	1985	1986	1987	1988	1989	1990	1991	1992	1993
Vada Pinson	1975		7	7	6					
Wilver Stargell	1982				1B					
Carl Yastrzemski	1983					1B				
Reggie Jackson	1987									1B
Bobby Bonds	1981									4

	Last Year	1994	1995	1996	1997	1998	1999	2000	2001	2002
Oliva		1	1	1						
Minoso			3	4	2	3	4			
Flood			4	3						
Pinson		2		5						
Jim Rice	1989		2	2	1	1	1	1	3	1
Dave Parker	1991				3	2	3	3	5	4
Dale Murphy	1993						2	2	4	3
Dave Winfield	1995								1B	
Kirby Puckett	1995								2B	
Andre Dawson	1996									2

	Last Year	2003	2004	2005	2006	2007	2008	2009
Rice		1	1	1	1	2	1	2B
Dawson		2	2	2	2	3	2	3
Murphy		3		4	4		5	6
Parker		4	3	3	3	4	4	5
Tony Gwynn	2001					1B		
Tim Raines	2002						3	4
R. Henderson	2003							1B

B—Baseball Writers Association of America
V—Veterans Committee

	No. with 10% or More	No. in Hall of Fame		Cumulative Total	
Year	of Votes	BWA	VC	(Different Individuals)	Non–Hall of Famers
1936	4	4	0	4	
1937	4	2	2	6	
1938	4	1	3	7	
1939	4	1	3	7	
1942	4	0	4	8	
1945	3	0	3	8	
1946	2	1	1	9	
1947	4	1	3	11	
1948	6	3	3	13	
1949	7	4	2	16	Pepper Martin
1950	6	4	2	16	

Year	No. with 10% or More of Votes	No. in Hall of Fame BWA	VC	Cumulative Total (Different Individuals)	Non–Hall of Famers
1951	6	4	2	17	
1952	9	3	5	18	
1953	9	2	6	19	
1954	6	1	5	19	
1955	10	1	8	23	Duffy Lewis
1956	9	1	8	25	
1958	11	1	8	28	Lefty O'Doul
1960	11	1	8	29	
1962	5	1	4	29	
1964	4	2	2	30	
1966	4	3	1	32	
1967	3	2	1	32	
1968	4	2	1	33	Terry Moore
1969	4	2	1	35	Tommy Henrich
1970	4	2	1	36	
1971	3	2	1	36	
1972	3	2	1	36	
1973					
Special	1	1	0	37	
1973	4	2	1	38	Dom DiMaggio
1974	6	3	2	41	Roger Maris
1975	5	2	2	41	
1976	4	1	2	41	
1977	5	1	2	42	Harvey Kuenn
1978	5	1	2	42	
1979	6	2	2	43	
1980	5	2	1	44	
1981	3	0	1	44	
1982	7	3	1	48	Tony Oliva
1983	4	1	0	48	
1984	4	1	0	48	
1985	5	2	0	49	
1986	7	1	0	52	Curt Flood, Orestes Minoso, Vada Pinson
1987	7	1	0	52	
1988	7	1	0	53	
1989	4	1	0	54	
1990	3	0	0	54	
1991	2	0	0	54	
1992	2	0	0	54	
1993	4	1	0	56	Bobby Bonds
1994	2	0	0	56	
1995	4	0	0	57	
1996	5	0	0	57	
1997	3	0	0	58	Dave Parker
1998	3	0	0	58	
1999	4	0	0	59	Dale Murphy
2000	3	0	0	59	
2001	5	2	0	61	
2002	4	0	0	62	Andre Dawson
2003	4	0	0	62	

Year	No. with 10% or More of Votes	No. in Hall of Fame BWA	VC	Cumulative Total (Different Individuals)	Non–Hall of Famers
2004	3	0	0	62	
2005	4	0	0	62	
2006	4	0	0	62	
2007	4	1	0	63	
2008	4	0	0	64	Tim Raines
2009	6	2	0	65	

Conclusions (Outfielders)

Twenty-nine of thirty-two outfielders who received 10 percent of the vote from 1936 through 1967 were eventually elected to the Hall of Fame.

Forty of forty-nine outfielders who received 10 percent of the vote from 1936 through 1985 were eventually elected to the Hall of Fame.

Of sixty-five outfielders who have received 10 percent of the vote through 2009, forty-eight are in the Hall of Fame (30 elected by the Baseball Writer's Association and 18 by the Veterans' Committee).

Four outfielders are under consideration by the Baseball Writers' Association: Tim Raines (2009; second year of eligibility), Dave Parker (2009; thirteenth year of eligibility), Dale Murphy (2009; eleventh year of eligibility), and Andre Dawson (2009; eighth year of eligibility).

The remaining thirteen outfielders are eligible for consideration by the Veterans' Committee.

Index

231